Sea
Diver

Sea Diver

A Quest
for History
Under the Sea

Marion Clayton Link

The University of Miami Press
Coral Gables, Florida
33124

TO MY HUSBAND
who first introduced me
to the wonders of
forest and sky and sea—
and now to that
new frontier, the bottom
of the ocean.

Contents

*Part
One*

*The
Florida
Keys*

1

o

o

o

Several years have passed since Ed and I first felt the lure of seeking the sunken remains of ancient sailing ships beneath the clear waters off southern Florida and the islands of the West Indies. When we made those first exploratory dives, we were as green as the moray eels which curled malevolently within the jagged coral reefs. Like most landsmen, if we had thought about sunken wrecks at all, we had envisoned them as hoary hulls still intact upon the bottom, and swarming with fish—dangerous and predatory fish, writhing octopi and huge rays with flapping wings.

We knew that up until the nineteenth century pirates had haunted these waters along the Florida coast, operating from their hide-outs in the complicated inner waterways of the Florida keys and the Bahama islands. We were vaguely aware that Spanish treasure ships had sailed in great convoys through these waters, laden with the wealth of the New World, on their way back to Spain. We knew that many of these ships had met disaster, not only from pirates, but more often from unexpected storms and hurricanes which had carried them into the reef-strewn waters along the Florida keys.

We had become increasingly aware of the hazards which these early mariners faced, as we sailed our forty-three-foot yawl, Blue Heron, up and down the Florida coasts, weaving in and out of the narrow passages which cut through the Florida keys, and navigating carefully about these same dangerous reefs which lay barely concealed several miles from shore, just at the edge of the Gulf Stream. And all along the coast of Cuba and in the lovely little harbors which we had found wherever we went in the Bahamas, we were reminded of the sailors who had preceded us, when there were no lighthouses or navigation markers, no accurate charts to indicate dangerous waters, and no auxiliary motors to help the awkward, square-rigged sails keep a ship out of trouble.

But little did we realize that spring of 1951, when we tied up at Bill Thompson's yacht basin at Marathon, where the Florida keys make a big swing toward the west, that we ourselves were about to become engaged in the most fascinating series of adventures we had ever dreamed of.

We had tied up at Bill's many times during our travels back and forth from the west coast of Florida to the east. This time we intended to stop over there before setting out on a cruise to the Bahama islands, to the east. We were accompanied by our two sons, William, age 13, and Clayton, age 9, who were spending their Easter vacation with us.

Bill Thompson, pioneer owner of one of the earliest yacht basins to be established between Miami and Key West, met us at the dock with a hearty welcome.

We greeted him. "What's new?"

"Come up to the office as soon as you can. I've got something to show you," he replied.

He had indeed. Coral-crusted cannon balls, a battered pewter cup and tanker, ivory tusks that were yellowed and flaking, worn and corroded coins and metal buttons—and a tale of diving on the remains of long-disintegrated sunken ships not far from the shores of Key Vaca, on which Marathon is built.

We sat with Bill and his vivacious wife, Ethel, far into that night, while they regaled us with their story of exploring these sunken wrecks together with a couple from Cleveland, whose hobby was skin diving with their children during their vacations. Bill said the pair were organizing a full-sized expedition that spring for a thorough investigation of three wrecks within the area, which he had spotted previously while fishing in the offshore waters.

"They have a cannon that they raised," Bill said, "and you should see the brass basins, and the coins and utensils they took home with them." He lowered his voice. "There are some metal bars out there on one of the wrecks, at Looe key. They look suspiciously like silver bars. We couldn't break them loose from the coral without some equipment."

Ed and I were both intrigued. We envied these lucky people from Cleveland who had stumbled upon this enticing adventure under the sea. I wished that I were a better swimmer. I wished that some such adventure might happen to us. I was only wishing.

Not so my husband. I had forgotten that, at the beginning of the season, Ed had stowed a heavy metal diving helmet and a crude hand-operated compressor in the forward hatch. He, too, had begun to consider the possibilities of diving, although I think his main reason at that time was the advantage of being able to make repairs on Blue Heron's hull or wheel when the necessity arose.

The next morning Ed hoisted the helmet to the deck. Calling on William and Clayton to aid him, he disappeared in the direction of the swimming pool. When I had finished the galley work, I donned my bathing suit and hastened after them. Close by the diving board, the two boys were taking turns working a wooden lever back and forth on a small platform, from which extended a rubber hose. The hose disappeared into the water, where, I inferred, it was connected to Ed, who was nowhere in sight. Sure enough, a few moments later he clambered up the steep side of the pool's coral bank, clumsily balancing himself against the weight of the helmet.

"It works," he proclaimed with satisfaction in his voice, "but I need more air."

I should have realized right then that one of those crucial times had arrived in Ed's life when it was essential for him to progress on to a new enthusiasm.

As a young man in the mid-1920's he had taken up flying. Those were days when there were few flying schools; equipment was elementary, and so was the type of instruction it was possible to receive from the barnstorming pilots who eked out a precarious livelihood from the grass airstrips scattered here and there about the country.

By the time Ed had learned to fly, he was well aware of the need for a better system of instruction. He designed and built the first Link trainer, a simple creation intended to give the student pilot familiarity with handling the controls of a plane before he left the ground. Throughout the years of the depression Ed made a meager living by using this device as the center of a unique flying school which he established.

It was some years later when his invention at last caught hold and was adopted by the Army Air Force. Today the Link trainer is well known, its complicated electronic successors simulating the very latest developments in modern aircraft.

Along with Ed's interest in flight training came a lively interest in exploring the possibilities for developing new and better methods of air navigation. He cooperated with Captain P. V. H. Weems, U.S.N., the navigation authority, and others in working out and adapting new types of aviation instruments and equipment, a bubble sextant for use in aircraft, and more efficiently arranged instrument panels and cockpits. During World War II his small company mushroomed until he found himself at the head of a booming enterprise which played an important role in the success of the whole Allied air effort.

His entire life pattern has developed in that way, his inventive mind and creative thinking carrying him along from one new project to another. It was not surprising that the conclusion of the war should find him seeking a change from the rigorous attention to business which the war years had demanded. From then on, he spent his free time sailing and racing our lovely forty-three-foot yawl in the waters around Florida, Cuba and the Bahamas.

Here, too, he was soon making innovations, this time in the ancient art of sailboat racing. By applying principles learned in the air to offshore navigation, using air navigation charts and a radio direction finder, he won the Havana–St. Petersburg race first in his class and second in the fleet, though he was a completely unknown newcomer in the field of ocean racing.

By 1951 the novelty had worn off this strenuous sport. Ed was fed up with the many weeks of careful preparation, the difficulties of organizing crews, and the terrific beating to which Blue Heron was subjected each time she raced. He was ready for a new activity. In the meantime he turned to more leisurely cruising, and we spent delightful days and weeks exploring the enchanting Florida keys clear to their western extremity at Dry Tortugas.

That is how we happened to be at Bill Thompson's place on the Florida bay shores of Marathon. Here we intended to prepare Blue Heron for a long-anticipated cruise to the Bahamas. When we were ready to sail, it would be simple to circle west and south, slice through the opening in Seven Mile bridge and head for Bimini, nearly 150 miles away.

But it was at this point that Bill Thompson succeeded in changing our entire outlook. Now he and Ed arranged for us to return to Marathon from the Bahama cruise at the end of May, in time to join the expedition which was slated to explore the three ancient ships that Bill had discovered lying on the bottom not many miles away.

The search was being organized by Jane and Barney Crile, the couple from Cleveland who had made the initial explorations with Bill. (The remainder of the time Barney was the very capable and well-known Dr. Crile of the Cleveland Clinic). Now they were recruiting equipment and a party of divers to continue their exploration of the three ships. Upon hearing of Ed's interest in the enterprise and of the Blue Heron, which would be available for their use, they were glad to welcome him into their group.

I realized that this new pastime of skin diving and searching the remains of sunken ships would necessarily make some changes in the way we were accustomed to spending our days aboard Blue Heron. But little did I realize that it would lead to the eventual disposal of our beloved sailboat and the substitution of a sturdy, sea-going shrimp trawler.

Neither did I foresee that I would soon be following Ed about the bottom of the sea in waters surrounding the most dangerous and frightening reefs in our part of the world, even to the most remote sections of the Caribbean.

In fact, at that time I did not even consider taking part in this underwater adventure, for I was a very poor swimmer. But I was keenly interested in the romance of an adventure involving sunken ships, the lure of possible treasure finds, and the sudden, mysterious disappearance of ancient Spanish galleons, pirate ships, slavers and square-rigged men-of-war into the sea. The finds which Bill Thompson had exhibited to us teased my imagination. What exciting objects might be found beneath coral and sand which had concealed them from human eyes these hundreds of years!

Having been unable to join the diving expedition at its start in the latter part of May, I finally arrived in Marathon on June sixth. The party had been at work more than a week. When the diver-explorers came in from the reefs that night, and we gathered about the outdoor grill to broil fresh-caught barracuda, which they had brought with them, I met nearly thirty men, women and children overflowing with enthusiasm and anticipation of what the next day's diving would bring forth.

I felt immediately as if I had always known the warm-hearted Crile family. I admired the way blonde, pretty Jane unconcernedly managed her brood of four, even as she and Barney performed a complicated sleight of hand with a half dozen cameras and underwater cases which they were reloading. And I was entertained at the masterly fashion in which Barney divided himself between assisting with the cameras and supervising the preparation of the barracuda, which was sputtering appetizingly over the fire.

Assisting Barney at the fire was a good-looking young man with rather bold brown eyes and a heavy shadow of beard on his mobile face. I was impressed to learn that this was Mendel Peterson, acting head of the Department of History at the Smithsonian Institution in Washington. He had joined the expedition as part of his summer vacation, to lend what aid he could in identifying the material brought up by the divers. It was his first venture in the realms of underwater archeology.

The others in the party were friends of the Criles, the men and children having the time of their lives with this submarine adventure; the women who had accompanied their families finding their fun in sunbathing, swimming and watching the activities beneath the water. They made a most congenial group.

We set out the next morning under a hot summer sun, three ill-assorted craft—a cruiser, which was used for sport fishing the remainder of the year; a sturdy LCP boat with two decks, which had been chartered for the expedition; and Blue Heron, whose sleek lines and delicate grace were never designed for hauling heavy cannon from the ocean floor.

The sea was calm. Now and then, from the deck, I caught glimpses of large fish gliding by. Once we sailed through a patch of hundreds of thousands of tiny fish, close-packed. Even as we watched, they spattered the surface like rain as the fringes of the school were raided by avaricious barracuda.

Vital, our French-Canadian deckhand, who had accompanied Ed south for the first time from our lodge in the Canadian bush, threw over a fishing line. It had barely hit the water when it was carried away in a wild rush. A few minutes later he pulled aboard a thrashing thirty-pound savage of the sea, one of those same barracuda. I shuddered at the thought of undertaking my first dive in the company of this toothy monster. And I looked admiringly, but also with perplexity, at the mothers and fathers in the party who were willing not only to face these underwater terrors themselves, but also to allow their children to go overboard.

About four miles out, not far from Sombrero lighthouse, the cruiser dropped anchor on what had come to be called the "ivory wreck" because of the number of ivory tusks which had been recovered there the previous year. Aboard with the Crile family was Arthur McKee, a professional diver and owner of the Museum of Sunken Treasure, a collection of underwater relics located at Plantation key, some fifty miles nearer Miami. Having made the initial discoveries on the ivory wreck the previous year with Bill Thompson, Jane and Barney were eager to explore it further.

Blue Heron and the LCP boat continued a quarter mile further on to Delta shoal, where Bill, in the years before the war, had discovered scores of cannon piled like matchsticks. Most of these cannon had been removed during the war years by professional salvagers and sold for scrap; but Bill, after long search, had finally relocated the spot by means of two cannon which the salvagers had missed, probably because the guns were buried beneath the shifting bottom sand at that time.

The divers had attached lines to one of these cannon the previous day, to prepare it for hauling. An empty bottle attached to one of these lines floated on the surface, marking the location. We anchored Blue Heron almost directly over it, and the LCP boat, manned by Bill Thompson and a lively crew of divers of all ages, cast anchor close by.

Soon the whole area was athrob with activity. Three

gasoline compressors blasted the air with sound on the LCP boat, and another labored on board Blue Heron. Red and green air hoses trailed from the boats and streaked the placid blue-green waters. Circles of white bubbles rose from the bottom in geyserlike shafts as the divers worked below, dimly glimpsed from the surface, colorful in yellow jerseys and black knit tights.

Swimmers splashed about on the surface with face masks, snorkels and fins as they viewed the bottom from above, seeking clues to new discoveries. Everyone was fully clothed. The veteran divers in the party wore black ballet tights or long ski underwear with bright-colored long-sleeved jerseys. The novices wore long-sleeved shirts, dungarees and shoes.

There were several good reasons for donning these costumes, I soon discovered. In the first place, the quiet waters of early summer had produced quantities of jellyfish, which, pale, ephemeral and ghostly, clouded the tepid waters. In spite of their protective clothing, many of the divers had come in contact with these jellyfish and were covered with a livid rash which looked and itched like measles. Also, the extra clothing acted as padding for the heavy lead weights which were worn across the chest or around the waist. And when the diver reached the bottom, he needed protection from the sharp coral rocks, which often caused poisonous infections, and from the many porcupine-like sea urchins which dotted the bottom.

I watched while two divers completed attaching lines from the winches to the cannon below. At last everything was ready. Two men manned the hand anchor winch; two others worked aft. They could make only a few turns at a time, for the pull of the heavy cannon was tremendous. At last they had it off the bottom. Long, lazy swells rolled in from the ocean. The swells, combined with the weight of the cannon, caused Blue Heron to roll badly. With each roll the cannon was lifted several feet and dropped back against the sharp coral on the bottom.

Ed put on a diving mask and went overboard to see how things were progressing. He found that the coral which coated the cannon was cutting through the ropes, which would undoubtedly be severed before the gun could be raised. He returned for some steel cable and departed below once more to reinforce the load. Sitting astride the iron barrel while fastening the cables, he plunged up and down with the motion of the boat as if he were riding a bucking horse.

With makeshift equipment and the well-intentioned but awkward efforts of the amateur crew, it was hours before the cannon was finally raised and secured to a spot in the curve of Blue Heron's bottom and keel, where it was made fast for the journey to shore.

It was then that Ed indicated the time had come for me to make my first dive. I had avoided thinking about it all day. I was eager to try it, and yet I was filled with trepidation. What if the air hose should kink, or the compressor cease operating? What if I should meet up with a shark or barracuda? What if I should get panicky and be unable to reach the surface fast enough? I had almost a phobia against putting my head underwater or getting water up my nose.

Outwardly calm, I donned jersey and dungarees over my swim suit, tied on my deck shoes and bathing cap and waited to have the diving mask adjusted—not the clumsy metal helmet which Ed had experimented with earlier in the year, but a Desco mask, a triangle of glass edged with black rubber, equipped with intake and exhaust valves and connected to a hundred feet of hose. Air, cool and comforting, poured in through the open valve as Ed tightened the fastenings of the mask about my face.

I climbed clumsily over the side of the ship and down a rope ladder into the water. As I had been instructed, I stuck my head into the water to see that the mask was tight and the air flowing properly. Little bubbles of air promptly left the exhaust valve and rose to the surface. I had been told to place the air hose under my left arm, and a circlet of lead weights had been hung over my right shoulder to give me additional weight on the bottom.

Ed went down with me. He wore an Aqualung, a self-contained diving unit, with a tank strapped to his back, for during the previous week he had acquired a much broader skill in the use of various types of diving equipment. Already a competent swimmer and diver, it had not taken him long to master the necessary techniques, for he also possessed the confidence and self-assurance which I so greatly lacked in this strange and unknown environment.

I felt my way down the life line suspended from the ship. Ed hovered close at my side. As the water closed in overhead, a lovely crystalline light sifted through it, and a steady path of bubbles streaked to the surface from my mask. Floating through the water to a depth of at least ten feet were innumerable transparent jellyfish. I was glad for the protection of many clothes. My ears hurt and popped. I slowed my descent, conscious of advice that I must neither ascend nor descend quickly, because rapid changes of pressure are dangerous.

Above me as I descended, the outline of Blue Heron's keel and bottom took shape, and I could see the cannon strapped snugly in its curve. The green light grew dimmer, for it was now late in the afternoon, though it was still sufficiently bright to make out the spectacular ocean floor below.

But there was trouble from an unexpected quarter. My feet, in their canvas shoes, insisted upon floating. As I descended the rope, I had great trouble keeping them lower than my head. When I reached the bottom, I could not get my feet down; they seemed determined to go off on an exploring trip of their own. Ed, seeing my predicament, surfaced and soon returned with extra weights, which he put in my dungaree pockets. That helped some, and I was able to put my feet on the bottom, but my efforts at walking were very unsteady.

I stood on the white-sand bottom twenty-five feet below and looked around me. A beautiful sea garden stretched out on every side, a world of waving sea grasses, fantastic coral formations and lacy traceries of sea fans. Here were cool caves from whose crevasses undulated the feelers of giant crawfish; beneath the sheltering ledges lay broken bits of coral and shells.

Ed touched my arm and beckoned me to follow him. He led me to a pit in the sandy bottom where lay a cannon crusted with coral and covered with sea growth. Scattered in the sand lay dozens of purple-tinged, porcupine-like sea urchins, forming a protective ring around the cannon. The spiny creatures frightened me, and I backed away, lost my precarious balance and wavered helplessly toward another pit, which was liberally dotted with more sea urchins.

It was only by a tremendous effort that I saved myself from tumbling among them. In my excitement I gulped great quantities of air and then found myself gasping for breath. The hose could not conduct air fast enough to satisfy my urgent requirements. My heart pounded. I felt stifled in the small confines of the face mask. Then, my feet once more safely on the bottom, I regained control of myself, and my breathing slowed to the point where the air hose could take care of the situation again.

I did not stay down long that day. After one more survey of that underwater world and its wonders, I inched slowly up the life line toward the surface and climbed back aboard Blue Heron, thrilled at what I had seen, my heart still palpitating with the excitement and adventure of it all. I was determined that I would learn more about this underwater skill before I went down again, so that I could really explore the bottom for myself.

We hoisted anchors and, with the cannon lashed to the underside of the boat, got under way, listing heavily to starboard, our speed cut in half by the additional drag. It was many hours later when we tied up at the dock, too late to examine our prize that night.

There was much curiosity and excitement the next morning as we gathered around the old gun while Mendel Peterson and Ed chipped away at the coral which covered it. Beneath the coral, upon its metal sides, we might find an answer to the identity of the ship which had foundered.

It was an interesting old weapon with many ridges, tapering to a small muzzle and ending in a heavy ring. The coral covering broke off in great chunks at the blows of the iron mallets. And there on its broad back was suddenly revealed, crudely cast in the metal, the inscription "anno 1617."

We couldn't believe it! Here was a real find, from a ship which must have sunk about the time the Pilgrim Fathers first came to the New World.

What kind of a ship had it been, Spanish or English? Was it on a mission of peace or war? What had happened to bring its sudden end upon this lonely reef? Had it been sunk in battle? Had it run upon the reef in a storm? Or had it been sailing along in seemingly clear waters, miles from shore, when suddenly it had struck the treacherous underwater coral?

Mendel Peterson gazed at it with particular interest. He had already identified the wreck on Looe key as an English warship. At this time, he could only assume that the ivory wreck had been a vessel engaged in the slave trade, of uncertain age and nationality. The third wreck, from which had come this early-seventeenth-century cannon, was Spanish, he was quite certain. More than that he could not say until he had had a better opportunity to identify the gun. It puzzled him that while each of the other two wrecks had yielded a variety of artifacts furnishing broad hints as to the country of their origin, so far nothing but cannon had been found at the location on Delta reef.

Pete, as we came to know Mendel Peterson, turned out to be an indispensable member of the expedition. His head was packed with a fund of historical facts and figures which were invaluable, as well as a broad knowledge of old armament, which was his special hobby.

It was Pete who was responsible for channeling Ed's developing interest in the underwater world into the field of marine archeology, for it was impossible to discover these ancient artifacts without feeling a tantalizing curiosity as to their origin. What had started out to be merely a new sport for the Links soon resolved itself into a consuming and enthralled interest in the past history of that part of the world. We questioned Pete at length.

It was early in the sixteenth century, soon after Cortez conquered the rich lands of Mexico, Pete told us, that the Straits of Florida, leading between the Florida coast and the Bahama islands, became the regular sailing path for most of the ships returning to Europe from the vicinity of the Caribbean. It had not taken the early navigators long to discover that while the best route to the New World led from Europe south toward the Cape Verde islands, westward to the vicinity of Trinidad, and then across the Caribbean with the southeast trades to the early seaports of Cartagena, Vera Cruz and Havana, the most favorable return route carried them northward through the Straits of Florida, then known as the Bahama canal, until they caught the westerly winds which would assist them back to Europe.

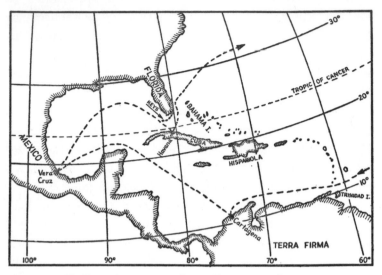

Early sailing route from Europe and return.

Unfortunately the narrow Straits of Florida, while providing both the helpful currents of the Gulf Stream and a normally prevailing southeast wind, also carried the hazards of a line of offshore reefs several miles from the almost invisible shore line of the Florida keys. For centuries, hundreds of ships were destroyed along these reefs.

It took only a brief glimpse at a chart of this area for us to understand why the waters in the vicinity of Marathon and the adjacent keys would be particularly rich in wrecks, for it is here that the line of keys swings from an almost north and south direction to east and west, the coral reefs following the same line several miles at sea. A ship feeling its way northward through the narrow straits, if it erred in its position even slightly, could find itself in these dangerous waters.

Add to that the hazards of hurricanes and violent storms, and it was easy to see why so many ships ended up on the reefs. Unfortunately most of these reefs are just underwater, so that they are not visible from the surface. And because they lie at the edge of the Gulf Stream, where the bottom drops suddenly to depths of several hundred feet, well beyond the reach of the average sounding line, their presence would be undetected until the ship suddenly encountered them. Because of the distance of the reefs from shore, there must have been many times at night or in poor visibility when they could be struck without any warning that land was near.

The three wrecks which Bill Thompson had come across while trolling a fish line about the reefs were no doubt indicative of dozens more which must lie along this 250-mile-long string of keys. However, were it not for the cannon, those coral-covered logs which Bill had spotted from the surface, the final resting place of the wrecks would still be a secret, for during the two to three hundred years these ships had lain on the bottom, they had completely disintegrated. It would not be easy to find the remains of other wrecks; almost impossible if the cannon had already been removed.

The wreck at Looe key, on which we were to dive the next day, had already been well worked over by the group. Ed, Barney, and Jane had labored a day and almost a whole night to raise and bring back to Marathon the two-thousand-pound cannon which now lay in a fresh-water bath near Bill's swimming pool. On it they found a crowned rose, insignia of British royalty.

In a protected enclosure near Bill's house lay charred pieces of wood from the ship's big timbers, corroded iron ballast, dozens of cannon balls of many sizes, bar shot and grapeshot. There was a copper hoop from a powder keg. There were bones, even part of a jawbone with the teeth still intact. There were bits from a Chinese porcelain bowl, the remains of a fine crystal unguent jar, a pewter mug, spun-copper plates and utensils and a brass door knocker.

These last had been found in one locale, indicating that they came from the aft section of the ship, the captain's quarters. At a spot some distance away had been found pieces of coarse, blue, salt-glazed eighteenth-century pottery; worn pieces of green-glass rum bottles, with the corks still in the necks of two of them; and the fairly complete remains of several clay pipes. This would appear to have been the crew's quarters.

Several worn and corroded coins of various nations, which had been found in scattered places on the wreck, were being carefully cherished by their finders. The latest date, 1720, appeared on a Swedish copper piece.

From these finds Pete had been able to reconstruct a fairly complete account of the shipwreck. He visualized a British warship of the larger class striking the reef sometime between 1720 and 1750. He said that it had probably met its end from natural causes rather than in battle, as the tompion was still in the mouth of the cannon which had been raised.

He felt quite certain that the ship was British because, in addition to the crowned rose which marked the cannon, many of the six-pound and twelve-pound cannon balls were engraved with a broad arrow indicating that they were British property. He figured that it was a warship rather than a merchant ship because of the number and size of the cannon and the large amount of ammunition it had carried, as well as the heap of iron ballast which was composed of bars molded to conform to the hull of the ship. A merchant ship would have carried only a few cannon of smaller size, and expendable ballast such as stone, he said.

It was these bars of iron ballast which had originally excited Bill Thompson and the Criles when they first dove on the wreck. I recalled Bill's hushed secrecy the night he had told us about them. He was so sure they had discovered a pile of silver bars. Today, with more experience behind me, I can understand his mistake, for it is very difficult on the ocean bottom to distinguish between silver and other metals, once they have become coated with a black corrosion.

Pete fixed the date of the ship's sinking between 1720 and 1750 for two reasons: the date of 1720 was the latest to be found on any of the coins which had been retrieved, and the cannon was marked with the crowned rose, an insignia which was not used after the death of Queen Anne in 1714. As the life of an iron cannon was only about thirty-five years, Pete figured that such a cannon would not have been aboard a ship later than 1750.

Subsequent investigation revealed that Pete was right in every respect. Returning to Washington with his data, he searched through the casualty lists of the British Royal Navy of the eighteenth century and found the entry, "1743 [sic] Looe 44 guns, Capt. Ashby Utting, lost in America."

Of course, that was how Looe key had received its name! Later we learned the complete story of the destruction of the Looe from the Admiralty records.

His Majesty's Ship Looe had sailed from England in August of 1743 under the command of Captain Ashby Utting, to carry Governor Clinton and his family to New York and then "to attend on the colony of South Carolina." She spent the remainder of the year cruising between Cape Florida and the northwest part of the Grand Bahamas, under orders to protect English and Colonial shipping from the Spanish, with whom England was at war.

Later this patrol was extended farther south to include the waters adjacent to Cuba and the Florida keys. On February 4, 1744, while cruising in the straits off Havana, Captain Utting captured a Spanish vessel and headed north through the Florida straits, followed by his prize.

Either the ship's navigator miscalculated, or unknown currents carried the Looe well off her course and to the west. In spite of frequent and careful soundings, shortly after midnight she found herself in the white breakers marking a small key which raised itself slightly above the surface of the water. She struck just as the officer on watch discovered their predicament. The ship first lost her tiller and then the rudder as she swung about in the tide. Water poured into the hull as she bilged, and the hold started to fill as she pounded upon the rocks.

There was just time to get the men ashore and to save twenty bags of bread and six barrels of gunpowder. It was fortunate indeed for her crew of nearly three hundred men that there was land upon which to disembark. The Spanish snow, which had been following the Looe closely, also piled up on the shore a short distance to port, where she soon began to break up.

It was not until morning that they discovered they were on a small key several miles off the "Martires," south of Cape Florida, for the navigator had been positive they had struck on Double Headed Shot cay many miles to the east.

Captain Utting realized that he and the men in his care were in a most desperate plight. They could expect only capture and imprisonment from their enemies, the Spanish, in nearby Cuba, and the hostile Caloosa Indians who inhabited the Florida keys were noted for their cruelty to shipwrecked mariners.

With both ships destroyed, they had only three small craft—a longboat, a yawl which was merely a double-ended rowboat, and the captain's barge. It was hundreds of miles to the English Port Royal in South Carolina, from whence they had come; and it was a considerable distance, with unfavorable winds, to the nearest English settlement of New Providence in the heart of the Bahamas.

There was no water available on the sandy islet upon which they found themselves; all they had were the few casks which they had been able to salvage from the wrecked ships. It was apparent also that a heavy storm would, in all probability, carry the seas completely over the surface of the low island. Their predicament was grave indeed.

As Captain Utting pondered their unhappy prospects, a lookout spied a sloop at sea, headed toward the northwest. When it failed to answer their signals, the captain commanded that the men arm themselves and take three small craft after it. He ordered them to use every means in their power to capture it, for it might well be their only means of escape.

The little flotilla did not return until the next morning, but they brought the sloop with them. Its Spanish crew, they reported, had escaped in the ship's lone boat and headed back toward Havana.

Captain Utting immediately set the men to work to equip the four available boats for their journey. The sides of the longboat were built up with timbers from the wrecked Looe, to increase its capacity and its safety, and all four boats were supplied as generously as possible with bread, water and ammunition.

By noon of the fourth day they were ready to start.

Sixty men were assigned to the longboat, ten to the yawl, twenty to the captain's barge, and 184 were crowded into the captured sloop which Utting estimated to weigh "not 30 tuns." As a last precaution to prevent the Spanish from salvaging the wrecked ships, the Captain ordered them burned. As the survivors pulled away in their heavily loaded craft, the Looe and her companion snow blazed up in flames. This explained the charred and blackened timbers which our party had found on the wreck.

Captain Utting ordered the boats to head for New Providence in the Bahamas, but by the next morning the three small boats had outstripped the sloop, with its astounding quota of passengers, and were no longer in sight. Finding it impossible to hold the heavily laden sloop on a course to the east against the prevailing wind, the men aboard yielded to necessity and allowed the current of the Gulf Stream to carry them northward toward Port Royal.

They arrived there on February thirteenth, five days later, thanking God for their safe passage. No one knew better than they that the overloaded vessel would have capsized in the slightest weather. The other three boats also reached their destination, New Providence, without mishap.

As Blue Heron glided along the ocean side of Looe key in still, clear waters, I stood on the bow scanning the bottom for signs of the wreck. I could feel the goose pimples rise as I looked at the cruel fingers of coral reaching seaward for new prey, for I saw that the reef was fashioned with alternate sharp ridges and declivities that extended from the solid bank of the inner side. Although this bank was now underwater, due to some past hurricane which had stripped it of vegetation and soil, it was here, I realized, that the survivors of the Looe had spent four anxious days.

Ed nosed Blue Heron in between two of the extending teeth and dropped the fore and aft anchors. I saw that the wreck had settled into the narrow valley between. Again, it was only because of the cannon lying on the bottom that we were able to relocate it so easily. The other two boats, which had followed us, anchored nearby.

As the morning wore on, I swam about on the surface with face mask and flippers, fascinated at the activities which I could glimpse beneath the water. In one place the coral came so close to the surface I could kick it with my flippers. Then it dropped off sheer to the ocean bottom thirty feet below, where the divers were working. I could scarcely wait to join them. It seemed hours before my turn finally arrived.

This time I was better prepared. Instead of weights hanging loose from one shoulder, I wore a weighted belt across my chest, for Ed was afraid that if it were fastened about my waist, I would not be able to remove it quickly enough in case of emergency. On my feet I wore those blessed flippers, which proved to be the means of making my feet do what I wanted them to.

I lowered myself slowly along the life line until my feet hit the edge of a wire basket placed on the bottom as a repository for the divers' finds. A heavy black air hose hung from the boat above; it was being used to clean away coral chips and sand from the objects on the bottom. I paused and looked around.

Towering high above the narrow valley on either side were coral cliffs and caves, from which grew beautiful sea fans and other branching Gorgonia. In my ignorance at the time I thought the animal-celled Gorgonia was vegetation.

Tiny, bright-colored fish swam about my feet. A huge pinkish-brown hog snapper hovered nearby. As I watched, three large, beautiful, black-and-gold angelfish sailed majestically past, waving their fins in slow and perfect rhythm, while just beyond, a single brilliant-blue angelfish shyly looked out from behind a pinnacle of coral rock on the valley floor.

This time, with the aid of the flippers, I was able to swim about this strange undersea ravine, floating up the steep sides of the coral rocks, peeping into eerie chasms and then gliding down to examine a nearly buried cannon, scarcely distinguishable under its disguise of coral. It was then I saw the giant anchor of the sunken warship, coral-covered and almost hidden under a jutting shelf of rock. Its huge ring was large enough to swim through. The shank, half buried in the coral, still revealed a section longer than myself. It must have weighed more than a ton. I hovered over it enthralled.

For more than an hour I explored this lovely spot, getting tremendous satisfaction out of playing fish. And the fish didn't seem to mind at all this clumsy, strange-looking creature from the world above. They swam about me, snouting out food from the bottom, playing tag with each other, completely oblivious of me.

With startling suddenness the realization came to me. I was no longer fearful of this strange environment. I was at last at home on the bottom.

2

o

o

o

By the time that first expedition was over, Ed and I were confirmed divers and treasure seekers. We had been afflicted with a contagion which was to lead us on strange and unexpected adventures. Following its onset we found ourselves unable to resist tales of treasure-laden ships lying upon the ocean floor, their contents still untouched. We felt sure that they only awaited our coming to surrender vast quantities of riches.

This virtually inescapable malady was to lead us to risk our boats and equipment many times, and even our lives, in treacherous reef-strewn waters, oftentimes far from sight of land. Before the disease had run its course, we had visited every part of the far-flung Bahamas, had followed the lure of sunken treasure clear to the Silver shoals, a forty-mile-square area of scattered reefs lying between the remote Turks islands and Hispaniola, shunned by every mariner since the time of Columbus. And off the southern shores of Jamaica we found ourselves battling the wind and tides which constantly assault the long, lean line of

Banner reef, scarred with the wreckage of many a ship headed across the Caribbean.

But, fortunately, though we fought a losing battle against this treasure-hunting disease, we built up a secondary infection—a consuming interest in the past history of this part of the New World. The ensuing years found us spending an increasing amount of time poring over old charts, government records and accounts of the adventurers of those early days.

Our awakened curiosity led us to ponder many questions. Just where did Columbus actually first set foot on American soil? Which path did he choose to sail the Santa Maria through the Bahamas before that ill-fated ship met her doom on a reef off the north coast of Hispaniola? Could we possibly locate the wreckage of the famous flagship? Would there be any evidence of it still in existence today?

We read about the notorious city of Port Royal, Jamaica, which sank beneath the sea in an earthquake one summer's day in 1692. From all we could gather, no real attempt had ever been made to salvage it. Eventually we were to feel compelled to explore these long-lost ruins. The urge was irresistible.

Thus it was that when we headed north in the summer of 1951 from our first adventure in the Florida keys, loaded with cannon balls, copper pans and twisted pieces of ship's rigging, we could hardly wait for the coming year, when we planned to return for further search in that graveyard of early ships.

Ed set the date for the end of the following January. By then the hurricane season, which spans a period from July through November, would be well over; his business would be sufficiently under control so that he could leave it for several months; and he would have had time to prepare the equipment which must be ready to commence operations in the spring. We even planned to place William and Clayton in school at Fort Lauderdale so that the family would not be so widely separated. They would be able to join us weekends and at Easter vacation.

During the June days that we had spent diving from the teakwood decks of Blue Heron, rigging block and tackle from her mast, and worrying over the damage that was inevitably done to her white sides and mahogany rails, Ed's ever-active mind had mulled over the problem of how to remedy these difficulties before our return the following winter. He was finally convinced that he would have to secure a boat more adequate for the job than Blue Heron had proved to be. A heavier and sturdier craft was needed.

An answer was not long in coming. One evening in New York, soon after we returned north, he was talking enthusiastically to a friend, Lee Warrender, about the results of his first diving venture. Before the evening was over, Lee had volunteered to supply his boat, Eryholme, a seventy-five-foot twin-diesel cruiser, for the task. We were also to have the services of her captain, Ray Budd, who was thoroughly familiar with the boat. The arrangement seemed ideal, and straightaway the two men started making plans for the necessary conversion.

A crane was erected on the forward deck for raising heavy objects, and the deck was reinforced. Davits were installed on the starboard side, where Ed planned to carry a glass-bottomed skiff he was designing. In the years to come, that small boat would prove to be one of our most useful possessions. It had two plates of Plexiglas in the bow just where it curved upward, so that a person could lie on the bottom and watch the ocean floor spread away on either side. Then, just in front of the aft seat by the outboard motor, another large panel was inserted, so that the bottom could be viewed straight down by either the pilot of the boat or a second observer.

With the clarity of those southern waters, it should be possible to see objects on the bottom without any difficulty. By plotting definite tracks back and forth within a limited area, we should be able to discover any evidence of the wreckage of sunken ships. We knew now from experience that the remains of any ship old enough to be of historic interest would not be lying there with hull intact, awaiting our discovery. We could only hope to find coral-encrusted cannon, possibly an anchor, a disordered pile of ballast stone, or even the round shapes of cannon balls, almost hidden in enveloping sand or coral.

We planned that coming season to make a further search of the three wrecks we had worked on near Marathon. We also intended to comb the waters along the reefs all up and down the ocean side of the Florida keys. Already we had garnered many tales from local fishermen who had seen cannon or piles of cannon balls on the bottom. Bill Thompson had discovered the first three wrecks seemingly without difficulty. We really anticipated little trouble in locating dozens of other wrecks, for there were treacherous reefs all up and down the coastline.

What we did not realize was that we had been blessed with a continuous streak of perfect diving weather the whole time we had spent at Marathon that first summer— a series of absolutely calm days without wind or waves, making it possible to anchor at will and to dive from early morning until dark. Furthermore, there had been no difficulty in locating the wrecks, for the calm waters were so clear that by standing on the bow of the boat it was possible to see everything on the bottom as if in a mirror.

We discovered, soon after our arrival in Marathon in 1952, that while winter weather may be ideal for sailboating, it is not the kind of weather one would select for diving, or even for searching in the vicinity of wave-roughened reefs. Day after day we experienced strong southeast winds, which occasionally veered into the south and west before developing into a full-blown winter "norther."

However, we found plenty to do the first two weeks in equipping Eryholme for her new activities and in testing the endless variety of equipment which Ed had shipped south. In addition to a small air compressor and three sets of Desco face plates, the paraphernalia included an outfit of self-contained Aqualung equipment and the large, clumsy white suit and lead boots of the so-called heavy diver.

But chief among the new equipment was an underwater metal detector which Ed had rebuilt from a type of land-mine detector developed during World War II. It consisted of a long black rod with a coil of wire sealed into a circle of clear Plexiglas at one end. In a waterproof tank at the other end were located the electronic gear and batteries and an electric meter to indicate the presence of metal. With this equipment Ed felt sure he would be able to locate cannon and other metal objects buried beneath the coral or under the sandy bottom.

We had flown to Marathon from our home in Binghamton, New York, in our five-place Grumman Widgeon, which Ed planned to use as part of his search equipment. It had already proved its worth the previous summer for spotting the outline of reefs and the most likely places for search. But we had also found at that time that it was next to impossible to make out objects on the bottom through the surface of the water. An airplane traveled too fast for such reconnaissance.

The amphibian definitely had its uses, however, as

we had discovered one morning when Ed set out with Jane and Barney to fly over the wreck sites on which they had been diving at Delta shoal and Looe key.

It was a calm, lovely day, and it seemed very possible that beneath the mirrorlike surface they might detect evidence which had hitherto escaped their search. The brown shadows of the reefs showed up in distinct patterns beneath the turquoise blue of the surrounding waters.

They flew low over the two locations near Sombrero light, quickly spotting the bottle markers they had left floating to identify them. There were no reefs near the surface at either of these places, and they found it impossible to see the cannon they had been diving on twenty-five feet beneath the surface.

Swinging the plane southwest, parallel to Seven Mile bridge and Bahia Honda bridge, they flew toward American Shoals light, twenty miles beyond, searching the water as they went for the pole marker which indicated Looe key. At last the reef appeared beneath them, the jagged coral fingers of its seaward side standing out plainly as they viewed it from the air.

Upon the surface, between two of these fingers, they saw a small boat, probably a fishing boat, for none of our party had planned to dive there that day. They had worked until well after sunset the previous night to raise a cannon from the Looe and tow it back to Marathon. Because of the dark, Ed had been forced to abandon one of Blue Heron's anchors, which had caught in the bottom coral. Now he looked for the buoy which he had left to mark it.

Then he realized that the fishing boat was on the wreck site. Circling the reef as he lost altitude, in order to have a better look at the area, he suddenly comprehended that the two men in the fishing boat were engaged in pulling up the long nylon line which he had left attached to his anchor. Three hundred feet of new nylon line! As he watched, one of the men took a knife from his pocket and, having pulled as much free line as possible into the boat, slashed it apart.

That was too much for Ed. With a muttered imprecation, he wheeled the Widgeon into a steep dive, leveled off in a quick approach to the calm waters off the reef, and before the startled fishermen knew what had happened, taxied up to their boat. As he cut his motors, he shouted indignantly, "Hey, that's my line you're taking. What's the idea?"

Salvagers there have been in the Florida keys for many centuries, both honest and dishonest. But that was probably the first time that two thieving fishermen, secure in the knowledge that there were no other boats in sight, were suddenly apprehended from the skies.

Sheepishly they handed over the severed line. They were too startled to find an excuse for their act. Putting on their motor, they quickly disappeared toward shore.

It was not until the second Sunday in February that the wind went down sufficiently for us to venture out. William and Clayton were with us for the weekend. We set out for Looe key early that morning, intending to anchor near the remains of the Looe. Captain Budd and Ed spent nearly an hour maneuvering Eryholme into a safe position, her stern anchored near the edge of the reefs, her bow headed out toward the Gulf Stream, so that it would be possible in case of emergency to pull up anchor and head seaward, away from the dangerous coral.

There was still a good breeze from the northeast, and the small, glass-bottomed boat bounced about in prodigious waves when we pulled her alongside to load her. Ed and the two boys piled into the boat and the three set out toward the reef to search for the cannon that marked the

Looe. William ran the outboard, while Ed and Clayton gazed down through the glass as they sprawled in the bottom of the boat.

They were back in almost no time. They had not found the Looe, but Ed had spotted a ship's bell lying in the deep crater of a coral head in another section of the reef. They had left a yellow wooden buoy bobbing over the spot while they returned to collect the air compressor, a diving outfit and a crowbar.

Captain Budd and I watched through binoculars as they returned to the reef. Soon Ed was overboard, his bright-blue canvas vest just visible through the surface of the water. Then all I could see was the rumps of the two boys as they watched their father through the glass bottom. Moments later the small boat leaned to the weight of the bell as it was secured to a line. Ed's head and shoulders emerged from the water, and he pulled himself into the boat.

Once the bell was aboard Eryholme, we examined it closely. It was slightly coated with pastel-hued sediment and sea growth. Coral had formed at the top, where an iron pin thrust through the ring was imbedded in a piece of black, moldering wood. Coral also encased the clapper, which was of iron and much deteriorated. We let it dry throughout the day, and then chipped off the protective covering that evening after we had returned to our dock.

The first lettering to appear was, "Gloria AO 1751." We had expected the bell would prove to have come from the Looe, but this date, seven years after the sinking of the British man-of-war, established that it had been aboard an unknown ship. Perhaps, we thought, we would find the ship's name on the bell. But when the lettering had been completely uncovered, it read only, "Soli Deo Gloria, AO 1751."

We could only guess that the bell had come from a

Spanish ship whose name, like that on the bell, was Soli Deo Gloria, for many Spanish ships carried similar religious names. There was little likehood that we could trace the identity of the vessel, for there are few available records of early Spanish shipping. We planned to go back another day to look for other indications of this mysterious ship.

Close by the dock at Bill Thompson's, where Eryholme was berthed, lay a heap of coral chunks which had been raised from the wreck of the Looe the previous summer and dumped for future investigation. Most of them bore reddish-brown stains, iron oxide from the cannon balls which they contained.

One morning soon after our recovery of the bell, Clayton was hammering out some of these cannon balls from the pile. Occasionally he would dash aboard Eryholme to show me a handwrought nail, some grapeshot, a bit of bone or some other evidence of the Looe's wreckage which he had found.

Finishing my housekeeping chores, I went out to join him and sit in the sun. I picked up a chunk which obviously contained two cannon balls and turned it over casually. On the other side I noticed the dull gleam of what appeared to be lead. There was something in this piece besides cannon balls. I called to Ed, who was experimenting with an air hammer to be used underwater. He turned the tool on the hunk of coral.

Two speedy cuts revealed a battered container. With a few more rackety strokes he freed a small, much-corroded teapot of dull metal. The rounded dome of the cover fitted smoothly and perfectly into the coral. It came out without a dent. The bottom, however, was crushed flat. The handle and the knob on the cover were missing; no doubt they were of bone or wood, long since disintegrated.

Later, after Ed had carefully straightened and restored the teapot, he turned it over to Mendel Peterson, who identified it as a rare pewter teapot of the Queen Anne period. He was delighted to add both it and the bronze bell to the growing marine-archeology collection at the Smithsonian. Ed and I like to think that the little teapot may very well have served Governor Clinton and his family while they were crossing the Atlantic on the Looe, en route to the governor's new job in the Colonies.

For nearly six weeks one norther followed another, and we were able to spend only three days diving, two of them at Looe key, where the water outside the reef seemed to clear more quickly. Only once were we able to dive on the wreck at Delta shoal, and then we found the sandy bottom so changed from these constant disturbances that we spent the whole day searching for the cannon which marked the wreck. There was no time left for exploration.

While Ed was busy equipping Eryholme and testing the new gear, he was more or less indifferent to the weather, but as day after day and week after week went by, his patience began to wear thin. We could not even spend our time cruising, for Eryholme, although a most comfortable boat when tied up at the dock, was too long and narrow to take to sea in rough weather. Not only did she roll uncomfortably, but her great expanse of glassed-in superstructure was dangerous in a big sea.

One morning while we lay at the dock, a strong wind beating at us from the southeast, two men appeared, asking for Ed, and disappeared into the wheelhouse with him. He introduced them to me, as they were taking their departure nearly two hours later, as Howard ("Webby") Webb and Robby Robinson, professional salvagers from Miami.

As they were disappearing down the dock, Ed said

to me in half-concealed excitement, "How would you like to go to the Bahamas?"

I was amazed; for if it was impossible to dive from Eryholme close to the Florida keys, how did he expect to take her across the Gulf Stream? And did he expect to find the water any less rough once he got there?

But when he had told me the story behind his question, I understood his enthusiasm.

The two men claimed to know positively of a wreck on the north Bahama banks, laden with brass cannon. There were at least fifteen cannon, perhaps many more, buried beneath the sand. They had a lead on a Bahamian who lived in West End, on Grand Bahama island, and who, they were certain, could guide us to the location.

It sounded too good to be true.

Old iron cannon were important in point of historical significance, and we had been happy to find them. If properly cared for, they possessed value for the collector. As scrap, they were worth very little. It appalled us to think of the hundreds of ancient guns which had been found by salvagers in these Florida waters and melted down for scrap during the war years. Not only because we grieved for the loss of the cannon, but because their disappearance also removed the only means of tracing the locations of many ancient wrecks.

Unlike the perishable iron cannon, which were usually abandoned once they had gone to the bottom, brass cannon were as highly prized several centuries ago as they are today, and every effort was made to salvage them at the time of their sinking. Consequently, today it is almost unheard of to find any on the Florida reefs. Not only would these brass cannon in the Bahamas be very valuable to the salvagers as old brass; they would be the choicest of finds for the Smithsonian collection as well as for ourselves, for their finely worked, gleaming barrels would be in as good condition today as when they had first disappeared into the sea.

There was even the possibility—Ed scarcely dared breathe it—that, if the brass cannon were of a certain period, they might contain platinum, which, unrecognized in the early days as a valuable metal, had often been used as an alloy with copper.

No wonder our imaginations were fired!

Ed also showed me a chart of the keys on which the two salvagers had indicated the locations of several piles of cannon balls or ballast stone, and of other areas where iron cannon had already been removed. These places were all further up the keys in the vicinity of Key Largo.

The temptation was great. On a beautiful Sunday morning in early March we left Marathon. There was just a pleasant breeze blowing from the east, and we decided the weather had at last given us a break. We intended to make our way slowly up Hawk channel, which leads between the keys and the line of outer reefs, investigating a few possible wreck sites on the way. The previous day Ed had reconnoitered this area from the air with the Widgeon. He had found that, while the water was murky off Marathon and north as far as Long key, from there on it appeared clear. If only it were smooth enough, we might be able to spot some of the wrecks.

We circled south under Seven Mile bridge and out into Hawk channel, where we set our course to the east-northeast. To our starboard was Sombrero light, guarding what was left of the ivory wreck and its companion wreck, from which had come the 1617 cannon. Not a thing could be seen beneath the milky green waters. Ahead of us was Washerwoman shoal, also marked on our chart as a spot where ancient cannon had been removed during World War II.

We passed Key Vaca and a string of other keys before coming in sight of Long Key bridge. There we commenced to see clearer water ahead. Opposite Matecumbe it was possible to make out the bottom fifteen feet below. About then, the wind, which had been blowing gently in from the sea, began to freshen, and light waves broke against our bow.

Ahead of us was the light that marked Hen and Chickens reef. In its vicinity, we had reason to believe, lay the wreckage of several ships from a Spanish silver fleet, which had gone down in the hurricane of 1733. Also in this same area, we had been told, was a pile of cannon balls lying on the sandy bottom in plain sight. It was here we hoped to make our first find.

Several fishing boats were making their slow way around the reef as we approached, but we found as we got nearer that the water so close to shore was too riley for us to distinguish the bottom. We changed course toward the open sea and, bucking ever-increasing waves, headed Eryholme toward a marker on a reef several miles out, which bordered the Gulf Stream. The cannon balls had been seen in a patch of white sand about a quarter mile inside the reef. We cruised near the reef and dropped the hook.

Ed and Captain Budd lowered the glass-bottomed boat—not without considerable trouble, due to the rough seas—and we started out. Ed ran the outboard and I stretched full length in the bottom of the boat, gazing through the glass. We bounced and cavorted over the waves. Every now and then the bow of the boat would come completely out of water, and then slap down upon a new wave with such a bang that I expected the Plexiglas bottom to splinter any moment beneath me.

Back and forth we plowed, from the reef to Eryholme and back again, each time steering for a different section and checking every little dark patch we could see against the white sand. But because our boat was set so low in the water, and because of the roughness of the waves, little could be seen except directly through the glass bottom. There I saw only wave-marked sand, patches of sparse sea grass, and, scattered over the sand at intervals, a sprinkling of small starfish. There was no coral, no shells, and I never saw a fish.

At last we gave up in despair. We would have to wait for calmer weather. We went back to Eryholme and headed her for the anchorage off Tavernier, a few miles away. There we spent the next two days tied up to a sunken barge in the middle of the shallow harbor while the wind howled in from the sea. Near us was tied Retriever, the battered workboat owned by our recent visitors, the salvagers Robby and Webby. It was half loaded with rusty iron girders which they had dived up from a sunken freighter at the edge of the Gulf Stream.

Our two days of idleness were memorable for long talk sessions with the two wreckers. We covered a multitude of subjects—the lore of underwater diving, various techniques for raising material from the bottom, for dynamiting and torch-burning under water, for frightening off barracuda when they became too thick and too curious, and for spotting wrecks from the surface.

But always the talk returned to the brass cannon on the banks of the north Bahama islands. If we would take Webby there aboard Eryholme to locate the cannon, they promised, Robby would then bring the salvage boat, with its heavy lifting equipment, to raise the cannon and transport them. We would take our share of the venture in brass cannon. At last it was agreed. We were to leave the following Monday from Fort Lauderdale for West End on Grand Bahama island. How we were to outwit our constant adversary, the wind, we did not figure. We could only hope.

As we pulled away from Retriever the next morning on our way to Fort Lauderdale, Ed shouted to Robby above the sound of the wind, "Have that junk boat ready to pull up the brass cannon when we find them." For Robby planned to stay on the job at Tavernier until he received a message from us to proceed to West End.

We had hoped to spend some time searching for two wreck sites off Key Largo on our way north, but the steady winds had made the seas too rough to spot anything on the bottom. We cruised over the streak of pale water which was White bank toward the outer reefs and the lighthouse tower on the Elbow, several miles beyond. This dangerous spot had received its name because here the reefs angle out into an unexpectedly sharp bend, which, in the days before navigational aids, was responsible for many a wreck.

Recently, at a salvage dock in Miami, Ed had seen an old anchor and some cannon which had been removed from this location. Like Webby and Robby, these salvagers had had no interest in what else might lie buried in the sand and coral close to the cannon. They had merely jerked up the guns and the anchor, leaving no visible evidence to mark the spot. We were in hopes that the wash of the heavy seas might have uncovered some other signs of the wreck that would betray its location, but we found the water too rough to do any searching in the small boat.

Interestingly, some of the cannon found on this site had borne markings similar to one found on the wreck at Delta shoal—the insignia of a tower, mark of the Amsterdam arsenal from which the Spanish purchased guns. Could this ship have been one of the same Spanish fleet which had scattered and sunk in the hurricane of 1733? we wondered.

Discouraged and more than a little seasick from our battle with the Gulf Stream, we finally headed for Angelfish creek, which cuts across the north end of Key Largo. From there we followed the Inland Waterway to Fort Lauderdale, loath to expose ourselves or Eryholme to further bouts with the disturbed seas.

At last the morning arrived when we had planned to leave for Grand Bahama island, eighty miles away. We did not even have to go on deck to know that the wind was still blowing strong, for Eryholme was rocking and tugging at her lines against the dock. A check with the weather man confirmed that it would be foolhardy to start out. Instead, Ed decided we should continue up the Inland Waterway to Palm Beach, which is almost directly opposite West End, our goal in the Bahamas.

At midnight two days later we set out to cross the Gulf Stream. Generally, both wind and sea are quieter at night, and the weather man had at last forecast slackening winds for the following day. With everything aboard well secured, and the crew fortified with doses of Dramamine, we left the shelter of the beaches and headed Eryholme east into the the turbulent waves. I gladly followed Ed's orders to go to bed, for the three men could easily handle the night watches.

They had already picked up Grand Bahama island when Ed called me at six the next morning. To my surprise, the wind had died completely. The surface of the water was glassy as we felt our way through the shallow channel leading into West End, on the inner side of the island. Looking down through thirty feet of water, I had the feeling that if I were to stick my finger in I would be able to touch bottom.

The men started taking soundings at fifteen feet, sure

that we were getting into water too shallow for our four-foot draft. Conch and other shells could be seen scattered over the bottom alongside large, fat starfish, very different from those I had seen in the Florida keys.

We felt our way cautiously in to the dock at West End. Now to find the man who would lead us to the brass cannon. If only we could get to the cannon site before this magic surface was broken up into rippling facets once more.

Webby went ashore and soon came back to tell us he had found his man. His name was Ceffy, and he owned a small bar ashore. Ceffy had insisted upon bringing along a companion. It would take about two hours for them to make arrangements, and they would be aboard at eleven thirty.

We waited impatiently. The glassy surface continued to hold. There wasn't even a stir of wind. I almost held my breath for fear I would break the charm.

At last the two black men arrived. Clad in ragged pants and undershirts and broken shoes, they were not very prepossessing. Ceffy was tall, with angular features and crooked yellow teeth. He talked in a peculiar singing nasal tone which was quite difficult to understand. I later found his speech to be typical of the island. His companion spoke scarcely at all.

We showed Ceffy our chart, asking him the approximate location of the cannon. The chart meant nothing to him. He could neither read nor write. He explained vaguely that the cannon lay somewhere north of us, across the shallow banks and well in from the line of reefs which mark their outer edge. Then he pointed to the northeast, where, he said, lay Mangrove key. We found it on our chart, thirty miles away, and set our course accordingly.

We were about to have our first lesson in bottom

navigation. For Ceffy, like most Bahamian fishermen, had been brought up to find his way about the banks without benefit of compass or other navigational aids. He knew the approximate locations of the surrounding islands, even though they were out of sight. He probably had a slight knowledge of how to use the moon and a few of the stars, gleaned from long nights at anchor on the native sloops.

But his chief means of finding his way was an uncanny familiarity with bottom contours. He knew where the sandy bottom had settled in wide windrows, where it was shallow and where it was deep. He knew which sections of the banks had a grassy bottom, and where these ended and the white sand began. When dark patches beneath the surface showed up ahead, he recognized them for what they were, either coral heads or bottom vegetation. He could find his way from the barest indications beneath the surface. This is possible only in certain areas of the world like the Bahamas, where the banks are relatively shallow and the water constantly clear.

It took us three hours to reach Mangrove cay, and then Ceffy indicated that we were to alter our course to slightly west of north. From here in, the course which Captain Budd traced on our chart, as he followed Ceffy's directions, looked like a corkscrew. Twenty miles farther on we changed course to east-northeast, while Ceffy, on the bow, glued his eyes to the bottom, searching for the edge of a certain bank. When he found it, we followed it west-northwest for several miles, then veered off to the southwest.

By this time the afternoon was well along, and the calm water was breaking into ripples which constantly became larger. No longer was it possible to see the marine life below.

Ceffy explained that we must stay on this last course until we reached the other side of the bank. We would find the cannon in deep water just beyond its edge, for it was here that he and a group of turtle fishermen had seen them, many years ago, near some caves formed by the edge of the bank.

This was encouraging. Webby began to take soundings. We were running in about two fathoms of water. Gradually it increased to two and a half and then, just as Ceffy had indicated, it dropped suddenly to four and a half.

This must be it! I peered over the side as Webby dropped the hook, half expecting to see the dull glow of the brass cannon we had come so far to find. The water was by now well covered with ripples, and the bottom was no longer visible. In every direction, as far as the eye could see, was an unbroken expanse of water. There wasn't a cay or a reef in sight. Beneath our boat, as I well knew, was a floor of white sand which stretched for miles—no coral, no rocks, scarcely any grass.

What a place to find a wreck! It looked hopeless. Nevertheless, having coming this far, it was no time to quit.

As soon as the glass-bottomed boat could be launched, Ed and Webby started out. They scoured the surrounding area for some time, then came back and took Ceffy along. It was getting dark by this time, and vision through the glass bottom was poor. At last they returned to Eryholme and dinner.

"Do you think we'll find them, Ceffy?" I inquired.

Ceffy looked vaguely across the water. "Oh, yassum, dey's got to be right here," he singsonged. "I'se seen dos barrels many times 'longside de boat."

We went to bed that night praying for a day of glassy water. Then we would chart the water, drop buoys for markers and systematically comb the surrounding area with both Eryholme and the little boat.

But early the next morning I felt Eryholme start to rock. The wind began its familiar song. When we arrived on deck, there was quite a sea rolling. It was no use.

We ate breakfast and disconsolately started back to West End. This time we took a direct compass course and found that, instead of the sixty-eight miles of hen tracks produced by Ceffy's bottom navigation, our return course was only twenty-eight miles long, leading us straight to the dock.

If we had any thoughts of going back for further search in that area, the wind's reappearance soon changed our minds. Eryholme remained tied up at the dock in West End for nearly two weeks while the anemometer registered velocities of from eighteen to forty knots. Webby finally left on the bi-weekly airplane to Palm Beach, to resume the less exciting but more remunerative business of diving up scrap iron in the keys. A few days later Ed and I flew to Miami, leaving Captain Budd and a Bahamian boatman to bring Eryholme back when the winds should let up sufficiently.

This was only the beginning of our search for the elusive brass cannon. We were to return many times in the coming years to these same banks, always with new clues. It was amazing how many different people had actually seen the heavy barrels, never twice in the same place, but unvaryingly somewhere within the confines of the northern banks.

3

o

o

o

It was the second week of April. Eryholme was anchored in the protection of Tavernier key, nearly halfway down the Florida keys. It was more than a month since we had set out to find the brass cannon on the Bahama banks. There had been plenty of time to pore over the old charts of the area which we had garnered. Time also to read of the exciting years when pirates lurked in every hidden cove; of French and English warships lying in wait to attack the stragglers of the silver fleets which Spain persistently sent through the narrow Florida straits; of the Indians who swarmed from the shores in their canoes to seize the cargoes of ships stranded upon the reefs; and of wreckers who gathered from the Bahamas and Key West to make capital of the losses of unfortunate shipowners.

This very spot where Eryholme was anchored had sheltered many of these marauders. The nearby islands of Tavernier and Rodriguez had been convenient landing places for their men and loot. Ashore, where a long string of buildings and countless neon signs now attested the modern town of Tavernier, savage Caloosa Indians once must have skulked, awaiting the unfortunate ship which storm or battle might bring to their shores.

For many years after Columbus's discovery of America, these long, low keys fringing the lower coastline of east Florida and continuing in a narrow chain to their terminus at Dry Tortugas were known only to the Indians who inhabited them, and to the unfortunate shipwreck survivors who became their victims. This was because no sailing ship dared venture very close to the dangerous line of reefs several miles offshore at the edge of the Gulf Stream. Eastward across the straits lay the Bahama islands, a collection of low cays and shallow banks which also warned off all shipping.

The Spanish did not at first realize the importance of these narrow straits. Their early journeys from the Old World had led them further south, to the environs of the Caribbean, which was soon dotted with their cities and fortifications and a network of sail paths set up between settlements by the early navigators.

It was not long before they found that the return route to Spain through the Straits of Florida was preferable, for it made best use of the prevailing southeast trade winds, as well as utilizing the aid of the powerful north-flowing Gulf Stream. The alternate routes to the east, either north of Hispaniola or diagonally through the channels of the lower Bahama islands, were made difficult because of almost constant winds from the east and southeast.

The Conquistadores had scarcely begun their exploring and colonizing efforts in the vicinity of Florida before the French began infiltrating into that area. Soon they were harassing their enemies, the Spanish, in the narrow confines of the straits. First French pirates and then French Regular Navy vessels made raids on the heavily laden merchant ships of the Spaniards as they pursued their slow way toward the homeland. Cargoes were filched, their crews killed or made captive, and the ships confiscated.

It did not take long for the brigands of other nations to discover the wealth to be gained by piracy on the Spanish ships. In self-defense the Spanish formed their merchant ships into organized convoys, protected by heavily armed galleons. These gathered at appointed times in the shelter of Havana harbor and then set out for Spain under the protection of their escorts. Thus one hazard was met.

But, as we have seen in the case of the Looe, the problem of successfully navigating the richly laden ships through these narrow straits, bordered on either side by coral reefs and shallow banks, was not so easily solved. Each nation—in fact, each navigator—guarded his handmade charts as a jealous chef would guard his recipes. There were no really accurate charts of these dangerous waters for many centuries, and every voyage was fraught with peril.

Even as late as 1763, Thomas Jefferys, geographer to His Majesty the King of England, wrote, in *An Account of the First Discovery and Natural History of Florida:*

> The navigation upon the extreme parts of Florida is remarkably dangerous, not only because it is within the course of the tradewinds but because the whole shore upon which the current for the most part sets is particularly low, flat, broken ground, and full nine leagues into the sea the water is in many places quite shallow, excepting some winding deep channels in several parts of it, which are the causes of frequent ship wrecks; for whenever a ship falls into one of these channels, she very rarely, if ever, gets clear of it; because, being deceived by the deep soundings, and having unwarily

entered so far within the banks, there is no returning by the same way, the vessel must inevitably be lost.

Storms and hurricanes did not lessen the problems of the navigator, for it was next to impossible to prevent the clumsy square-riggers from being carried off their course by heavy winds and currents, and there was no means of ascertaining their position when out of sight of land. Consequently, through the years, many of them never reached their destination, but piled up on the Florida reefs instead.

What struck me as remarkable was that over the years the Spanish did not seem to learn that hurricanes occur only in the summer and fall months, nor did they schedule their convoys to sail at other times of the year. Instead, almost invariably, they sailed from Havana in the summer months, calmly inviting disaster.

By 1565 Pedro Menéndez, the Spanish explorer, had driven the French out of northern Florida and had founded St. Augustine to protect his country's interests in that area. Spain now had some control over the waters to the north of the Florida straits.

Although the Florida Indians were always wary of the Spaniards, Menéndez did succeed in making friends with them by pretending to marry Doña Antonia, the sister of the Indian chief, Carlos. Throughout these early years this liaison paid off, for the Spaniards were able to enlist the aid of the natives in salvaging the wrecks along the coast and in establishing a limited amount of barter between Havana and the keys. But people of other nations were always at the mercy of the Indians.

Seemingly the Spanish should have had complete control of the Florida straits, for they had possession of Florida, Cuba and the Bahama islands to the east. But because they were interested only in the quick riches to be obtained in Mexico and South America at that time, they failed to secure their hold on the seemingly valueless lands of Florida and the Bahamas by colonizing them.

They did not realize their mistake until it was too late. Before their first century in the New World had passed, the Spaniards had given up attempting to settle the Florida peninsula, with the exception of St. Augustine and its environs. And by the beginning of the seventeenth century, the Bahamas had become a hiding place for the enemy ships of other nations, as well as pirate ships, both of which preyed upon Spanish shipping. From then on her ships were forced to run the gantlet of the straits without benefit of protection from either shore.

During these years, hundreds of ships, alone or in convoy, were destroyed on the reefs along the keys. Whenever they foundered in such shallow water that they could be reached from the surface, they were salvaged—not only by the Spaniards, who hurried from Havana to reclaim their property, but also by the Key Indians, who swarmed from the shores in their dugout canoes. These Indians were amazingly good skin divers, and anything of value which they could reach by skillful and successive dives of three to four minutes did not remain long on these wrecks.

Whatever they left was later picked over by roustabout pirate crews looking for salvage and, still later, by wreckers from the Bahamas and Key West, whose livelihood depended on what could be scrounged from the misfortunes of passing ships.

It was apparent that there could not be much left for the treasure seeker of the present day. Our greatest hope was that, with modern diving paraphernalia, we could stay down and work the wrecks an indefinite period of time. With the additional advantage of up-to-date salvage equipment and explosives, we would be able to penetrate formerly inaccessible wreckage. But, were it possible for us to locate them, our best opportunity would still be in diving on wrecks which had gone down in water so deep that they could not be reached at the time of their sinking.

Tracing back the story of shipwreck and salvage in those early centuries, I found records of fleet after fleet of plate ships which had been caught in hurricanes and cast up on these unfriendly shores. Early in the eighteenth century, two entire fleets were destroyed by hurricanes along the coast of Florida. The first large fleet met its end in the summer of 1715, off Cape Canaveral in the vicinity of Palm Beach. In 1733 a second plate fleet, under the command of Admiral Don Rodrigo de Torres, was lost, the ships being scattered all up and down the reefs off the Florida keys, from Key Largo to Key Vaca.

From his office in the Smithsonian, Mendel Peterson had sent us an old chart detailing the names of the ships under Admiral de Torres's command and the approximate locations where the original nineteen had foundered. One account of the disaster noted, "With the help sent from Havana the people were picked up, some silver was saved and the fifteen ruined ships were burned." * The Spaniards made it a practice to burn whatever superstructure remained above water once they had salvaged a wreck, so that it would not be seen by any of their enemies.

All up and down Los Martires, as the Spanish called the keys, English ships and the ships of other nations also found a watery grave. Today the names of many of the reefs commemorate these early warships which were lost.

* Another account, which contradicted the above to some extent, reported, "The ship La Florida of the fleet of don Rodrigo was shipwrecked on the shoals of Matecumbe. Fifty-five were drowned. Fourteen more ships foundered, three of which capsized, disappearing beneath the waves with all hands."

In 1695 the sixty-gun H.M.S. Winchester, returning from a raid on Cap Haitien with two other ships, was wrecked in a storm off Key Largo. Some years after, as we already know, the H.M.S. Looe and the snow which accompanied her foundered on what is now Looe key, and the brig Ledbury sank in a hurricane near Elliott key. Ledbury reef is northeast of the key. In 1770 the Carysfort was wrecked on what is now Carysfort reef; and in 1822 the U.S.S. Alligator, having pursued eight pirate vessels and taken five of them, struck and sank on the reef now marked by Alligator Reef light.

As late as 1850 there were only three aids to navigation in the Florida keys. Lighthouses were placed on Cape Florida in 1827, and at Key West in 1823. A light boat, which could not be depended on to be on its exact station, marked Carysfort reef until 1852, when it was replaced by a 110-foot lighthouse.

Even with these three markers, ships continued to pile up on the reefs throughout the nineteenth century, aided and abetted, it was said, by wreckers from the thriving island community of Key West, where Federal courts had been established to administer the law of wreck and salvage. These courts reached the peak of their activity during the ten years from 1850 to 1860, when it is recorded that 499 vessels were salvaged.

By the time we had finished studying these accounts and poring over copies of old English, Spanish, French and Dutch maps which Pete had obtained for us from the files of the Library of Congress, we were steaming with impatience to continue our explorations. But still the wind continued to blow.

We now realized that we were every bit as handicapped with Eryholme as we would have been with Blue Heron, but for different reasons. Eryholme was not designed to weather the heavy seas which we would be called upon to face many times in the future, as we pursued our explorations to the Bahamas and the Caribbean islands. If we seriously intended to continue this historical salvage, we must have more adequate equipment.

So I was not surprised when, at breakfast one windy morning, Ed said, "Let's take the bus up to Miami and look at boats. Perhaps we can find a larger sailboat than Blue Heron that would do the work for us. At least we would have a ship we could go to sea in when the wind is blowing. That's more than we can do with this cockleshell."

He was still thinking sails, for he had never been won over to the lure of high-powered diesel cruisers. So, later that morning, when we explained our problem to our yacht broker in Miami, it was sailboats we asked to see. We spent the day looking at sail, but none seemed to meet our needs. Toward the end of the day we were returning from inspecting a boat in Coconut Grove, south of Miami, when our discouraged companion had a hunch.

"There's a sixty-five-foot diesel trawler near here," he said dubiously. "The owner finished her up from a shrimp-boat hull built at Miami Shipbuilding last year."

We weren't at all impressed. We were looking for sail. But we allowed ourselves to be driven to a nearby dock where lay Sea Diver, then known as St. Christopher.

There she sat, solid and sturdy, all sixty-five feet of her; she was eighteen feet in the beam, with a high, straight bow that sloped steeply toward the aft deck. The cabin was all shrimp boat. To this day, whenever I think of her, I am reminded of the early Popeye cartoons, for there wasn't a straight line in her entire construction. The deck sloped, the pilothouse curved, the window frames were all angles, the door frames conformed to the sloping deck and roof, and everything inside had been constructed accordingly.

But I didn't see all this with my first look. I saw only a typical shrimp boat, dressed up with an extra-tall mast and radio antennae, a low cabin top on the aft deck, and a deep, wide seat built across the fourteen-foot stern. She was painted with a wide band of gray-blue around the bulwarks, and the wooden deck was gray. The rest of her was white.

We went aboard. She seemed tremendous after the close quarters of Blue Heron, and the narrow beam of Eryholme. The deckhouse was cut up into several small cubicles in typical shrimp-boat fashion—a wheelhouse forward; the captain's quarters at center, furnished with a small table, bunk and stool; an adjoining head; and a small, badly arranged galley aft.

But there was a stainless-steel electric refrigerator, and a small stainless-steel sink. In the wheelhouse there were an automatic pilot; a very good seventy-five-watt, ten-channel radio receiver and transmitter; and an RCA radio direction finder, in addition to a large, clearly readable compass. I could see that there was also room to install the myriad of other navigational aids and instruments which were Ed's delight.

We walked forward up the sloping deck and found a sturdy electric winch to haul the 150-pound anchor and its hundred fathoms of chain. This immediately made a hit with two sailboat people who were used to hauling in the anchor with a hand winch. We could also see the possibilities of the six-foot pulpit that extended high into the air from the bow, wonderful for cruising in unknown waters and for searching. This brought to Ed's mind the advantages of a crow's-nest for this same purpose. He examined the tall mast, considering the feasibility of installing one there.

At the rear of the deckhouse, where the heavy steel mast towered upward, was a hatch to the engine room and an electric hydraulic elevator designed to carry heavy objects up from below. There was also a power winch driven from the main engine, designed to handle the steel boom attached to the mast and extending to the stern of the boat. This was the customary shrimp-boat gear for handling nets and catch. Heavy standing rigging supported the mast to port and starboard. Here was the perfect rig for hauling cannon off the ocean floor, or for swinging overboard the heavy wooden boat which sat upon the raised deck of the aft cabins.

We went down a wide, roomy ladder through the companionway on the aft deck, to the place where the shrimp hold would ordinarily be. We found ourselves in a large master cabin, twelve-by-eighteen feet, furnished with two bunks, a chest of drawers, writing desk and dressing table. It opened forward into a passageway, on either side of which was a smaller stateroom, and a large head with a roomy shower stall and generous linen locker. All three cabins had a great deal of locker space. Aft of the master cabin was a lazaret with an amazing amount of storage room, extending clear to the stern planking.

A door opened from the passageway into a light, spacious engine room in the heart of the ship. What an engine! It was an eight-cylinder Caterpillar diesel rated at 150 to 300 horsepower, and it filled the center of the engine room. On either side were four large storage tanks for fuel oil, with a total capacity of sixteen hundred gallons. A large workbench, two sets of storage batteries, small engines for various purposes, and a hot-water tank filled the extra space.

Forward of the engine room we found the crew quarters. These had been retained as in the original shrimp-boat design, with bunks for four men, an adjoining head and a large locker. A steep ladder led upward to the forward deck.

As we progressed through this capacious, well-designed boat, I could feel a mounting sense of excitement. A similar feeling transmitted itself to me from Ed. Here was everything we needed for our purpose. It only lacked the trim lines and billowing canvas of our favorite sail.

After spending a tense, exciting evening weighing the pros and cons of sail versus power, we went back the next morning to take another look at the trawler. As I had sensed it would, right from the beginning, the highly practical, efficient shrimp boat with the Caterpillar diesel won out. Within a matter of days we were the enthusiastic owners of Sea Diver, renamed to symbolize her new purpose.

Sea Diver spent the next two weeks in a shipyard in Miami, undergoing some structural changes we felt necessary to adapt the boat to our needs. The many little cut-up rooms of the deck cabin were replaced by a single large, airy room separated into three sections by four-foot-high partitions—a pilothouse, a lounge with folding table and two bunks, and a galley aft. This would allow the free circulation of air so essential to operations in southern climates. It would also make it possible, when we were cruising short-handed, to combine the functions of wheelhouse, galley and lounge. It would be of particular value at night, as one person could be on duty with the help of the autopilot, while his relief slept nearby, ready to help or take over if the occasion demanded.

The new cabin was paneled in natural pine. The heavy plank table was flanked by two combination seat-bunks covered with durable green nylon. A small ship model on one wall and a glass-covered display case for some of the more interesting objects which we had re-covered from the ocean bottom lent atmosphere. Split-bamboo shades covered the windows, shutting out the hot sun rays but allowing air to pass through.

A metal crow's-nest was added thirty-five feet up the mast, with a welded-metal ladder leading to it. Lockers were built along the starboard side of the deckhouse, for storing the diving equipment. And davits were placed astern, where the glass-bottomed boat could be carried and dropped into the water at a moment's notice, in the protection of the larger boat.

4

o

o

o

Old King Neptune must have set out in 1952 with the avowed intention of discouraging us from our purpose. Not only did the winds continue to blow and the seas to churn up sand and powdered shell until it was impossible to see the bottom, but on our very first trip from the shipyard in Miami we had a most unexpected accident.

We had no crew aboard, just another couple and ourselves. We had been combing the waters within the reefs off Key Largo, searching an area where we had been told cannon had been seen on the bottom. Now it was nearly noon, and we realized that, if we were to get to Marathon that night, we would have to leave immediately. We could make better time by cutting between the reefs and taking the outside route bordering the Gulf Stream than by following the intricacies of Hawk channel, close to the keys.

Checking the chart, we found that we could safely set a course through the reefs and out to sea by passing just south of a red nun buoy "C," which served to mark the division between the Gulf Stream deeps outside and the shallower waters behind the reefs. I took my turn at the wheel while the others went below.

A half hour later, as Sea Diver approached the red nun, I studied the chart to check our position, then disengaged the automatic pilot and took hold of the wheel to guide the boat past the marker. The chart showed a depth of eighteen feet from Sea Diver's position south of the marker to the deeper water outside the line of reefs. I headed the boat in this direction about fifty feet from the marker.

Suddenly Sea Diver was brought to a violent stop. We had hit something so solid that I could feel the deck under my feet assume an abrupt slant as the bow came out of the water. I immediately threw the engine into neutral, and as I leaned out of the door to see what we had hit, large and small pieces of wood from the bottom of the boat floated aft. Ed came running, and so did the others on board.

Sea Diver had by now drifted off the obstruction, and we were floating clear. From the bow we could just make out the angular shape of some sort of submerged metal framework, lying with its top about three feet beneath the surface.

We dropped anchor and Ed hurried below decks to set the pumps going. When he returned to where we were hanging over the starboard rail, attempting to make out what we had hit, he reported that there were no signs of damage inside the hull, as far as he could see, and that the boat did not seem to be taking on an undue amount of water.

He set the air compressor going and got into his diving gear, for he wanted to have a look at the damage to the outside of the hull. He had been overboard only a brief interval when he returned to the boarding ladder and asked for a crowbar.

"There's a lot of loose wood hanging from the worm-shoe," he said, "and some big bolts sticking out."

He worked beneath the boat for some time, chiseling off splinters of the hull, which bobbed to the surface and floated off. When he had completed the job, he handed up the crowbar and then swam toward the obstacle which we had hit, now a hundred feet off our port bow.

We were relieved to hear, upon his return, that the damage was apparently superficial. The heavy wood stem had been stripped partially from the bow, and the keel was gouged the whole length of the boat, but the hull itself seemed to be intact. We might expect some leakage through sprung seams, he said, but otherwise it would be safe for us to go on.

The obstruction which we had hit was an iron tripod marker which had evidently been jettisoned in these waters when the red nun was installed. Ed stormed at the carelessness of a government agency that would install a new marker without removing or destroying the old one, or at least indicating the location on the official charts as a hazard to navigation.

We decided then and there that our sturdy shrimp boat, elegant or not, was really built to take it. She had survived her first testing. However, as the days went by, we found that she was taking on more than the normal amount of water in her bilges, and we finally returned to the shipyard in Miami to have her hauled. A new worm-shoe and some paint and calking soon had her as good as ever.

When we started forth again a few days later, we had two worth-while additions aboard the Sea Diver. The Bendix fathometer which Ed had ordered some time previously had been installed and was now ready to chart the exact depths of the waters which we would traverse upon our voyages, and be of aid when we were coming into strange ports at night, or when approaching an unknown shore. And we knew from previous experience on the shallow Bahama banks that, with no land in sight, the fathometer would help us to fix our approximate location by allowing us to compare actual water depths with those marked on the chart.

This time we also had a competent new crew member —Robby Robinson, the salvager, who had joined us to assist with the diving and the deck work. Unfortunately, during the stormy weather of the past month, he and Webby had sunk their salvage boat, Retriever, upon one of the reefs near Key Largo, where they had been working. It now reposed on the bottom, awaiting salvage in its turn; and Robby, who had appeared at the shipyard one day, had been easily talked into joining us.

The record of the following two months was one of frustration and disappointment, spiced with just enough success to keep us going. Day after day we met with high winds and consequent murky water. In spite of a seaworthy boat, we still found ourselves tied up at docks or anchored in the shelter of reefs and islands, for it was impossible to locate anything on the bottom as long as the water around the reefs was so roiled.

It was particularly aggravating because, soon after we had left the shipyard, Mendel Peterson and his wife joined us for a two-week period. The Smithsonian curator, who had kept us supplied all year with a constant bombardment of charts and records, was as eager as we to locate some of the old wrecks and to dive upon them. He had great plans for developing the marine-archeology section at the Smithsonian, which had had its inception the previous year with the discovery of the Looe and the other wrecks near Marathon.

Together, he and Ed had worked out an arrangement whereby, with Pete's knowledge and help, Sea Diver would be used to search for and dive upon whatever wrecks the two men might consider of historical value. Pete planned to spend his vacations and as much additional time as was necessary collecting relics from these discoveries, to augment those from the previous expedition, which had already created a tremendous interest among the thousands who had viewed them in the rotunda of the Smithsonian.

Actually, Pete was the complete answer to what all directors of modern museums are looking for. He was young and enthusiastic, an inveterate collector of everything, but especially interested in coins and old armament. His head was packed with an impressive fund of historical facts and figures, which he produced freely and easily upon demand. In addition, we found him to be a willing and helpful crew member and a most entertaining companion.

Nellie, his plump, pretty wife, a member of the staff of the Museum of Natural History at the Smithsonian, where she spent her days classifying sea life, made the final perfect member of our crew, for in addition to her other talents she liked to cook.

Two unsuccessful efforts to explore the reefs off Key Largo in high winds proved the futility of trying to do any searching until the seas calmed, so we headed Sea Diver for Marathon and spent the next few days at Bill Thompson's dock, chafing at our ill luck. Pete and Ed were indeed discouraged, for Pete's allotment of time was fast dwindling away. Their spirits brightened, however, when Ed received a phone call from a diving acquaintance, Jack

Brown. He had located some cannon on a reef off Key West and wanted Ed to join him with our equipment. Jack had only his "duck," an amphibious trucklike vehicle, relic of the war years, which he was using to work the reefs, he said.

He explained that he had need of a few old cannon barrels to add interest to an aquarium he was planning to open in the keys. He did not know the vintage of the wreck, but from the amount of coral on one of the cannon, which could be seen on the bottom, it was a very old one. He was not interested in the smaller artifacts that might also be a part of the wreck, he said; once the cannon had been raised, he was willing to turn over the remainder of the salvage to us. He assured Ed that, although the wind was strong in that vicinity, and the water was rough, it was also clear, so that it was possible to work on the reefs.

That was enough to give new hope and enthusiasm to Pete and Ed. We set out at the crack of dawn the next day, rolling in the big waves which hit us broadside as we paralleled the string of islands leading westward toward Key West. By the time we arrived at the Gulf dock where we planned to meet Jack, the wind had picked up to twenty-five knots, and the sea was much too rough to think of approaching the reefs that afternoon.

We had been in only a short time when Jack appeared, with the news that he had raised and brought ashore three cannon—a small swivel gun, a carronade and a six-foot heavy barrel. He was eager to have Pete identify them. He took the two men crosstown in his car to the spot on the opposite shore where the "duck" was based.

When Ed and Pete returned, they were quite excited at the prospects. It appeared that Jack had located a British ship whose armament indicated that it was late eighteenth century. Pete said that, oddly enough, the bore of the large cannon went only partway through the barrel and ended in a big air bubble. He figured that it must have been carried as ballast on the ship after it had been rejected for other use, upon the discovery of the flaw in the metal.

We were to meet Jack's party and his "duck" at Sambo reef, some six miles offshore from Key West, the following morning. We found the water behind the reefs reasonably calm so early in the day, but once we had rounded the last buoy and turned east to follow the outer edge of the reefs, we encountered a fairly rough sea. From the distant shore we could see Jack's "duck" making its way toward the reef, and we slowed our approach, timing our arrival to correspond with his in order to ascertain the exact location of the wreck.

We were hardly settled, and Pete and Ed returned from looking over the bottom, when Jack hailed us from the "duck," which was anchored a scant fifty feet away. We would have to move Sea Diver, he informed us, for he was going to set off a charge of dynamite to loosen the visible cannon and cannon balls from the coral. This was discouraging, but necessary, we realized, and after some careful jockeying, Sea Diver was eased away from the reef. We waited for the dynamite sticks to be placed.

When Ed saw the amount of dynamite Jack intended to use, he was appalled. "It'll blow the whole wreck to Kingdom come," he said.

But Jack wanted to be sure of accomplishing the job. We waited for the muffled boom of the underwater explosion and the sharp, hard impact against the bottom of the boat. Then we spent another hour returning Sea Diver to her original position in waters now roiled and muddy from the explosion. We might as well have skipped the whole procedure, for when our boat was once more in place, the men found the water still so murky that it was impossible to distinguish anything below.

We gave up for the day, but hurried back at daybreak the next morning to get Sea Diver placed before the wind should come up. To our joy the surface was calm and the water on the reef clear and transparent.

Robby was the first to go overboard. He had been down only a few minutes when he appeared suddenly at the foot of the ladder, pulling off the face mask as he emerged. His face registered bewilderment and surprise.

"You should see what that dynamite has done," he shouted in his excitement. "The reef is all on a slant, and there's a hole right through the bottom. I'd have disappeared completely out of sight if I'd ever stepped into it. There's the strangest look to everything down there."

He insisted that Ed put on the mask and go down. Ed disappeared down the ladder. He was gone for a long time, but when he came back his face wore the same bewilderment.

"You feel as if the whole bottom is topsy-turvy," he said. "It looks as if that explosion had turned the reef right up on its side."

By this time, Pete had hooked up another mask and was hurrying over the side to have a look at this amazing phenomenon. Ed followed him down.

Nellie and Robby and I waited impatiently for them to reappear. When their two heads bobbed out of the water once more, they could hardly wait to remove their masks.

"What's wrong with things?" Pete queried. "There's a huge pile of rubble down there, but I didn't see any steep cliffs or yawning chasms."

Ed started to argue with him, then was struck with a sudden thought.

"Here, let me see that mask again," he said. He picked up the mask he had just removed and examined it carefully, holding it up to the light.

"Here's our trouble," he exclaimed. "Look at the plastic in this mask. It's all warped out of shape. Someone's left it in the sun."

Jack and his party had arrived by this time, and the "duck" was anchored near us. The men returned to the bottom, where they helped rig tackle to the cannon which had been freed by the blast, so that they could be raised on the "duck." By afternoon Jack was ready to set out for shore, the overloaded duck listing heavily to port, staggering through the big seas with its burden of three cannon, a pile of heavy cannon balls and five people. We watched its slow progress toward shore, fascinated, expecting any moment to see it swamped. To our relief, it reached the quieter waters near shore without mishap.

We stayed to salvage what we could, hoping to find some smaller objects which would give us further clues to the identity of the wreck. At last I was able to secure a mask and air hose long enough to go down for a look. The bottom was indeed a shambles. Broken coral and rubble lay in piles, punctuated with a scattering of cannon balls. A large gun barrel lay in two pieces, broken apart by the blast, and the mouth of a second cannon protruded from a heap of coral, its muzzle showing black against the surroundings, for the coral crust had been cracked away from it by the concussion.

The three men worked the remainder of the afternoon to free this cannon and bring it to the surface. It was quite a different shape from the others, and when we finally had it on deck and had removed the coral from its back, we discovered that it bore the date of 1657. Pete said that the barrel was Spanish.

Thus we learned that beneath the wreck of the English ship which had gone down nearly two hundred years ago, lay the remains of a Spanish ship which had struck this same dangerous reef at least a century earlier. We later came to realize that this was not surprising, for wherever reefs thrust themselves into the sea beyond their fellows, or strong currents carry ships off their course, it is not uncommon to find more than one wreck.

We went out to Sambo reef again the next morning, hoping to bring up some of the smaller objects, although Ed said that without some sort of dredging equipment to move the rubble, there was little chance of finding much.

He and Robby went down with the metal detector. They had not been working long when they surfaced, complaining of headaches and nausea. It was an extremely hot day, and we figured that the heat, plus fatigue from the efforts of the past days, had combined to upset them.

So while they stretched out on the shady side of the deck, Pete put on one of the masks and, picking up the detector, went down to continue the search. He was back in a short time, also feeling sick.

With his return, all endeavor came to a halt. The three men lay about the deck, wondering what had happened to them. When they had recovered sufficiently to get the anchors aboard, we headed back to our dock in Key West, where they spent the remainder of the day resting quietly in their bunks. Their conclusion was that the air compressor had picked up exhaust fumes from the generator, and had pumped the poisonous air down through the hoses into the face masks. No one had thought of such a contingency when the portable compressor had been set down in a sheltered part of the deck, where there was no circulation of air to carry off the fumes. It was a lesson none of us would forget.

A few days later, Sea Diver was back at her dock in Marathon. Pete and Nellie had left for home; and Ed, Robby and I, with Bill and Ethel Thompson, were about to start out on an exploring trip to the ivory wreck. As soon as Robby had finished filling the two gasoline barrels on top of the deckhouse, we would be ready to take off.

Ethel and I were chatting on the aft deck when we heard a muffled shout forward. I looked up just in time to see Robby tumble head first from the deckhouse roof. He struck the outer rail as he fell and crumpled on the deck. We rushed to him to find him grimacing with pain as he tried unsuccessfully to rise. An hour later our unfortunate helper was on his way to a hospital in Miami. Later that day we learned that Robby had broken three ribs, close to the spine, and would be laid up for some time. So, minus our helper, we left Marathon that evening and anchored behind Little Sister island, where we would be only a short distance from the wreck site and could make an early start the next morning.

We found the location without any difficulty, thanks to Bill's knowledge of the bottom in this area. The two men first made a thorough search of the now-familiar spot with the metal detector. They had worked out quite a system for their explorations, Ed swimming along with the detector while Bill followed behind, marking each spot that showed the presence of metal with a brick. When they had thus charted many places, they started uncovering them one by one, digging into the sand with a crowbar, or if they suspected something fragile, scooping it out with their bare hands.

In the course of their survey they came across an ivory tusk which had been overlooked the year before. They also brought up the bronze shoulder plates from two old muskets. All that could be found of the guns themselves were two blackened, hollow, cylindrical sticks of coral sand, for the metal barrels of the guns had completely disintegrated due to the corrosive action of the salt water over the years. The detector also led them to a brass door lock and, surprisingly, nearby, a large, heavy key.

The second day, Bill climbed on deck from a trip to the bottom, and after he had removed his face mask, reached into his breast pocket and carefully brought forth a small piece of coral. He showed it to Ethel and me proudly.

"I'm pretty sure it's something valuable—maybe a piece of jewelry," he said. "The metal detector picked it up, and I dug it out from deep down in the sand with my hands. After I discovered how small it was, I didn't dare use any digging tools."

He placed it in a china cup from the galley and poured acetic acid over it. This would dissolve the coral composition covering it without damaging the object itself, he said. All through our lunch hour we eyed it curiously. What would it prove to be?

By late afternoon, when we were on our way back to Marathon, Bill could wait no longer to find out. Carefully tapping at the coral with the handle of a screw driver, and rubbing it with his fingers to loosen it, he finally succeeded in uncovering the object which it enclosed.

To his chagrin and our unkind laughter, it turned out to be the key of a Spam can, tightly wound with a strip of tin, as it had come from the can. We thus learned that under salutary conditions it does not take very long for coral encrustation to form on a metal object underwater.

Indeed, Ed's metal detector worked so successfully that much of the time the men found themselves digging beneath the sand only to uncover a variety of beer cans discarded by thirsty fishermen as they trolled about the reef in their boats. Unfortunately, there was no dial on the detector which would indicate "gold," "silver," "iron" or just "tin cans," and it was imperative to examine each separate indication for fear of missing something of value.

During the previous month, while Pete was with us, he and Ed had been negotiating with the Navy to obtain the loan of a magnetometer-gradiometer. This instrument had been developed during World War II to aid in the detection of wrecked ships and other equipment which had gone to the bottom. It was a very sensitive device, with much greater power than the metal detector we had been using. The hand detector which Ed had contrived performed only within a few feet of an object, whereas Ed hoped this new instrument would pick up the presence of wrecks on the bottom when towed on the surface of the water behind Sea Diver.

The magnetometer finally arrived, a four-foot-long cylindrical aluminum tube, larger at one end than at the other. There was also an indicator box, its face dotted with dials and switches. Ed and Bill spent several days attempting to put it in adjustment. It was a very delicate instrument, one which the Navy technicians had long ago given up in despair, we learned later. No doubt that is why they were so willing to let Ed experiment with it. Had he known then what he knows so well today, he probably would have shipped it right back to them.

I should have no reason for complaint; I was only an interested bystander. But of all the things that have tried my patience throughout our years of diving, that magnetometer threatened it most.

In the first place, the weather was stifling hot that summer. Without the magnetometer to delay us, we would have been at sea, where, even though the temperature was high, the winds would have served to evaporate the sticky perspiration which enveloped us constantly at the dock. With the sun beating down upon her painted decks, Sea Diver became unbearable. At night it was impossible for Ed and me to sleep in our bunks below decks; yet when we moved to the wide seat on the aft deck, we were soon driven below again by swarms of pesky mosquitoes. Often we slept on the floor of our cabin to catch the least little stir of air.

The hot wind blew ceaselessly, now and then stepped up by sudden squalls, sweeping in from the sea. Waterspouts moved swiftly across the troubled surface of Florida bay. One night a waterspout passed so close to Sea Diver that every movable object upon her decks was carried off into the harbor.

I welcomed the day when Ed at last proclaimed the magnetometer ready to be tested. With Bill and Ethel accompanying us, we headed for the ivory wreck, and soon had the long tubular instrument overboard, lashed to the bottom of a rubber life raft. As we towed it around the wreck area within cable length of Sea Diver, the boxlike indicator on deck registered some very definite reactions.

Marking one of the spots where they had received an indication, Ed and Bill dove upon it, and after digging deep in the sand, came upon a cannon. It was a new location, some distance from where we had worked before. They decided to raise the cannon and disappeared underwater with crowbars and hauling chain. Ethel and I went overboard for a swim and watched them through our face plates as they wrestled with their crowbars to free the cannon from the sand.

We were back on deck when Ed came up to ask for a hoe. While he was waiting at the foot of the boarding ladder, Bill's head popped up beside him.

"What do you suppose it is?" he said to Ed as he pulled the mask away from his face.

"Looks to me as if it might be a silver bar," Ed replied.

"It's certainly buried deep enough under that old cannon. Must be several hundred years old." The two men again disappeared beneath the surface, and their bubbles trailed across the water toward the spot where they had been digging.

Ethel and I looked at each other in great excitement. Had they really come across some early treasure? Perhaps the magnetometer was worth all the time and trouble.

A little later Bill came up again to see if we could find him some gloves. His hands were raw and bleeding.

"We're having a devil of a time digging out that bar," he said. "But it looks promising." His eyes beamed happily at us as he sank once more beneath the surface.

Some time later, when both men appeared at the foot of the ladder and handed up a metal bar, about 12 by 4 by 1½ inches, into our waiting hands, we were as excited as they. The bar was extremely heavy for its size and black with corrosion. When Bill knocked off a quarter inch of the crumbling outer layer from one side, a silver-gray metal was revealed which appeared to be hand-hammered. It gave a solid ring when struck.

The four of us examined it minutely, passing it from hand to hand. Then Ed brought a magnet from the engine room. With great ceremony he held it over the bar. It was attracted to the magnet. Our hopes faded, for silver would not respond to such a test. Soon after, the section of silvery metal which was exposed to the air began to turn a red-brown. Yes, it was iron, and it wasn't very old.

The iron bar remained a puzzle for some time to come. How had it arrived in the location where they had found it, deep beneath a cannon which must have lain there close to three hundred years? Some time later, Bill ascertained that metal plates of similar size had been used in the construction of the Overseas highway bridges. Perhaps some fisherman had used the bar as an anchor for a crawfish trap, and it had hooked under the cannon and broken free from its line, gradually sinking into the sand beneath it.

We spent the remainder of the month experimenting with the magnetometer, which we now familiarly called "Maggie." When the weather allowed, we took our temperamental partner out to sea, towing her both on the surface and below, lashed to a thick wooden plank at the end of a heavy line. However, there were many days when our prima donna flatly refused to perform, and then Ed and Bill worked patiently ashore to restore her to a more co-operative attitude, while I sulked in the heat and wished I had never seen her.

We made one final effort at Looe key, hoping, with the aid of "Maggie," to locate the remains of the Spanish snow which had been wrecked the same night as the British Looe, and also the mysterious vessel from which had come the bell marked "Soli Deo Gloria." We wondered if we might also come across other wrecks, for we knew that Looe key had proved fatal to many ships in past centuries.

We arrived there just before dark on a calm, lovely evening, and anchored behind the key, ready to search the outside of the reef early the next day. But by morning it was blowing hard, and breakers were rolling across the reef from the sea. It was impossible to approach any closer to the jagged coral with Sea Diver. By afternoon the wind was even higher.

We waited over the second night, vainly hoping that the next day would be better. Instead, the wind became constantly stronger. On the afternoon of the second day we headed back to Marathon through heavy rain squalls and wind up to fifty knots. Back at Bill's dock that night, the wind held steady at fifty with squalls of even higher velocity.

The weather man on our radio said this was hurricane-breeding weather—high barometer, hot and sticky air, dull red sunsets and hundreds of squalls constantly building up at sea. All that was needed was a circular movement blowing into a low-pressure area to turn the squalls into a full-fledged hurricane.

Fortunately the hurricane did not develop, but the disturbed weather continued for the duration of our stay. Sea Diver was finally put up for the rest of the season without our getting another opportunity to go out to the reefs. King Neptune had won the first bout in his battle to protect his own. But we were not discouraged. We had big plans for the coming year.

5

o

o

o

Shortly after our return to Florida in February, 1953, we made our first dive on a wreck which, even today, after several years of exploring, still stands out in my mind as the most picturesque, the richest and most interesting of all the old wrecks near the Florida keys which it has been our privilege to investigate.

Although our efforts of the previous year had produced relatively little in actual articles recovered, or even in wrecks discovered, we had added a great deal to our knowledge. We felt that we now knew how to go about locating the elusive remains of long-sunken ships. Once having found them, we certainly had improved our techniques of salvaging them. These things we had learned mostly by trial and error, always an expensive procedure in both time and equipment, but there were no textbooks to enlighten us on the subject.

We had also learned enough about the weather to realize that it is impossible to prognosticate what may be expected. We had been harried with strong winds from start to finish during the previous year. Unpredictably, it had blown just as hard in the usually calm late spring and early summer months as in the winter.

Sea Diver had undergone considerable transformation since we had left her in Miami, for in the brief weeks we had used her following her purchase, we had discovered the need of many additions for our comfort and convenience. Rolling chocks had been installed on both sides of the hull, for while the time-tested shrimp boat, with its six-foot draft and rounded bottom, is a most seaworthy design, it has, as we soon found out, a great tendency to roll.

I was the proud custodian of a commodious stainless-steel freezer, which had been placed just outside the galley door on the deck. It was encased in a plywood chest to protect it from sun and weather. And, remembering our discomfort during the extreme heat in Marathon the previous summer, Ed had had a number of ventilators and power-operated fans installed, in addition to an air-conditioning system in the aft cabins below decks. Now we could look forward to a good night's sleep no matter how hot the weather.

These were the things of immediate interest to me. Ed bragged that, with the addition of extra bilge pumps, Sea Diver could now rid herself of 13,500 gallons of sea water per hour. The three pumps now on board could be started separately or run together. As he had also installed a high-pressure jetting pump, which would pump six thousand gallons per hour, to be used for moving sand on the bottom, he felt that we were more than adequately prepared against foundering at sea.

With the installation of three more water tanks, Sea Diver now had a total capacity of thirteen hundred gallons of fresh water. This would take care of all our needs for long periods at sea, and even allow for shower baths and quantities of fresh water to rinse the salt from our diving equipment.

Ed had installed a loran, a long-range radio air-navigation instrument developed during the war, in the wheelhouse. Although it was used chiefly in airplanes at that time, Ed figured it would be helpful in our searches of waters beyond the sight of land, because with it we would be able to pinpoint a spot and return to it within very close limits. This instrument would augment the Bendix fathometer installed the previous year.

The diving paraphernalia now included a twelve-cubic-foot air compressor, its 120-pound capacity enabling us to use air-driven tools either on board or underwater, as well as providing ample air for three divers at one time. Ed had put considerable thought into choosing and arranging his diving equipment so that it could be put into operation quickly, with a minimum crew. The air hoses had been wound on reels so that, after attaching the diving mask, the diver could go overboard and without assistance from the deck pull out any length of hose he might require up to two hundred feet. He could reach a still greater distance by connecting the hose from the permanent reel on deck to a second reel on one of the small boats, which could be anchored two hundred feet from Sea Diver. This reel, in turn, would allow two divers to operate from it with air supplied from the first hose.

Sea Diver now carried a pair of small, flat-bottomed boats, sixteen by four feet, with a high freeboard. Each boat was equipped with a two-foot-square glass panel for underwater observation. The smaller of the two boats nested perfectly inside the larger one when stored on deck, and it was fully equipped with a diving reel, air tank and reduction valve, so that with the addition of a compressor it would always be ready for use. The two boats could be bolted together into a catamaran-type platform which would be useful in shallow water or among shoals.

We now felt that we had in Sea Diver a boat that we could operate indefinitely, by ourselves if necessary, yet one that would house comfortably a crew of as many as ten, should more hands be needed. She was equipped to take any weather and could cover two thousand miles without replenishing either fuel or water supply. Furthermore, she could carry an extensive larder of fresh food in her deep freeze and refrigerator.

With nearly every kind of navigational aid at our command, we would always be able to ascertain our exact position. We could depend on Sea Diver's powerful radio equipment to keep us in touch with the world ashore. With her complete and versatile power and diving gear, she was ready for any job that might appear. With the many conveniences of her living quarters, we would always be comfortable, no matter what the temperature or the length of time at sea.

In short, we felt that we now had the perfect boat for our purpose.

Earlier that winter of 1953, in Binghamton, with the snow flying outside the windows of our home, we had studied the meager records which Pete had been able to ferret out of the destruction of various Spanish treasure fleets in the environs of the Florida keys. One account in particular caught our fancy—that of the silver fleet of 1733, under Rear Admiral Don Rodrigo de Torres, which was overtaken by a hurricane soon after it left its rendezvous point in Havana harbor.

As I studied the ancient chart showing the approximate locations of the fifteen ships which were lost, my imagination caught at the drama of that terrifying holocaust of wind and storm as it attacked the doomed flotilla. In my mind I pictured the sequence of events which must have occurred starting that hot, still summer morning in July.

An orange-red sunrise spread itself across the eastern sky, reflected in shades of palest peach in the transparent waters of Havana harbor. From the grim stone bastions of Morro Castle overlooking the entrance to the port issued a series of heavy cannon blasts in long and continuous salute, startling the eager crowds which had gathered on the opposite shore to watch the silver fleet of Rear Admiral don Rodrigo de Torres begin its long, hazardous journey back to Spain.

Led by the admiral's galleon and squired by three additional two-decker warships bristling with guns, the remaining fifteen heavily laden merchant ships maneuvered awkwardly in the fitful breezes of early morning to take the places assigned to them. One by one, as they reached the harbor mouth, they broke out full sails to take every advantage of the increasing breezes from the southwest.

Many hours later, the patient watchers on the shore could still discern the flotilla on the far horizon, making its slow way toward the Bahama canal to the north. With that distant fleet went the hopes and prayers of all Havana, as well as those of the scattered Spanish colonists; for close family ties bound those left behind to the nearly three thousand souls aboard; and many were the fortunes that would be won or lost, depending on the safe passage of the convoy.

There was a special urgency to their prayers that year of 1733, for the silver fleet bore one of the richest treasures which had ever been sent off to Spain, and its successful arrival was depended upon to recoup many of the disastrous losses of the past two decades.

Beginning with the destruction of the plate fleet in 1715, when the entire company of ships was swept aground on the Florida coast by a hurricane, the bad luck of the Spanish had continued. No sooner had they contrived to salvage some of the precious cargo from those of the wrecked ships which were accessible, than that wicked Englishman, Henry Jennings, commanding a crew of three hundred men and three ships out of Jamaica, swooped down upon the Spanish salvagers and made off with more than three hundred thousand pieces of eight.

In 1730, a terrifying earthquake had shaken Chile and brought down the cities of Santiago and Concepción in ruins. That same year, a hurricane sweeping across Matanzas province and the plantations of Cuba had completely destroyed the homes and crops in its path. But worst of all, it had caused the shipwreck of the frigate Genovesa, on which the fortunes of the mainland were being shipped to Spain. The wreckage of the galleon had later been found on the shoals off Vibora in the Florida keys.

But now at last the fleet of 1733 was on its way, and the admiral's navigators nodded with approval as the strengthening southwest winds carried the clumsy square-riggers on a course which would lead them safely past the treacherous Cay Sal banks to the northeast, and well away from the even more dangerous reefs along the Florida keys on the western side of the Bahama canal.

But their joy was premature, for unfortunately the wind did not hold in the southwest. As the day advanced, it went quickly past the west and into the northwest. By evening, increasingly strong northwest winds were carrying the ships much too close to the Cay Sal banks for safety.

Finally, as the wind, blowing ever more vigorously, moved on into the north, Admiral de Torres was forced to order a change of course to the west. The fleet must of necessity keep under way, for there was no anchorage to be found in the deep waters of the Gulf Stream.

All that stormy night, with shortened sail, the fleet pointed west, the navigators making every effort to chart their unorthodox course, greatly disturbed lest they strike the Florida reefs. As dawn broke, their anxiety was somewhat relieved. The now gale-force winds had swept to the southeast, and with this change the fleet was able to point more and more to the northeast. There was still time to escape—by a narrow margin—the long line of reefs which fringed the far edge of the Gulf Stream.

But as the day advanced, ships' officers conferred in worried groups, and the passengers, confined to their quarters, shrank in fear at the strength of the wind and the ever-increasing waves, which were now mountains of heavy green water topped with flying spray and foam. Sails were reduced to the minimum. There was a constant check of water depths, which unvaryingly showed no bottom, for the fleet was still in hundreds of fathoms of water. A sharp lookout was maintained for signs of land or breakers.

Those concerned with the navigation of the fleet soon realized that the relentless southeast winds and the increased velocity of the Gulf Stream were carrying them in the direction of the reefs against their will. To add to the admiral's troubles, it was becoming increasingly difficult to hold the fleet together because of the large variation in the sailing speeds of the many types of ships.

Here and there a line gave. Sails blew out with staccato reports. Some of the ships had already lost masts and topsail rigging. On the galleons the gun crews worked feverishly to fortify the lines which held the guns in their places, for if ever one of these iron monsters broke loose on the decks, there would be grave trouble.

The winds increased to hurricane strength. Admiral de Torres, aboard the flagship, Rubi, which had been constantly signaling its charges in an effort to keep them together, finally realized the impossibility of the task. He ordered the ships still in his vicinity to make what way they could to the east, and appointed a place of rendezvous farther up the coast when the storm should be over.

As dusk approached, the despairing admiral, through driving rain and tossing seas, could make out only two of his fleet of nineteen. Whatever lay ahead of the flotilla that menacing night, there was nothing more that he could do. Their fate was in the hands of the gods.

By morning the hurricane was ended, though strong winds still flagged the tumultuous seas. The admiral, perhaps by superior navigation and a manageable ship, more probably by great good luck, had managed to keep Rubi clear of the reefs. Driven far north by the storm, he set out to seek the remains of his fleet. By midday he had succeeded in rounding up three badly beaten merchant ships. At his orders two of them limped off toward Havana for help. With the third accompanying him, he set out to learn the fate of the other fifteen.

As the Admiral sailed Rubi south along the line of reefs, a short distance below Tavernier island he was able to make out the battered remains of five of the fleet, scattered inshore. As he sailed closer, he was startled to see that the nearest ship, now lying on her side well beyond the line of foaming reefs, was El Capitana, no longer the proud galleon that had so recently started out from Havana in gleaming splendor.

Unable to approach any closer to the stricken vessels until the seas had calmed, Rubi continued her sad tour of inspection toward the southwest. As she sailed past the mass of rocks now known as Alligator reef, four more battered merchantmen could be seen in the shallower water, well in toward shore. Ahead, just off Viper key, the admiral was shocked to come across the barest indication of a sunken galleon, the Almirante, her broken masts protruding just above the surface of the water.

By the next morning the wind had subsided, and the sea was slowly resuming a more normal look. From his overnight anchorage off Viper key to the lower end of Key Vaca, the admiral counted four more wrecks. At the far end of Vaca he came upon a third galleon, which had been delegated to bring up the rear of the merchant fleet. She was well aground on an outside shoal. But this time signs of activity could be discerned aboard. As Rubi approached, those on board could see that the hull of the ship was whole and seemed to be riding fairly high in the water.

The admiral gave orders to bring Rubi about, and a way was carefully sounded in to an anchorage near the stranded galleon. The merchantman, still following, anchored close by. A longboat was launched, and soon the captain of the stricken ship was aboard Rubi.

The galleon was stuck fast on the shoal, he reported, but still in floatable condition. Fortunately she had not struck on a coral reef, where disaster would have been almost certain. By manning the pumps, the captain was confident he could get her to Havana if only she could be moved from the bar. Now, with Rubi's help, this might be possible. How fortunate if they could save her and her cargo of treasure.

The two officers concluded that it would be necessary to get rid of her cannon before attempting to kedge her off the shoal. So all through that night, while the stars twinkled in a calm, clear sky above, and the waters of the Gulf Stream flowed more and more placidly on their way north, the crews of the two ships struggled and sweated and strained to jettison the seventy-odd cannon, each one of which weighed from one to two and a half tons. Another portion of the crew worked feverishly from the smaller boats, setting anchors to seaward, their lines attached to the windlasses of the stranded ship, to assist in kedging her off as her load was lightened.

By morning more than seventy cannon lay on the bottom of the sea in two heaps, one to port and the other to starboard of the ship; lay there in piles like matchsticks, vaguely discernible from the deck in the murky waters below. It seemed a heavy sacrifice, but if the ship could be saved it was well worth it.

It was nearly sunset when at last the galleon floated free once more. Although leaking badly, she was able to get under way toward Havana, leaving behind on the ocean floor to mark the place of her near destruction only two useless masses of cannon barrels and a scattering of ammunition.

Could these be the same two piles of armament which Bill Thompson had come upon in recent years on the sandy bottom of Delta shoal? Was this why, after many forays upon the spot to find other evidences of the wreckage of a ship, we had never come upon a single artifact other than cannon barrels and ammunition? Although it seemed quite likely, we realized that, without other objects to identify the ship, we would never know.

Now, more than two hundred years later, Ed and I hoped to find the locations of some of the wrecked silver fleet. Aboard Sea Diver, highly prized and closely guarded, were two modern charts of the Florida keys, the first from Fowey rocks to Alligator reef, the second from Alligator reef to Sombrero key. On these charts we had marked the approximate locations of fifteen of the plate fleet as they had been charted by a Spanish navigator who had visited the area a few years after the disaster, when many of the hulls could still be distinguished beneath the water. They were scattered from the Martires rocks off Key Largo to Key Vaca. We had also noted on the same charts the known locations of cannon and ballast which had been seen upon the bottom in recent years. This information we had gleaned from many sources.

The most promising area, where both ancient and modern indications overlapped, was in the vicinity of the reefs east of Hen and Chickens light, near Plantation key, where we had attempted searches many times before, only to be driven off by rough seas and murky water. Here, when the weather had become more amenable later in the year, we hoped to return for a thorough search.

A new problem had arisen, however, since the previous year, when we had paid our first visit to the little Museum of Sunken Treasure which Art McKee had established on Plantation key.

We had become acquainted with Art on our initial diving venture out of Marathon. He was the only professional diver in the party, and I had been very much impressed by the heavy diving equipment which he wore and his evident familiarity with the bottom. Ed, too, had learned many valuable pointers on underwater salvage from Art at that time.

The visit to his museum had proved most interesting. In addition to two weighty silver bars, labeled mysteriously as having been found "east of Key Largo," we had seen a huge anchor at least fifteen feet in height, rows of ancient cannon, bar shot and cannon balls, a black iron kettle as big as a bathtub, and many smaller artifacts which Art said came from "his" wreck out on the reefs.

He told us in a confidential tone of voice that he thought he had discovered a Spanish galleon. He was busily salvaging it from his boat, Treasure Princess, whenever he could find free time and the weather was cooperative. He had invited us to spend some time diving on the wreck with him when we returned in 1953. From his description of its location, it appeared to be in the most promising section of our chart. We felt almost certain it would prove to be one of the ships from the 1733 plate wreck.

Now we learned that Art had purchased a lease from the state of Florida for exclusive search, diving and salvage rights in an area reaching from Key Largo well south of Hen and Chickens and extending seaward to the reefs. The law had been passed the previous year, and he was the first diver in the area to acquire such a permit. This would effectively end what hopes we had of finding and exploring any of the wrecks in this area. Art, however, repeated his invitation hospitably when he learned that we were back in Miami.

Thus we found ourselves, one unexpectedly quiet day in March, between trips to the Bahamas, rendezvousing with Art and his Treasure Princess at Hen and Chickens light. After an exchange of greetings from the decks of the two boats, he indicated that we were to follow him and headed seaward in the general direction of Crocker reef. We fell in behind his boat, brimming with curiosity. Sure enough, his course led us directly to the area which we had searched so diligently from time to time for that heap of ballast or cannon balls which had been described by our various informants who had seen them there.

It was evident that Art was a frequent visitor to the spot, for, although there were no visible signs to mark its location, he headed confidently seaward. While his assistant operated the boat, he took bearings on the shore and distant Alligator light, finally directed the course changed slightly to the left, brought Treasure Princess about in a tight circle and dropped his hook. He signaled for us to anchor nearby.

When our anchor was down and Sea Diver had drifted to her natural position in relation to wind and tide, we found ourselves side by side with the Treasure Princess.

Across the intervening water, Art called, "There's the galleon. You can see the ballast from your deck."

Beneath the calm water created by the shelter of the two boats was plainly evident a spreading heap of ballast stone topped by an elongated object—a cannon.

We hurried into our diving gear and were soon on the bottom. The first thing that caught my eye was a large sign anchored many feet beneath the surface. "Private property of Arthur J. McKee. Keep off." Art had placed it there to warn away skin divers who might poach on his wreck or spear the numerous beautiful fish which swarmed around it.

The wreck lay beyond the sign, a lengthy pile of coral and ballast rock surrounded by depths of white sand. The cannon which surmounted the ballast had been dug from the sand and hoisted to the top of the wreck so that it would be visible to sight-seers through the glass bottom of the Treasure Princess. Near one end of the ballast was a small section of timber which Art had uncovered with his jetting hose. However, most of his finds, as he had already told us, came from the soft sand near the wreck.

Beneath these ruins, no doubt, reposed the jewel coffers of great ladies, luxurious appointments from the captain's cabin, and unknown treasures which had gone down in the baggage of the returning voyagers. Undoubtedly there had been quantities of gold and silver, too, although it was doubtful how much had survived the salvage operations which must have gone on for years while the hull was still more or less intact beneath the water.

As the centuries passed and greedy teredo worms chiseled the ancient beams until they broke into pieces and were swept away by the sea, I could imagine the contents of the upper cabins gradually sifting down through the moldering timbers to lie atop the ballast pile. Meanwhile the more prosaic furnishings aboard, pots and pans, pottery and glass and china, must have settled downward also, to be crumbled and broken beneath the heavier wreckage of the ship.

Now all that remained visible was this pile of crusted stones, resting on heavy broken timbers buried in sand. And even these few timbers would have disappeared long ago had they not been protected over the centuries by their covering of sand.

Between the piles of rounded ballast stones, cemented securely together through the years with a binding of coral sand, were crevasses in which now lived huge black sea urchins, spotted yellow and black morays and pinkish, thick-fingered anemones. Over the ballast pile hovered drifts of small silver bait fish, impelled first in one direction and as suddenly in another by some unseen force; and at my approach, myriads of bright-colored little fish darted into their holes within.

Through the screen of milling fingerlings, at the far side of the wreck, I could see the slower, more ponderous movements of yard-long black groupers, which inhabited the wreck-fashioned coral reef in numbers. Constantly in evidence, like sentinels patrolling the wreck's perimeter, were a half dozen king mackerel, identifiable by the fine black line which marked their white sides laterally.

After we had inspected the 150-foot length of the ballast heap, Ed returned topsides to get the metal detector.

Later, as he swam over the white-sand bottom beneath our boarding ladder with the instrument extended before him, the indicator hand kept up a mad jig. The bottom, between Sea Diver and Treasure Princess, was seemingly filled with metal objects. Yet when he applied it to the sandy area on the far side of the pile of ballast, he was unable to secure any indications at all.

The galleon must have lain on its side and spilled its contents in only one direction. The barren side was perhaps close to where the ship's bottom had reposed.

By the end of the brief afternoon, the two men poking away at the coral-cemented ballast stone and the white sand beneath it had recovered many interesting objects, for this was the first time that a metal detector had been used on the wreck. Ed was especially proud of a well-preserved sword which he had unearthed at the edge of the ballast. There were cannon balls galore.

Back on the deck of Sea Diver, as we headed once more for Miami, we reviewed the events of the afternoon. After checking the location of the wreck with our chart, we came to the conclusion that we probably had been diving on the remains of the galleon El Capitana. If this were so, it was one of the larger warships which had guarded the silver fleet. It had carried the general in charge of the expedition, according to the records, and most of the 225 persons aboard, including the general, had been lost in the tempest.

If Art had really stumbled upon El Capitana, we realized that this wreck should be unusually rich in findings, for at that time the galleons generally carried the bulk of the valuable gold and silver, while the smaller ships were loaded mainly with bulky merchandise, ores, logwood, precious woods, cochineal and the like. Also, because the larger vessels were safer and more comfortable, they were more apt to have had as passengers important church and government officials and other well-to-do travelers, returning to the mother country. No doubt their personal baggage had contained many articles of value which would have ended up on the bottom.

Working alone and with inadequate equipment, as he had begun, it would take years for Art to make any appreciable progress with "his" wreck. We were delighted that he had invited us to return in July to work with him.

During the summers of 1953 and 1954 we spent quite a little time on Art's galleon wreck. Mendel Peterson was with us much of the time. That first summer we were able to supplement Art's equipment with an additional jetting hose and the metal detector, which had proven so valuable. Following the wavering needle of its indicator over the white-sand bottom with the two jetting hoses, the men uncovered, in addition to several cannons, a fascinating array of old swords and battle axes, pewter and silver plates and utensils, and small pieces of jewelry.

They also found scores of pieces of eight, all black and corroded save those which had lain in contact with another piece of metal. These were still solid, the full arms of Spain on a crowned shield and the square cross showing distinctly after they had been cleaned and treated. The date 1732 was distinguishable on many of them.

Yet all the time they were uncovering these objects, Ed and Art had a stricken feeling that the jetting hoses were driving far more relics than they were salvaging deeper into the seemingly bottomless bed of sand. It seemed that almost as fast as the streams of water washed the sand away from an object, the sand at the sides of the hole thus formed would slowly but inexorably creep back until, by the time the operator had finished, there was very little trace of his efforts. The divers could go on forever in this way without ever reaching many of the valuables which must be there.

What they needed, Ed said, was an air lift. Then they could suck the sand up to the surface through a big pipe and redeposit it at a safe distance from the scene of operations. With this device they could successfully remove the sand from around the wreck and at the same time uncover whatever objects were buried there. If they put a screen across the mouth of the pipe, it would prevent it from clogging and also keep any object but the smallest from being carried away. These small pieces could be salvaged as they emerged from the far end.

But wouldn't it take a very special piece of equipment to operate such a contrivance, I asked?

Yes, Ed said, it would take a powerful compressor to do the job. There was room for one in the lazaret of Sea Diver, and he intended to have one installed before we returned the following year.

I loved to watch the men at work on the wreck as I floated by the hour on the surface above them, a face mask covering my eyes and nose. I became so engrossed at times that I would suddenly find myself in the very uncomfortable situation of being completely out of air. Frequent experience of this sort of thing finally trained me to long intervals of holding my breath, for I would almost rather have strangled than turn my head for a gulp of air just as some fascinating object was being uncovered down below.

Occasionally my view would be obscured by one of the great columns of bubbles which rose obliquely from the masks of the divers beneath me, causing my skin to prickle wherever the little pockets of air burst against it. And often the clouds of sediment stirred up by the jetting hoses blotted out the entire scene from my sight if the tidal currents were not moving swiftly enough to carry it away.

While Pete and Ed, in Desco face masks and swim trunks, looked like ordinary mortals on the bottom, Art, in his heavy iron helmet and long-sleeved black sweater, appeared to be a man from another world. While the others swam here and there and worked most of the time in a horizontal position, Art strode upright about the bottom, his muscular body supporting the grotesque, formidable-looking metal head covering, which emitted spasmodic clouds of bubbles; or he knelt over his labors, unable to tilt his body beyond a certain degree.

Ever since Art had begun diving as a sandhog in his native New Jersey many years before, he had used a helmet and the heavy diving equipment that went with it. Now he conceded to these warmer southern waters only to the extent of omitting the bulky waterproof suit and lead shoes, but he still clung to the helmet. It gave him lots more air, he said, and furthermore he was used to it.

I was constantly amused at the almost daily under-water comedy staged by a huge pinkish hog snapper which the divers had adopted as their mascot. This friendly denizen of the wreck could be seen whenever the men were at work, hovering like an affectionate puppy close beside them, and waiting to devour the tasty tidbits which the jetting hoses dislodged from the sand and coral. Behind him, more timid but just as hungry, hovered his two devoted wives, slightly smaller than their lord and master.

Occasionally one of the divers would interrupt his work long enough to clutch at a wriggling worm uncovered by the jet stream. He would hardly have time to extend it toward the waiting snapper before it disappeared down that lordly sultan's throat. One wondered when the patient retinue behind him fed, for they never presumed to snatch an offering as long as their mate was around.

One day as I watched, while Ed manipulated the jetting hose and Pete and Art pawed among the rubble at its mouth as the sand melted away before its attack, there was a sudden gleam of gold. All three dove at it at once, but Pete managed to fasten his fingers upon it. It was a heavy, tear-shaped glob of the metal.

We examined it closely when they brought it to the surface. What could it be?

Pete had the answer. "I'll bet it's a melted gold doubloon," he said. "It could have been melted when the Spanish burned the superstructure of the ship after they salvaged it." As I turned it over in my palm, I could see upon its back the impression of the wood which it had lain against as it resolidified.

Later Pete was able to substantiate his supposition, for the gold was of the same fineness and color, and weighed almost exactly the same, as a gold doubloon of the 1730's. The slight difference in weight could be attributed to the heating process it had gone through, he explained.

I was delighted when the men decided to present the gold piece to me to add to my charm bracelet, for it was the first bit of gold we had ever found on the bottom. Their only stipulation was that I must lend it to the Smithsonian for an exhibit of underwater artifacts which was being planned for the following summer.

As for the pieces of eight which were being turned up almost every day, we found that those which were still in good enough condition to be identified bore the dates 1731 or 1732. Pete, who is a coin collector in addition to his many other interests, told us that coins of these dates were very scarce and therefore of unusual value. This was because practically the entire production of the Mexican mints during these two years had been aboard the Spanish fleet when it was destroyed, and consequently had never gotten into circulation.

Also, he said, the same year that the disaster took place, the mints discontinued producing the "cobs" which had been the coin of the realm for many years, and replaced them with minted coins, the machinery for which had been shipped to Mexico in 1732.

These new coins bore the well-known Pillars of Hercules on one side and the laureated bust of the ruler on the opposite. They later became known by collectors as "Pillar dollars." The divers found only a few of these on the wreck, the bulk of the coins recovered being the cruder "cobs." They even found some rare pieces of four.

I inquired where the word "cob" had originated.

"It came from *'cabo de barra,'*" Pete said, "which means 'cut from a bar.' It was called a piece of eight because it possessed the equivalent value of eight reales."

He told us that the melted gold doubloon which had been found was probably also a "cob" rather than a milled coin, for although before 1679 all gold from the New World was shipped to Spain in bulk and minted there, from that date until 1732, doubloons were struck in "cob" form in Mexico. The new machinery of 1732 had made it possible to issue the fine-appearing milled doubloons which are so much more common today.

Ed later performed an interesting experiment which satisfied him as to the scarcity of the 1732 pieces of eight. Wherever he went in Europe or the United States, he dropped in at coin collectors' shops asking for Spanish pieces of eight of that date. Never was he able to find any. Several times he was told that if he would leave his name and address, the dealer would attempt to get one for him. He was warned that if any could be located, they would be very costly. Ed did not need to worry. He never heard from any of these dealers again.

When we returned to the keys in the summer of 1953, we headed straight for Art McKee's newly completed Museum of Sunken Treasure, which he had designed to house his rapidly multiplying underwater finds.

Mendel Peterson was with us again, as well as our younger son, Clayton, who had turned into a very capable diver for an eleven-year-old. We had not been able to persuade his brother, Bill, to join us, for Bill was spending the summer on a ranch in Wyoming, thus fulfilling something he had dreamed of all through his childhood.

We found the museum to be an impressive structure of gray block simulating an early Spanish fort, with battlements and towers. It was situated on the Overseas highway on Plantation key, its sixty-five-foot tower overlooking both the Gulf of Mexico and the Atlantic. From its top, with the aid of the telescope he had placed there, it was even possible for Art to police the site of his galleon wreck far out at sea.

On the greensward inside the moat which surrounded the museum, separating it from the road, Art had placed the huge anchor which was one of the first things he had raised from the sunken galleon. Overhead, from the battlements, fluttered the flags of all nations, and from the tower high above waved a black-and-white Jolly Roger.

In the main display room of the fort we found an imposing array of artifacts from the Spanish plate ship and from other wrecks which Art had worked. In the picturesque courtyard behind the museum were displayed anchors, ballast rock, numerous cannon and cannon balls, and all the larger objects which had been secured from wrecks up and down the keys. There was even a replica of the ocean floor, with a diver in full heavy-diving gear at work upon a cleverly simulated wreck.

But the most interesting exhibit of all was housed in a heavily constructed vault in the interior of the fort. Here we found the accumulated results of Art's long search for treasure. On display were two of the three silver bars which Art still insisted he had found "east of Key Largo." There were some fine examples of gold doubloons and pieces of eight, and a few pieces of gold jewelry, including a pair of gold filigree earrings set with emeralds.

Reposing upon a black velvet cushion was a rare and finely worked gold religious medallion, which had been discovered on the galleon wreck only recently. According to the legend, the medal had been struck in honor of the canonization of the Peruvian Archbishop, Turibius, in 1726. It seemed quite possible that it had been part of the baggage of some high ecclesiastic aboard the plate ship when it sank.

Out on the wreck the next day we found that Art, over the past winter, had succeeded with much effort in uncovering a great many more of the ship's timbers. It was now definite that she was lying on her side, for it was even possible to distinguish gun ports at points beneath the ballast where the timbers had been exposed. Reposing, slightly uncovered, in the sand were the four cannon which we had located with the metal detector the previous summer.

Art was delighted to have us arrive with the air lift which Ed had promised, for he was sure that with its help we would be able to reach a great many more objects than had been possible previously. He was also counting on the help of Sea Diver's lifting equipment to move the heavy cannon, once they were uncovered, to the top of the ballast pile, where they would be safe from the shifting bottom sand, and where they could be viewed by Art's patrons on the glass-bottomed Treasure Princess.

The men spent the better part of the day in rigging the new air-lift equipment. After joining the large sections of galvanized pipe together on Sea Diver's deck, and connecting a long section of heavy rubber hose to the air compressor, which had been installed in the lazaret, the divers maneuvered the long, gleaming pipe to the sea bottom in the vicinity of the cannon. It was placed at an angle so that, as the sand was sucked up, it would be deposited in a location far removed from the wrecked ship.

The air lift worked like a charm. For the next few days Ed, Art and Pete took turns guiding its greedy mouth into the white sand which almost covered the four cannon. As one diver held the long tube, the other two placed themselves where they could remove the hunks of coral, ballast stones, and the occasional pieces of wreckage which were revealed by the air lift.

Every now and then, just often enough to keep everyone's interest stimulated, a prize of worth would appear —a pewter plate or goblet; a bronze mortar; a bent, blackened silver table fork or spoon; an occasional moldered piece of eight clinging to a cannon ball or to a bit of the ship's metal rigging.

No man would ever have worked as hard as those three for the mere purpose of making a living. They toiled happily, without ceasing, disappearing below as soon as it was possible to make out their surroundings in the morning, continuing until the low slanting rays of the late-afternoon sun forced them to quit.

While they concentrated on the area around the cannon, Clayton and I placed ourselves on another section of the ocean floor, where the debris which emerged from the upper end of the pipe showered back into the water and sank to the bottom. In addition to the sand, there was a continuous rain of bits of pottery and glass, an occasional coin or silver button, shells and bits of wood and stone.

By the end of the second day a huge hole had been dredged about the base of the four cannon, which lay cemented together with more than two hundred years' encrustation of coral sand. They would have to be dynamited apart before they could be moved. It would be a delicate operation to set just the right charge that would loosen them from one another, yet not damage their metal, which was undoubtedly weak from centuries of immersion in salt water.

So next morning, with Sea Diver anchored directly above the cannon, Ed and Art disappeared over the side carrying a fuse attached to a roll of fine insulated wire, and the necessary sticks of dynamite. As soon as they had climbed back on deck, Sea Diver's anchor chain rattled through the guides as Pete allowed her to slip back a scant fifty feet.

With a flashlight battery, Ed made contact with the end of the coated wire. Almost instantly we felt a sharp blow on the bottom of the boat as the concussion wave radiated upward from the explosion. Just off the port bow there was a slight disturbance on the surface of the water.

Sea Diver's winch whined as she was moved back to her original position. A scattering of small fish floated on the water surrounding her. As I looked over the side, I saw hundreds more of the silvery minnows which ordinarily hovered deep in the water over the wreck, darting crazily about near the surface, the perfect pattern of their mass drills completely disrupted.

As soon as the water had cleared a bit, Art and Ed went overboard again, soon returning to report the complete success of their effort. The four cannon, freed from the bondage of centuries, now lay separate yet unharmed, they said. The water below was still murky from the explosion, and the bottom was littered with tiny fish. However, not one of the large groupers or snappers which inhabited the wreck had been hurt, for, fortunately, the two men had remembered to chase them away just before coming up to set off the charge.

Clayton and I followed Art overboard to watch him prepare the cannon for moving, while Ed stayed aboard with Pete to operate the deck tackle. After Art had secured a grappling hook and chain about each cannon and had attached it to Sea Diver's boom, the men planned to raise the barrels a few feet from the bottom and then to alter the vessel's position sufficiently to swing the guns over the top of the ballast pile. When Art considered that each one had reached the correct position, he was to send Clayton or me to the surface to signal the others to lower the boom until each barrel was properly placed on the pile of rock.

It took a good while to transfer all four cannon. Meanwhile I lazed about on the bottom, making an occasional trip to the surface with messages from Art, who was busily rigging and placing them. Clayton was everywhere at once, poking into the ballast pile, hovering over the cannon, darting to the surface to watch proceedings on deck and then descending to swim playfully toward the circling fish.

Near me, Art's lucite camera box, perched on its weighted tripod, gleamed softly through the hazy water. There was an answering gleam from the silver bodies of the dead bait fish scattered upon the bottom as they reflected the penetrating rays of the afternoon sun.

Undaunted by being so rudely driven from their former haunts, the hog snappers had returned, poking their ugly pink noses into the excavation, where Art labored over the cannon. A huge sting ray, which had been napping quietly in a nearby patch of grass, finally roused itself and glided past me to inspect the proceedings. At the far end of the ballast pile I could just make out the hovering black shapes of the more timid groupers, which had fled the explosion.

As soon as the fourth cannon had been placed, Art and I returned to Sea Diver's deck, while Pete and Ed went below to inspect the completed job.

When they reappeared a half hour later and were removing their masks, I said, "Where's Clayton? Isn't he coming up, too?" for I suddenly realized he had been down a very long time.

I went to the rail and gave his air hose a few sharp tugs. Nothing happened. After waiting a few moments, I took hold of the hose again, and this time started to haul it in hand over hand. My tactics finally brought a protesting boy to the foot of the ladder.

"Oh, Mother, do I have to come up already?"

He was disgusted and spared no pains to show it as he pulled himself up the ladder and removed his mask and flippers.

Ed, who had been watching, suddenly exclaimed, "Where is your belt? Didn't you wear one?"

It developed that eleven-year-old Clayton had been on the bottom for more than three hours without any weights to help keep him down. It is hard to imagine the amount of effort this required, unless one has tried it; for human lungs, fortified with a generous supply of air from the compressor, create a high degree of flotation in the body. While Clayton had remained on the bottom with no weights whatever, I had found it necessary to wear a twenty-pound lead belt to permit me to stay down without exertion. Needless to say, he was tired. But next day he was his usual busy self, much to my relief, for such a long and strenuous immersion at that depth could have had serious consequences.

Before leaving the wreck of the Spanish galleon toward the end of July, Ed rigged the magnetometer behind Sea Diver and carefully patrolled the area between the wreckage of the unfortunate vessel and the outer reef, where she must have first hit. Wherever there was the slightest indication of the presence of metal, a yellow buoy was placed. Later the men followed the course laid out by the yellow buoys, tracing their path on the bottom with the metal detector.

It was apparent, from the frequent indications of

metal which they found, that the ship must have dumped part of her deck cargo on the outer reef, including the cannon which had been salvaged earlier. She was then driven by wind and sea, either on her side or listing heavily to one side, to her present resting place, spilling stuff from the decks all along her path.

The magnetometer was also used in adjacent areas, where there was reason to think there might be other wreckage. To their delight, the men came across two more piles of ballast stone which showed signs of the presence of metal. These they carefully charted for future search.

We have never been back. Since that summer Art McKee has continued to salvage his wreck. Today he wears a Scott mask instead of the heavy iron helmet which formerly seemed a part of him, and uses the air lift, which Ed left for him. He has continued to gather a fascinating collection of artifacts for his Museum of Sunken Treasure.

During the next two years, our own quest for elusive shipwrecks led us increasingly toward the Bahama islands, to the east. What we found there so intrigued us that we lost interest temporarily in the more familiar keys.

But in spite of the adventure and excitement that we found while sailing the Bahamas and the adjacent Caribbean waters, where we explored and dove upon a goodly number of reefs and banks, we have about come to the conclusion that in these waters off the Florida keys, route of the Spanish plate fleets and for centuries chief highway from the New World to Europe, there undoubtedly still lie the greatest number of promising wrecks this side of the Atlantic.

Part Two

The Bahama Islands

1

○

○

○

Back in our sailing days with Blue Heron, Ed and I had found the Bahamas to be the most delightful of cruising grounds. From one-hundred-mile-long Andros island to dozens of the palm-fringed, white-beached little cays which dot the seventeen-thousand-square-mile area, we had explored an endless succession of varied and fascinating places. Nowhere else in this part of the world had we found waters of such luscious hues. Nowhere else had the beaches seemed so white, the skies so softly azure, yet vibrant with the snowiest of cirrus or cumulus fluff. From the northernmost point opposite central Florida to the southernmost island closest to Hispaniola, a span of nearly eight hundred miles, we learned that this archipelago consists of some seven hundred islands and twenty-four hundred cays.

As we sailed across the shallow banks which join most of these islands, divided here and there by underwater canyons as much as three miles in depth, we tried to conceive what natural phenomenon had once shaken the earth to create this widespread archipelago in the vastness of the early sea.

Skirting the outer shores of many of these islands and fringing the edge of the banks, we found long necklaces of dangerous coral which made the approach to the shores they guarded a hazardous experience. In those days on Blue Heron we took good care to maintain a safe distance from their reaching talons.

It was here in the Bahama islands, on the outer shores of an island the Indians called Guanahani, that Christopher Columbus first set foot on the soil of the New World and made the acquaintance of the Lucayans who inhabited it. Although we had discussed visiting this historic area many times, it had somehow failed to become part of our itinerary. But at least it served to arouse our interest in the early history of the Bahamas.

We found that not many years after Columbus's first visit, the islands had been stripped of their Indian inhabitants by the Spanish settlers on nearby Hispaniola. In almost no time the captive Indians had disappeared from existence, victims of forced labor in the Spanish mines or of strange and terrible diseases brought from Europe by the white man.

For the next few centuries the Bahamas were inhabited only by buccaneers and wreckers, for whom they served as a remote and rewarding hideout. Close to the outer edges of the archipelago these ruffians lay in wait to pounce upon the heavily laden treasure ships that passed or to salvage what they could from unfortunate vessels carried up on the reefs.

In the fastnesses of secret inner harbors a succession of pirates hid their marauding craft, safe from the occasional gunboat which might be sent in pursuit. Thus for many years the Bahama islands existed under no proper law, a refuge for runaway slaves, wreckers, pirates and other unsavory characters. New Providence island, where Nassau is situated, became the pirate headquarters.

Conditions finally became so intolerable that early in the eighteenth century the British government sent a force headed by Captain Woodes Rogers to establish order in the islands and subdue the brigands. Rogers succeeded in persuading them to lead a quieter life by hanging many from the gallows. Those who did not take to the new order soon left for more hospitable areas. It was not long after this that the islands were settled by English colonists, later augmented by American Tories who had fled the newly created United States at the end of the Revolution.

Although agriculture and fishing were the accepted way of making a living during those early days, the wrecking trade also flourished. Gradually the string of reefs fringing the seaward islands accumulated more than their normal quota of wrecked ships, many of them victims of the wreckers' tricks. Wherever Ed and I sailed in the Bahamas with Blue Heron, we heard tales of pirates and wreckers, and booty which still lay on the bottom or was hidden in secret places on land.

So when we later became enamored with diving and the exciting prospects offered wherever coral reefs and treacherous bars exist, our minds naturally turned to these widespread Bahama banks and cays, where it seemed certain we would be able to locate many worth-while diving prospects.

Our first attempt made with Eryholme in search of the brass cannon on the north Bahama banks had ended in failure. A number of Bahamians later told us similar stories of brass cannon which had been seen lying on the sandy bottom of these extensive, shallow banks; but whenever we tried to pin down these tales as to exact location, we learned only that the cannon were in the vicinity of the Lily banks.

So we had ceased to get very excited over the prospects of finding the cannon until one day we picked up a copy of an old chart that Mendel Peterson had sent us, labeled "A description of the Bahama Banck," which had originally been drawn up in the mid-seventeenth century by a Mr. Charles Salmon, under the command of a Captain Phips.

On the western border of the same banks we had searched for the brass cannon, three wrecks had been charted. They had most intriguing names: the "plate wreck," the "Genuees wreck" and the "copper wreck." The latitude of each was plainly indicated, and although the map was rather crudely drawn, we found upon comparing it with our present-day chart that whatever landmarks still existed matched very well as to latitude. There was no longitude given, for in those early days of sailing, the navigator had no means of determining it while at sea.

We believed the plate wreck must have been part of a Spanish treasure fleet. The Genuees wreck had perhaps received its name because it contained gold from the west coast of Africa, transformed by the British into guineas for their trade; while the copper wreck, no doubt, had carried a valuable load of that much-prized metal.

We soon discovered that the Captain Phips who had caused this chart to be drawn and who had evidently located and attempted to salvage these wrecks was the same Captain Phips who, a few years later, wrested a treasure of millions from a Spanish galleon which had been wrecked on the Silver shoals earlier that same century. Ed and I had often read and talked of the Silver shoals. What treasure hunter has not? For the story of Captain Phips's sudden elevation to wealth and fame by his finding of the Spanish plate wreck has lived to this day to spice and encourage the plans of treasure seekers the world over.

Perhaps, then, this seventeenth-century chart held the

clue to a similar discovery. If we could locate even one of these three wrecks, perhaps we, too, would come upon wealth untold. Or if these wrecks had already been thoroughly salvaged of their valuable cargo, we might yet find a most complete collection of armament and artifacts representative of that early century in the New World.

At the mention of armament, Ed said, "You don't suppose—? Could those brass cannon we were looking for with Eryholme have come from one of these ships?"

It seemed very possible. Taking the latitudes from Phips's chart, Ed plotted out the position of the wrecks near the edge of the banks. He found that both the copper and the Genuees wrecks lined up exactly with particularly dangerous shoal reefs along the western edge of the bank, while the plate wreck appeared to be somewhere on Matanilla shoal, which forms the curve of the bank to the north. Here his theorizing came to an abrupt halt, for there was no longitude given, and this wide shoal, curving off into Lily bank, presented an area of miles which might contain the wreck. This presented a most exciting possibility. Perhaps the brass cannon we had sought were part of the plate wreck, and perhaps Phips's chart would furnish just the clue we needed to locate the cannon.

So we decided to include a search of these northern banks in the cruise to the Bahamas we were planning with Jane and Barney Crile that summer of 1953. During two trips which we had made to Nassau and the islands the previous winter, we had garnered possibilities of many likely wrecks. From these we had mapped out a summer adventure which would take us across the banks in the vicinity of the Berry islands to Cay Gorda at the eastern end of Northwest Providence channel. Now we planned to end our excursion with a search for the three wrecks which Captain Phips had charted.

It seemed scarcely possible that the solid-rock monument which reared itself like a small fortress from the water on Sea Diver's starboard bow was the only terra firma to be seen in any direction. Yet there it stood, alone in all that vast expanse of ocean. This was Memory rock, designated on Captain Phips's chart as "the Rock"; the same rock which our treasure-hunting predecessor had used as a key to map the locations of the three wrecks we had come to find.

We had left West End, on the tip of Grand Bahama island, late that morning. Setting a course approximately north-northwest, close to where the turquoise waters of the shallow banks meet the deep blue of the Gulf Stream, we had sailed past a few small cays and reefs which gradually dwindled, then disappeared entirely, leaving only the contrasting color of the deeps and shallows to mark the division between the banks and the deep water of the Bahama canal.

There were six of us aboard—Jane and Barney, enthusiastic as always over this new underwater adventure; Dick Burrows, part Spanish, part Indian, whom we had picked up at Sandy Point earlier on our trip to guide us to some wrecks with which he was familiar in the vicinity of the Abacos; and Clayton, as much at home beneath the water as in his own back yard.

Now, as we gazed at the rock, we planned our strategy. According to Phips's chart, the copper wreck lay a few miles north of the Rock, well inside the outer edge of the reef. Eight miles north of it, the Genuees ship had come to grief. Another ten miles beyond, somewhere in the area of Matanilla shoal, lay the plate wreck. Within the line of reefs, our chart showed sufficiently deep water to allow Sea Diver to pass, but we had not traveled these waters long before we realized we must be constantly on the lookout for numerous places where the sandy bottom had shallowed up, and for the occasional coral heads which might appear.

It puzzled me how Ed expected to know when we had reached the latitudes Captain Phips had indicated, for once we had left the rock there was nothing to indicate our position. I soon learned the answer, for Ed, having assigned me to steer the boat while Dick Burrows watched from the pulpit for any hazards ahead of us, sank to his knees before the loran, his head covered with a dark cloth to shut out the daylight, observing its intricate lightninglike patterns. Within these trappings, he was able to pinpoint our exact latitude and longitude.

By the middle of the afternoon we had voyaged north to the edge of Matanilla shoal and then back to the reef which Ed had picked as the location of the copper wreck. Far to the south, Memory rock was dimly visible on the horizon. Although the day was nearly gone by the time we had our anchor down, and the sea, even behind the reef, was choppy from a brisk northwest wind, we could not resist a brief exploratory trip in the glass-bottomed boat.

Jane, Barney, and I had hardly left Sea Diver before we spotted on the bottom a large, coral-crusted anchor and an attached section of chain. We relayed our discovery to Ed on the deck of Sea Diver and then went on our way, but without the excitement usually attendant upon such a discovery, for we realized that the presence of the chain marked it as a product of the past century. Until that time only rope had been used for anchor cable. A cruise along the outer edge of the reef for several miles revealed nothing further, and, as the sea had become rougher, we headed back to Sea Diver.

When Ed and I arrived on deck the next morning, we found that the rest of the party had already embarked on a before-breakfast survey of the shoal. They returned shortly with news of the discovery of two more anchors halfway down the reef. These were also equipped with chain, they said, and fashioned with metal stocks. They had seen no other evidences of a wreck in the vicinity of the anchor. Ed reminded us that the metal stocks, like the chain, were an indication that the anchors had not lain on the bottom long, as only wooden crosspieces had been used until about the middle of the nineteenth century.

After breakfast Clayton, Ed, and I set out with the glass-bottomed boat. We had not searched long before we spotted a large metal windlass rearing up from the bottom about twelve feet below us. As we circled to have another look, we could see anchors, a second, smaller windlass and a long length of chain trailing across the bottom from the large windlass, which was still wrapped with a heavy section of it. Nearby lay a heap of the chain, just as it had reposed in its locker when the ship went down.

"Well, this certainly isn't the copper wreck," Ed said, "but it looks like a good spot for Jane and Barney to get the underwater pictures they're after."

It was afternoon by the time Sea Diver was anchored near the wreckage and the equipment prepared for diving. The sky had clouded over several times, with accompanying deluges of rain, but between showers the sun shone bright and beautiful, and we took turns exploring and photographing the bottom. I stayed on deck with Dick to tend hoses and to hand down cameras and equipment as they were needed.

The afternoon was nearly over before I took a turn below. By this time the tide was running out, and as I climbed down the ladder I found Sea Diver riding within a few feet of the bottom. The coral-coated windlass of the wrecked ship was only a few yards away, and I saw that Ed and Clayton were holding on to it. Ed motioned me to swim their way.

I released my hold on the ladder and launched myself

in their direction. But I was not prepared for the force of the tide, which immediately seized me and carried me feet first toward the stern of the boat. I swam against it with every bit of strength I could muster, for the surprise attack had carried me well aft of the ladder and there was nothing within reach to hang on to. I succeeded only in preventing myself from being swept farther astern.

Ed, who, I now realized, had attached himself to the windlass to brace himself against the surge, saw my predicament and allowed the current to carry him my way. I grabbed at his air hose and clung to it, still kicking wildly with my flippers, as he towed me to where I could get a purchase on the windlass. I hung on for dear life, breathing heavily, and consequently adding to that stifling feeling which seems to accompany extreme effort or emotion underwater.

How was it, I stormed to myself, that everyone else was able to handle himself without difficulty, whereas, had it not been for Ed's assistance, I would have been swept away with the tide? Of course there was the comforting thought that my air hose would have brought me up short when I reached the end of it. Had I been wearing self-contained equipment, however, I might now be struggling helplessly against the tide, far out at sea. There was still a lot I had to learn about this underwater swimming, I decided.

I was far from enjoying that interval. I stayed close beside the windlass while Jane and Barney took turns diving down with their cameras to photograph the Link family underwater. Now and then I ventured a quick foray to some other piece of wreckage to which I could cling. When I saw the pictures later, I was surprised at the ease with which I appeared to be handling myself, one arm outstretched with careless grace as if I were examining something on the face of the wreckage. Such is the effect of a fluid environment, for in its grasp it is impossible to make an awkward movement.

I was still breathless when I climbed back on deck, and it took me the rest of the afternoon to recover. The other divers soothed my injured ego a little by assuring me that earlier in the afternoon there had been no difficulty. I had been unfortunate enough to join them just as the outgoing tide reached full force, and they, too, had had to exert every effort to carry on with their picture taking.

I now realized the meaning of those little arrows on our chart flanking "1½ knots" at the edge of the bank. I am sure the outgoing pull was much stronger than average that particular afternoon.

It really was not so surprising, I thought, that a sudden, shelf-like drop from less than two fathoms to the 150 fathoms at the edge of the Bahama canal should create such a condition. As a matter of fact, it probably explained why all that we had been able to find on these wreck sites at the edge of the bank were such heavy things as cannon, windlasses, anchors and chain. With such a current flowing twice a day over the years, anything less weighty must soon disintegrate and be carried off.

My experience that afternoon taught me a healthy respect for the power of tides such as I had never experienced along the shores and reefs of the Florida coast. Many times thereafter we encountered a similar situation as we explored the shoals and reefs of the Bahama banks, yet in other deep-water sections of the Bahamas we had no difficulty.

Before the afternoon was over, a wind from the northwest had sprung up and Ed suggested we seek an anchorage for the night on the Lily bank, in more protected waters. If this same wind continued on the morrow, he said, it would be too rough to search the outside reefs, and perhaps we had better start our survey for the brass cannon and the plate wreck, farther in on the bank.

When we woke the next morning, we found that the wind had returned to its normal summer position in the southeast. It was already blowing ten knots, roughing the surface of the water and destroying the clear visibility of the bottom. As we were already on the location, we decided to continue with our plan to search for the brass cannon and the plate wreck.

We had been told that we would probably find the cannon forming the center of a dark patch of coral, its grassy perimeter separated from the black center by a stretch of white sand. So Barney, Dick and Ed took turns watching from the crow's-nest as we followed carefully calculated compass courses back and forth across the banks. Each time the watcher spied a black patch, we cruised hopefully toward it, eyes peeled to catch a glimpse beneath the water of those loglike objects which would be brass cannon.

We found the entire Lily bank to be harmless, deep sand, but toward the middle of the afternoon, in the vicinity of Matanilla reef, we came upon some wicked-looking coral formations. After Sea Diver was anchored at a safe distance, Jane and Barney took the dinghy to examine them. They found a wild, awesome underwater wilderness, its brown, tumbled, rocky surface broken by deep crevasses full of seaweed and milling masses of fish.

When they were once more on board, we retreated southward a mile or so to the safety of the bank, where we anchored for the night. The day had passed without a glimpse of what we were seeking. Ed acknowledged the difficulty of the task we had set ourselves. It was all very well to know the latitude of the plate wreck, but with no longitude to assist us, Ed figured the wreck could lie anywhere within a ten-mile-long area. He retreated under the black hood once more to consult the loran. He found that Sea Diver was some distance north of the latitude which Captain Phips had designated on his chart. As she was also well east on the bank, he figured that by traveling due south in the morning until we reached the latitude of the plate wreck, and then heading directly west until we reached deep water at the far end of the bank, Sea Diver would be within the area of the lost ship.

Fortunately, the following day proved perfect for our task. The sea was so calm and clear that it appeared to have no depth at all. We explored every black patch which came within our vision as we slowly patrolled the bank. We finally reached deep water without even the thrill of a false hope. Then, finding ourselves in the deep water of the Bahama canal, which signaled the end of our course, we circled southward and started back across the banks in a southwesterly direction. The sea was as still as the extremely hot air which surrounded us. The day was ideal for our search, but our spirits were low, for it seemed most unlikely that what remained of the plate wreck would be exposed to view in such deep and shifting sand.

We had traveled on this last course for about a half hour when we glimpsed something sticking out of the water far ahead. By turns we looked at it through the binoculars, but could only make out that it was an open pyramidal structure set on a slant—perhaps some ship's wreckage or a drifted marker, we speculated, for there was no beacon indicated on our chart anywhere in this remote area of the banks.

We headed toward it in glassy water only two fathoms deep. Soon there was a cry of joy from Clayton, who was straddling the plank flooring of the pulpit. A school of porpoises had discovered Sea Diver and were sporting about the bow. To a man, the whole ship's company grabbed cameras and began photographing while the frolicsome animals raced and stunted and showed off before us like Hollywood veterans.

Snorting and cavorting, they would swim alongside, then make a sudden lunge into the white foam which curled up at our bow. In formations of three and four they raced along just beneath the surface, then with one accord leaped gracefully into the air. As they dove back into the water, we could hear their squeals of glee, and the peculiar sound of their breathing through the blowholes in the top of their heads. They stayed with us until Sea Diver approached what now appeared to be the remains of a drifted marker beacon. Then suddenly they were gone, and in their place we caught glimpses of hundreds of rapier-like barracuda swimming in easy, wide circles about the wreckage, their silver-and-black bodies gleaming against the brightly lighted white bottom sands. A school of smoothly curved "horse-eyes" slowly and deliberately circled Sea Diver. And as we paid out our anchor, a dozen amber jacks gathered at our stern; beyond them a churning mass of houndfish awaited the pleasure of the larger fish for supper.

I looked toward the numerous barracuda, ranging in size from two to six feet, as they milled about the waterlogged structure, and thanked my stars that I was on deck. Not so Jane and Barney.

"Come on, Jane. Here's our chance to get some pictures of barracuda," Barney called to her. The anchor was hardly down before they were over the side, armed with nothing more than a camera apiece. Barney struck out toward the fish and Jane followed. Now they were midway between the marker and the boat. The barracuda retreated before them, fanning out to each side as they approached. We called to them not to allow themselves to become encircled. They were taking pictures, maneuvering to get shots of each other in company with the fish. Barney was nearly to the marker when Jane called to him to come back.

"Barney, you don't have to get that far from the boat," she shouted, with just a hint of panic in her voice. "They'll follow you if you come *this* way."

And they did. But the savage-looking fish kept a respectful distance as the two swimmers retreated slowly toward the boat taking pictures all the time. They climbed back on board while scores of curious barracuda clustered only a few feet from the ladder.

With only one day left before we must return to Florida, we decided to abandon our nearly hopeless search on Lily bank and return to the reef north of Memory rock. Perhaps tomorrow we might come across the four cannon which had been seen by a fisherman at West End, and we figured it was just possible that these guns might mark the location of the copper wreck. We got Sea Diver under way and set our course southward. Just before sunset we anchored once more behind the reef where Phips had indicated the copper wreck was to be found.

Our last morning on the banks dawned hot, with little wind. Jane and Barney wanted to spend the day skin diving, so they took the small skiff, planning to tow it along behind them as they took turns swimming and diving along the outer edge of the reef. Ed, Clayton, and I started out with the glass-bottomed boat.

We searched the entire morning without coming across a single encouraging indication. Reaching the south end of the reef, we turned back toward Sea Diver. We could see Jane and Barney in the water some distance away, near where they had anchored the small boat. Suddenly they began to wave at us. They were shouting, too, but we could not make out their words over the noise of the outboard. We headed their way, thinking they were in trouble.

As we approached them, Jane gasped, "Cannon. Dozens of cannon. All over the bottom."

In the quiet which followed the cessation of our noisy outboard, they told us how Jane, who had been swimming along the surface gazing down through her face plate, had suddenly spied a cluster of cannon. When she and Barney dived on them, to their amazement they discovered there were more cannon lying in every direction.

We quickly cast anchor beside them, and soon were in the water, where we could observe the coral-crusted guns from the surface. There were indeed dozens of them. A series of exploratory dives failed to reveal any other signs of the wreck, though there might be many objects hidden in the coral growths which partially covered the bottom. Could it be we had found the copper wreck? We decided to bring Sea Diver to the spot so that we could use the air equipment and examine the bottom more carefully.

When I reached the bottom of the ladder in my diving gear that summer afternoon, I looked down upon a golden underwater world. The sun beaming through the translucent water in slanting rays turned the sandy bottom to purest gold, and illuminated the scattered cannon and coral formations until they, too, shone, their surfaces ornamented with the vivid reds and greens and purples of numerous sea growths, which gleamed like jewels against the gold encrustation. Yellow and purple sea fans and snaky lavender Gorgonia waved to and fro in the tide.

We made the most of our few remaining hours. When there weren't enough air hoses to go around, those who were left without them spent their time floating on the surface, from whence they made numerous dives to examine or photograph whatever caught their eye below. Ed and Barney combed the bottom with the metal detector, and we all searched the area carefully, hoping to come across other evidences of the wrecked ship.

By the end of the afternoon we were convinced that, as in the other wrecks we had found on the same reef, whatever may have lain there originally had long since been swept away in the powerful tidal flow of decades. There were left only about thirty heavy cannon and a scattering of rock ballast. The cannon, Ed said, were mostly British carronades of the early nineteenth century. The metal detector had failed to reveal any hidden metals in the coral and sand which surrounded them.

We returned to the protected waters behind the reef to anchor for the night, our search at an end. We had found no sign of the copper wreck; yet we felt sure that it was upon this very reef that Captain Phips had found and salvaged it. Could we but look long and hard enough, we might still come across some trace of it.

But we were now convinced that if either the Genuees wreck or the copper wreck should be found on these outer reefs, they long since would have been swept clean of any worth-while artifacts. As to the plate wreck, it was probably buried in the shifting bottom sands of the Lily bank, to be revealed only at some rare moment when an unusually disturbed sea might uncover it briefly. It was scarcely probable that fortune would favor us to such an extent.

We put Jane, Barney and Dick Burrows ashore at West End the following afternoon. The Criles planned to catch the plane from Nassau to Palm Beach on its semiweekly stop at Grand Bahama, for Barney had to be in his operating room in Cleveland the following morning. Dick was to hop an island freighter for Nassau. This left Ed, Clayton and me to crew Sea Diver across the Gulf Stream to Miami, where we planned to meet Mendel Peterson the next morning and then proceed to Art McKee's wreck in the Florida keys.

We felt very much alone after the fun and excitement of the past two weeks, and not a little disappointed that we had failed to turn up anything of consequence in our meanderings. But I had forgotten the odd-shaped chunks of coral-covered metal which we had picked up at Burrows cay until I stubbed my toe on one of them as I hurried forward to help get Sea Diver under way for the all-night crossing to Miami.

"What do you suppose is under that coral?" I questioned Ed as I took the wheel, while he and Clayton made ready to haul in the anchor. It was not the first time we had speculated over the identity of these salvaged objects which we had dynamited loose from the shallow bottom off Burrows cay.

Dick had taken us to the wreck on our way from Cay Gorda to West End. He told us that a remote Spanish ancestor of his had been shipwrecked on the island and that this was how it had received its name. We had anchored Sea Diver some distance from the small cay and gone in on the skiff, for the remains were in only about a fathom of water. There was little wreckage to be seen, but in the coral rock which formed the bottom we could faintly discern a few stubby cylindrical shapes which appeared to be short pieces of pipe or broken sections of cannon.

Ed and Barney had blasted out two of them and laboriously transferred them aboard Sea Diver. They were heavily encased in coral, which we had left on to protect the inner metal until we reached Florida and could immerse them in fresh water. They were apparently very old, for a chunk of coral which had broken off from one end was more than an inch thick.

Although the night's crossing was uneventful, the summer sky dazzling with stars above the fluorescent surface of the sea, it will always linger in my mind. We were barely out of sight of the Bahamas when we first picked up the luminous flush in the western sky which was Miami and the Gold Coast. I slept for a brief two hours in the heart of the night and then took over the watch, anticipating that breath-taking moment when the man-made glow of the Florida coast would be matched by the dawn light in the east.

I was not disappointed. Wrapped in a steamer robe on the foredeck of Sea Diver while the faithful automatic pilot guided us steadily toward home port, I watched the first faint light creep upward in the east, paling the stars and giving a faint apricot tint to the edges of the scattered clouds hanging heavily over the now-vanished Bahamas. Then, as the sun rose above the horizon, the apricot deepened until the whole eastern sky was filled with brilliant orange. Only the delicate cirrus clouds in the south bore remembrance of the apricot dawn.

Ahead of Sea Diver the medley of lights which was civilization gradually disappeared in the dawn; the sweeping beam of Hillsboro light beyond Fort Lauderdale was no longer visible. The blinking colored lights on the tall towers, which had previously indicated to us the location of Miami, had vanished. Ahead could be seen only a dim, low coastline. A few miles more and it would be possible to distinguish the tall hotels along the water front of Miami Beach.

Ed and Clayton, awakened by the morning light, joined me on the foredeck and together we watched with binoculars for the first clue as to our position. At last we were able to pick out the thickened horizon which was Miami Beach. With a slight change of course we continued toward the stone jetties guarding the entrance to Miami, skirted the now-towering white façades of Miami Beach, picked up the navigation markers of the outer harbor entrance and then swung into the long approach to Miami. Quickly inspected by quarantine authorities as we halted briefly in the channel, we went on to customs clearance, and by nine o'clock were in the yacht basin in downtown Miami.

We were just tying up when Pete hailed us. Tossing his duffle aboard, he helped to set the spring lines, then joined us on deck. We showed him the few pieces we had recovered from the Bahama waters—the iron balustrade that looked like a bedpost; the stubby, cylindrical-shaped iron pipes which might be broken gun barrels; a battered grenade; and some metallic ballast from the wreck off Cay Gorda.

To our surprise he evinced a great interest in the cylinders. "Where's a mallet? Let's see what's under this coral," he said.

As the coral fell away, we saw what appeared to be the muzzle end of a small cannon. The piece was so short I felt sure it was broken, yet both ends were as smooth and finished as the ends of a pipe. The second piece proved to be similar, though larger in circumference.

"Are these all you have of it?" Pete queried, as he laid the two pieces on the deck with a space between.

"Well, there were some other pieces in the coral on the bottom," Ed said, "but we didn't know what they were, and they were apparently all alike, so I only brought a couple of them along."

"You could get the rest of it then?" Pete seemed relieved. I wondered at his constant use of the singular.

"Do you know what you have here?" he questioned.

He told us that these pieces were part of an ancient cannon called a lombard, which was in common use until the middle of the sixteenth century. After that time it was replaced by the type of barrel we know today, which is molded all in one piece. The earlier guns, he said, were made exactly like a barrel, the wrought-iron bars bound together with metal hoops which were shrunk around them to hold them in place. The particular lombard we had found was broken into sections. Apparently we had failed to recover the one or two additional sections which would make it complete.

Just such a piece of armament had announced to Christopher Columbus aboard the Santa Maria that land had been sighted from the Pinta, as his small fleet approached the Bahama islands on that historic voyage westward in 1492. Pete said that these parts which we had found probably dated back to within sixty years of Columbus's discovery of America and, as far as he knew, represented the only lombard in existence today which had been found within the American continents.

He was insistent that at the first opportunity we must return to Burrows cay to see if we could recover the missing parts of the gun. In the meantime he would send the two pieces to the Smithsonian, where the long process of curing and preserving them could be begun.

Pete also examined with interest other things we had found at Burrows cay: broken bits of brown pottery, now-crumbled bits of tarred hempen line, and a misshapen hollow metal ball with a fuse hole in the end. From these various small artifacts he deduced that there were two separate wrecks upon the same spot, the earlier wreck bearing the Columbus-period lombards, and the later one, probably eighteenth century, containing the grenade, the tarred line and the pottery.

So our voyage had not been a complete failure after all. Ed was sure we would be able to recover the additional section of the lombard, although, he said, we probably would not be back in that part of the Bahamas again until the following year.

Unwittingly, we had found a sample of armament long since relegated to history. Thus were sown in us the first seeds which were to result in the climaxing voyage of

our explorations with Sea Diver—a voyage during which
we would seek the place of Columbus's first landfall and
his route through the Bahamas when he discovered the
New World, and during which we would search for the
unknown reef off the north coast of Haiti where the Santa
Maria met her doom. The voyage would also include the
faraway Silver shoals beyond Turks island, where Captain
Phips made fame and fortune with his discovery of a
treasure-laden Spanish plate ship.

2

○

○

○

Pete's identification of the sixteenth-century lombard made us eager to return to Burrows cay to secure the missing section. But although we spent the entire winter of 1953–54 in the Bahamas, it was not until summer that we anchored once more near the site of that disaster.

We found the place undisturbed since our previous visit. It was plain to see how the ship had ended up where its ballast now lay, in scarcely six feet of water just off the island's rocky shore. It had wrecked on the edge of the Little Bahama bank, just where a ship caught in a storm, heading through Northwest Providence channel, could easily have been swept into the shallows near the shore. The fact that there were also remains from a more recent wreck on the same spot was proof of its hidden menace.

We searched the site with great care, hoping to find other evidences of worth, but aside from the scattered stone ballast there was nothing left but the odd pieces of cannon.

It required another small charge of dynamite to loosen

the remaining sections from the bottom. These Barney and Ed quickly transferred to Sea Diver. This time, knowing their value, they hastened to submerge the two sections they had retrieved in a barrel of fresh water to prevent their deteriorating further before delivery to the Smithsonian.

We made Nassau our headquarters that year, berthing Sea Diver at the Yacht Haven, a popular center for yachts from every part of the world. We planned to track down a score of stories we had heard of wrecked ships and sunken treasure in widely scattered parts of the Bahamas.

We were better equipped than ever before, for Sea Diver was now fitted with radar and sonar as well as specially designed plates to keep her from rolling when at anchor. We also looked forward to a permanent crew of two—Vital Jetty, the French-Canadian who for many years had looked after our place in the Canadian bush; and Edward Kemp, a native Bahamian from Andros island who had crewed for us during our visits to the Bahamas the previous winter.

When Vital had accompanied us to Marathon on our initial diving venture, his first time away from the familiar forest life of lumbering, hunting and trapping, we had been amazed at the readiness with which he had adapted himself to living on a sailboat, and his versatility in handling the many strange tasks which confronted him. He had heartily disliked the summer heat of the Florida keys, but in spite of this he must have found sufficient interest and adventure in that first job to make him willing to set out with us again.

Although he could neither read nor write, and his English was an amusing blend picked up in the lumber camps and colored with outcroppings of his native French, he had a very keen mind. He need only watch Ed start a motor or repair a piece of equipment once; from then on he was able to repeat the process. He liked to keep things clean and tidy, which was a most welcome attribute aboard Sea Diver; and he could cook like a French chef.

We had wondered when we set out that winter how Vital and Edward Kemp would get along together, for Kemp, an equally adept member of his part of the world, was possessed of an entirely different temperament. He had grown up in the little village of Nicolls' Town on the eastern shore of Andros island, close to Morgan's bluff at its northern tip. From early boyhood he had been schooled in the seamanship of the banks, accompanying the older fishermen of the community on long trips in the native sailing sloops in search of fish and crawfish. Now in his own village Kemp was kingpin. He was an official of the government and a warden of the church. He owned extensive property and a crawfish boat of his own which he rented to his fellow villagers. As Captain Ed Kemp he was well known throughout the Bahamas.

He was a good-looking black man, tall and well built, with an affable, easygoing nature which wore well. He was very religious, and it became a familiar sight to see him perched on the stool behind the automatic pilot, a pair of little steel-rimmed spectacles clinging to his bony features, carefully tracing out the words of well-worn religious tracts which he carried with him faithfully on all occasions. He was a most abstemious man, who never took a drink and seldom smoked. Kemp was handy in the galley, too, where he produced some delicious Bahamian dishes.

But his chief value to us was his uncanny ability to find his way about in the shallow waters of the Bahama banks. With Kemp watching from the pulpit, we did not need a fathometer—in fact, he was much more dependable, for his quick eyes picked up the shallow places long before we had reached them. And many times his outstretched arm motioned us in careful detours about coral heads and shallow sandbanks which we otherwise might have hit.

We were indeed fortunate in the respective abilities and personalities of our crew. But it was not until we had lived aboard ship with them for some time that we came to appreciate how favored we were. The two men, so different in appearance and temperament, were soon fast friends. This, in spite of the fact that after many weeks they were still not always able to understand each other —the broken English of the French-Canadian and the heavy Conch accent of the colored Bahamian.

Vital, with his quick Gallic wit, constantly twitted the slower-minded Kemp, who nevertheless always managed to hold his own in his good-natured way with a dignified and often apt reply.

We were entranced at the colorful interchange of conversation which went on between them—comparisons of winter in the bush with year-round summer on the banks; of fishing in Canadian lakes and streams with deep-water fishing and crawfishing in the Bahamas; of dangerous hurricanes which Kemp had experienced, and the perils of blizzards which Vital had met while following his trap line, miles from civilization. They discussed their respective Catholic and Baptist faiths, marriage and children, the technique of canoe construction as compared to that of the sturdy Bahamian dinghy; and so on and on and on.

As there was only the one cabin on the deck of Sea Diver, around which the whole life of shipboard centered, from navigating the ship in the pilot house to preparing the meals and doing up the dishes in the galley;

and as three times a day all on board must of necessity gather here to eat and drink, our voyages were continually enlivened by this interesting pair.

Kemp, the previous winter on Sea Diver, had been well indoctrinated with our enthusiasm for sunken wrecks and treasure ships. So when we dropped anchor in Pleasant Harbor behind his home at Nicolls' Town in January of 1954, he was there to meet us. He hurried aboard, bursting with stories which he had gathered of piles of ballast and cannon upon the banks. Our chart of the area in the vicinity of Andros island was soon sprinkled with dots and notes describing what was to be found in the various locations. He promised us that when we were ready to look for the wrecks, he could produce the men who had told him of them.

Unfortunately we found ourselves once more beset by the same high winds and heavy seas which had characterized the winter months in previous years. And although the fishermen Kemp brought along were sure they could lead us directly to the wreck indications which they had seen on the banks, we combed these waters day after day whenever weather permitted without coming across a single objective.

Several times we were endangered by heavy seas in the Tongue of the Ocean, which skirts the Andros island reefs. And once, when our anchor dragged, we found ourselves aground in Conch sound, with east winds of twenty knots blowing us ever harder upon the solid coral bottom near the shore. It took the arduous labors of all hands over an anxious period from sundown to the following noon, plus the help of some fifteen villagers, to get Sea Diver off. Fortunately, she escaped with only a chewed-up wormshoe and a slightly bent wheel, which Ed, working underwater, was later able to straighten.

After many days of fruitless search, hampered by the rough seas, we decided to head south by way of the Tongue of the Ocean for the poorly charted and almost unknown banks south of Andros. Here we hoped to come upon two wrecks which Kemp advocated enthusiastically. We had only to follow the directions which he had obtained from a Curly cay fisherman, he assured us, to cast our anchor beside the cannon which distinguished them.

It was a long trip to this area, and we spent the first night at Fresh creek, halfway down Andros, so as to arrive at our goal with plenty of daylight left to find an anchorage. It was well that we did, for upon our arrival the following afternoon we found our chart was useless. Once inside the banks we would not have dared to move had it not been for Kemp's careful piloting.

There followed several days of picking a route for Sea Diver through a maze of coral heads, and of searching without success for the cannon which were supposed to mark the two wrecks. We spent one frightening night among the reefs while thunderstorms, one after another, raged past us with winds up to forty knots threatening to tear us from our anchorage.

During our sojourn on this remote spot, Ed and I took time to indulge ourselves in some fascinating hours of diving upon bottom which we were sure had never before been explored. We raided shallow beds of finger coral, spreading the smelly stuff all over Sea Diver's upper decks to bleach. Ed dived up quantities of conch and crawfish, which abounded on the banks, while Vital and Kemp amused themselves by filling the freezer with a limitless variety of fish which they had caught from the small boat.

Then we headed for Nassau. We had found no trace of wreckage, although we had followed every clue. At Nassau we spent considerable time tied up at our dock, for the winds blew almost continuously for weeks. Once word got around of Sea Diver's purpose, we were besieged by a continuous stream of islanders, some diffidently, some boldly, attempting to sell us information as to locations of cannon or ballast stone on the bottom.

At first we listened with eagerness, convinced that when the weather improved, we would have a number of wrecks to search out. We jotted down the names of our informers and where they could be located, and we arranged to get in touch with them to guide us at the proper time. Between storms we even managed to search for two piles of ballast within short runs of Nassau. We spent several days combing the areas which our guides indicated, but we never came across a clue.

After a few experiences of this kind Ed decided that rather than pay a set sum a day for these men to guide us, he would offer them only their keep while they were aboard, but if they were able to take us to the site, he would double the usual daily wage. He also promised that if we found anything of value, we would share with them on an equal basis.

It was remarkable what a difference this made in the number of candidates and the length of time they were willing to put on a project. I am sure it was responsible for weeding out many a speculative Bahamian who had nothing to lose but his time, and yet could gain, almost for the asking, a pleasant trip on Sea Diver with pay.

One morning there appeared on the dock alongside Sea Diver a graying old colored gentleman with a most patrician manner. He inquired for Ed in a soft, pleasing voice. He was from the Abaco islands to the north of Nassau, he said, and he told us a fascinating yarn of buried treasure on the outer shore of one of these islands. Like most of our callers, he seemed sure that we would be able to go ashore there with our metal detector and locate the pirate's trove without any difficulty. He was most disappointed when Ed told him that we were interested in investigating only underwater treasure.

But then his face brightened. He lowered his voice mysteriously. "I knows a wrack, sir, not very far from here. They's always finding silver on the shore. I've even picked up some myself."

He went on to say that a pile of ballast lay in the water a few hundred feet from land, and that many times following a storm the villagers had found pieces of eight on the beach. This sounded most interesting and we questioned him eagerly.

"They says it was a Spanish treasure ship, and those brass guns at Government house was taken off it. I dunno, sir. Maybe there's still silver there on the bottom."

"Where is the ballast? How deep is the water? Can you show us the spot?"

Our questions came thick and fast. Perhaps at last we would come upon a worth-while wreck. But when he said Cay Gorda, our hopes were dashed. It had indeed been a rich find. It was here that Art McKee and Charlie Brookfield, several years before, had come upon three heavy silver bars, two of which were now on display at Art's museum.

We had thrilled at Art's story of their discovery—how the two men had culled the leadlike bullion from a pile of ballast rock which lay in a scattered heap near Cay Gorda. Working from a small boat in heavy diving gear, they had sorted over the ballast, which lay in water only about ten feet deep. They had seen no other signs of the ship, and it was their belief that after knocking out its bottom in the shallow water, the hull had been carried out to sea, where it had sunk in the deeper water farther offshore.

We had headed eagerly for Cay Gorda on our first

trip to the Bahamas with Sea Diver in March, 1953, accompanied by the retired Canadian Air Marshal, Robert Leckie, and his wife, Sally, both of whom were enthusiastically indulging in their first diving experience.

Cay Gorda turned out to be a pretty, palm-sprinkled island with a scattering of rude thatched huts facing on a small, almost landlocked harbor formed by a rocky outer cay. We anchored Sea Diver offshore and approached the settlement in the glass-bottomed boat, not wishing to risk putting the larger boat aground in the narrow entrance. We found only a fisherman, his wife and two children on the island. They explained that no one lived on Cay Gorda any more; that they and some of the other villagers from nearby Sandy Point used the island to raise some small crops and occasionally spent a few days there cultivating their gardens. The man knew of the ballast we were seeking and obligingly skulled us to its location in his heavy native skiff.

It lay only a few hundred feet beyond the southern entrance to the harbor, in water of not more than two fathoms, just at the edge of a shelf where the bottom dropped off sharply into much deeper water. Through the fisherman's glass bucket we took turns looking at the ballast, which lay in a scattered pile on the bottom. It seemed likely that some of these irregular shapes might turn out to be silver. Without a detector, how could Art and Charlie have been sure that they had retrieved all of the valuable bullion?

We decided to return to Sea Diver and bring her in where we could anchor her close to the ballast pile.

"This should be easy," Ed said hopefully, as he guided the vessel toward the yellow buoy which we had left to mark the spot. "When I turn the metal detector on that pile of rocks, it will soon tell us whether or not there is any silver left there."

As soon as our anchor was down, he and Bob disappeared eagerly over the side with the metal detector. Sally and I followed them into the water and watched from the surface as they scanned the rock pile with the instrument. About a quarter hour later I saw Ed pick up a piece of the ballast stone, and he and Bob headed for the ship. I swam back to the boarding ladder to meet them.

Raising his face mask, Ed said, "There's something peculiar about that wreck. I think the stones have a metallic content. The detector goes crazy wherever I point it."

He carried the piece of ballast aboard and he and Bob examined it carefully. Sure enough, it contained a slight sprinkling of a foreign substance which looked like zinc, and it responded definitely to testing with the detector.

"Well, there's a pretty how-do-you-do," said Ed, disgusted. "How are you going to pick out silver when the whole pile is jumping?"

The detector was useless. There was nothing to do but handle each piece of ballast separately in hopes that a bar or two of the bullion might have been missed by previous searchers. Ed and Bob spent the remainder of the afternoon at this arduous task.

They climbed wearily aboard just as the sun was sinking, convinced that whatever silver bars may have lain there in the past, the carcass was now picked clean. Furthermore, Ed said he felt sure that on such a hard and rocky bottom there was little chance that anything else of interest would have survived the constant action of the sea, which surged in and out of the cove with strength even upon a calm day. There was one more chance. With the aid of the magnetometer and the glass-bottomed boat we might be able to locate the remainder of the wreck, which must have been swept into the deeper water offshore.

So after rigging the magnetometer behind Sea Diver

the following morning, Ed spent the next two days combing carefully back and forth over the deep water adjacent to the ballast site. To make sure that we did not miss a clue, Bob Leckie patiently guided Sally and me in turn over the same territory in the glass-bottomed boat, hoping to glimpse some sign of wreckage which the magnetometer might miss. But there was not a trace of anything. The whole bottom was as clean as if it had been swept with a giant broom. The arrival of a "norther" on the third day forced us to give up our search and head for Nassau.

We did not abandon our hopes of Cay Gorda with that one attempt, however. That same summer, on our way to Burrows cay with Jane and Barney, we stopped off there again. In the meantime we had come to the conclusion that if coins had been washed up on the beach in such numbers over the years, there must still be some in the sandy bottom between the ballast pile and shore.

Sure enough. After a morning of scrounging at the edge of the rock pile, we managed to find three heavily encrusted coins. Only one of them was in sufficiently good condition to permit identification, and that was only after Jane had patiently sanded away at the encrustation over a period of several days. It proved to be a Spanish silver coin of the seventeenth century, a crude cob with a shield upon one side and a square cross with castle and lions in alternate corners. We later ascertained that this coin coincided with the authenticated period of the silver bars which had come from the same site.

While we now felt that we had explored every possibility at Cay Gorda, there still remained one facet of this interesting wreck to be followed. Since our first visit we had heard tales of fishermen obtaining ballast for their boats from this convenient spot, where the water was so shallow that the bars could be hooked up from the bottom. Lead ballast was particularly prized in this world of scarce rock and metal, and it was said that several of the boats now carried "lead" ballast in their holds. No doubt by now these vessels were scattered all over the Bahamas. In fact, three of them, we were told, had been sunk in hurricanes, two on the shallow banks to the north, and a third on the banks beyond Northwest Channel light.

It was these tales which had inspired Ed to return to the Bahamas in September with the Widgeon. Kemp had told him that it was then, during the hurricane season, that the owners of the boats pulled them up on shore to recalk and paint them. Necessarily the ballast was removed and cleaned at the same time.

Could it be that among the worthless ballast might be some of the "lead" bars from Cay Gorda? Of course Ed realized that at the time Art and Charlie had found the three silver bars, every piece of lead ballast in that section of the Bahamas must have been hopefully scrutinized by its owner. Still he felt it was worth a gamble, for with the plane he could canvass any number of fishing villages in a few days' time. Should a hurricane suddenly materialize, it would be easy to outstrip it and fly to the safety of the mainland.

This venture yielded a most surprising result. In several of the villages he was told that an American in a small cruiser had appeared during the hurricane season the previous year on a similar mission.

We were never able to trace down the story of this American who had preceded us. Because of the strict rules of the Bahamian government on treasure-trove, we felt certain that if any silver had been found, it had been spirited quietly away; for neither the ultimate owner nor the natives who had profited by the transaction would have admitted it and thus been forced to share their gain with the government. This has proved most unfortunate for the preservation of much memorabilia, as in consequence many precious objects which have been recovered must have been melted and recast into anonymous shapes of gold and silver before being placed upon the market.

The Bahamas abound in tales of the discovery of caches of old coins in abandoned wells, in the foundations of long-destroyed houses and outbuildings, and in caves and rocky pits. Many of these stories are true, for in the early days of pirates and desperadoes there was no other way for the householder to secure his valuables.

The shrewd natives coming upon these caches over the past century have learned to keep their discoveries secret, for their prosperity is short-lived once the acquisitive government learns of their finds. Instead they hoard the coins, exchanging them one or a few at a time where they will create the least attention; delighted when they can find a visiting American who will give them good present-day currency in their place.

There still remained to be located the three fishing sloops bearing "lead" ballast from Cay Gorda which had foundered in hurricanes upon the banks. While we were based at Nicolls' Town, Kemp produced a fine-looking young fisherman named Yorick, who claimed he could take us to the location of the foundered sloop which had carried the Cay Gorda ballast on the banks north of Andros. We made several trips, with Yorick as our guide, in search of it. Always we seemed to run into foul weather or heavy seas before the ballast could be located. But because Yorick was so sincere in his efforts, and Kemp was so sure that he would eventually take us there, we kept on trying.

Even in May of 1956, en route to Jamaica by way of Nassau, we stopped off once again in this area and spent the afternoon in a fruitless search for this wreck. To the best of our knowledge it still lies undiscovered somewhere in the vicinity of Northwest Channel light. Somehow we have never found the time to search for the other two victims of the hurricane on the banks near Cay Gorda. So perhaps someday, even yet, these piles of worthless rock will yield a harvest of silver bars to the happy explorer who comes upon them.

3

○

○

○

It was our finding of the old lombard dating from the time of Columbus which first sparked our interest in the wanderings of the Great Explorer. For the question was immediately raised as to whether the ancient gun could have come from one of Columbus's ships.

Consequently we sought out Columbus's account of his voyage to the west in 1492, in which he described the first land he saw in the New World, the Bahamian island known to the Indians as Guanahani, which he called San Salvador. We found from other sources that while there existed a great deal of controversy as to the identity of this island, it was the general consensus that his first landfall was upon Watling island, about halfway down the chain of Bahamian islands which front on the Atlantic.

There was no reason to think that any of the ships under Columbus's command during the four voyages he made to the New World ever sailed anywhere near the area where we found the lombard. Instead, we learned, subsequent voyages led him more and more to the south. After

that first expedition, the Bahamas were completely neglected for the more lush and profitable lands in the vicinity
of the Caribbean.

While we were debating the question of where Columbus's sailings had taken him, we came across a small
book, *Guanahani Again,* which questioned whether Columbus had in fact made his first landfall on Watling island.
It had been written by Captain Pieter Verhoog, an officer
of the Holland-America Line, who had made many voyages through Bahamian waters. Captain Verhoog maintained with careful, well-documented arguments that Columbus had first set foot on the island of Caicos, farther
to the south. As his study was backed by years of research among the original manuscripts dealing with all
aspects of Columbus's voyages, it seemed to us that his
selection of the Caicos archipelago and the consequent
route which Columbus took through the Bahamas was
worthy of consideration.

But then I recollected having read, several years before, a fascinating account of Columbus's voyages, *Admiral
of the Ocean Sea,* by the well-known naval historian, Rear
Admiral Samuel Morison. The book was aboard Sea Diver,
and we reread it thoroughly, meanwhile comparing Morison's picture of Columbus's first voyage with Verhoog's
account. Necessarily, because of the selection of different
islands for the first landfall, the two scholars had traced
radically different courses for the little fleet through the
Bahamas to Cuba.

From then on, in our spare time, Ed and I pored over
the writings of various historians from Columbus's time
on, not neglecting to read and compare the various translations of Columbus's *Journal.* Instead of solving the problem to our satisfaction, we became more confused.

Navarrete, the first historian to render the early Columbus documents available to the world, in the early

nineteenth century, had selected Grand Turk island as Columbus's San Salvador. Washington Irving, soon after, in the *Life and Voyages of Christopher Columbus,* sited Cat island as the first landfall, while others had selected Watling and Atwood islands. Of course, the variety of choices had resulted in the selection of completely different paths which the Santa Maria might have sailed through the Bahamas before her tragic end on an unknown reef off the north shore of Hispaniola.

None of these earlier writers had ever visited these Bahama waters. Their theories had been evolved only from reading Columbus's *Journal* and from a study of the very unreliable charts of the centuries following his discovery. Captain Verhoog, on the other hand, had the advantage of having sailed these same waters, although from the high deck of a fast-moving steamer. And Dr. Morison had made a special voyage from Spain and later through the Bahamas, where he had traced out the course which he believed Columbus had followed, checking each leg of the route with the *Journal.*

Here again there was much chance for error, for there are no charts in existence today of the track of the original voyage; and the early maps of this area were grossly inaccurate, the islands being charted in most unrealistic positions, their names bandied back and forth in a welter of confusion.

Furthermore, we learned, Columbus's *Journal* as it exists today is not the original but a rendition from the original made by Las Casas in his *Historia de las Indias* many years later, in which he abridged most of the original log, quoting in detail only the day of the first landfall and the following twelve days. Las Casas condensed all other entries, and recorded them in such a way that references to Columbus are generally in the third person.

Forced to remain tied up at our dock in Nassau by bad weather, we found plenty of time to mull over these controversial facts. Then one day our very good friend, Philip Van Horn Weems, retired United States Navy officer and founder and head of the Weems System of Navigation, arrived on board Sea Diver for a brief stay. It was Captain Weems who had first introduced us to Verhoog's theory, and we soon found ourselves involved in long debates with him as to the relative merits of Morison's and Verhoog's arguments. It was during these discussions that the idea first occurred to us to go and see for ourselves.

After all, it should not be difficult to take Sea Diver south to the vicinity of Caicos island and trace out the course championed by Verhoog. Upon our return journey we could carefully go over the course from Watling island selected by Dr. Morison. Sea Diver was particularly well adapted to such a trip, for she did not differ too greatly from the original Spanish ships in size and speed, and we should be able to take her wherever Columbus might have gone.

Captain Weems enthusiastically agreed to go with us. We could have chosen no better companion, for he is without doubt the outstanding navigation expert in the world today, and a man who plunges heart and soul into whatever he undertakes. A man of nearly three score years and ten, his broad shoulders and powerful muscles bear testimony to a lifetime of physical activity. From early youth in the Naval Academy, when he won the Olympic wrestling championship for the United States, to the present, he has maintained a high level of physical health and dexterity. With his years of experience in navigation and seamanship, the practical diplomacy acquired from his naval career, and his strength and experience in the water, he would be a most valuable member of our team.

It was while we were discussing plans for this trip that Captain Weems fairly took our breath away with another idea.

"What chance do you think we would have of finding the remains of the Santa Maria?" he said. He told us that he had been reading a treatise of Morison's describing the loss of the Santa Maria when it struck a reef in the harbor off of Cap Haitien at midnight on Christmas eve of 1492.

"Morison went down there and investigated that area," Captain Weems continued. "He even picked out the exact reef where he thinks the Santa Maria sank." He brought forth a copy of Morison's paper, and we examined the chart which was included, showing the harbor off Cap Haitien and the wreck reef which Morison had selected as the last resting place of the Santa Maria. We spent an exciting evening as we reviewed the possibilities of finding the lost ship.

Ed figured that some of the metal ship fittings, anchors and armament would still exist, as on many of the old ships we had searched. Even though Columbus had salvaged what he could of the wrecked Santa Maria to construct a fortification ashore, there must have been parts of the ship which were inaccessible to the salvagers. These must still be on the bottom, heavily coated with coral and much corroded after the centuries. We had never examined a wreck as ancient as the nearly five-centuries-old Santa Maria, but if the lombard which we had found in the north Bahamas had endured since that early time, it was most probable that the metal remains of the Santa Maria would still be intact. With our metal detector and magnetometer we should have a good chance of locating one of the most historic ships of all time.

The next day Captain Weems returned to Sea Diver from a visit to town, brimming over with enthusiasm. He had been to the Haitian consulate to talk over the possibilities with them. They had assured him that arrangements could be made for us to explore the waters off Cap Haitien, and that their government would be most interested in encouraging the search.

We considered the situation, for we knew nothing of sea and weather conditions in that area. We recalled from talks in the past with some of our sailing friends that big seas were usual along that coast. We knew that this was an area where there was a rainy and a dry season. We must be sure to plan our trip at a time when the water would be clear, and there would be the least number of storms to disturb our work. We seriously considered the possibility of leaving that very spring, but when we added up the requirements that must be met, we finally decided that the expedition must wait until the following year.

In the meantime another possibility presented itself and grew with fascinating urgency and appeal. Ever since we had perused William Phips's charts and realized the exciting possibility of locating the remains of the Spanish treasure ship on the Silver shoals, we had toyed with the thought of someday visiting these remote waters and attempting to secure the riches which Phips had indicated still remained beneath the coral. For although the New England sea captain had been fortunate enough to remove more than a million and a half pounds' worth of gold and silver from the wreck, he had noted in his log that his divers had been unable to penetrate a large section of the hull which had become heavily encased with coral in the years it had lain on the bottom. He had intimated that it still contained a substantial portion of the bullion which he was forced to abandon.

To me, an expedition to the Silver shoals seemed only a dream—a dangerous adventure in far-off waters, which, while it tantalized my imagination, I had no real desire to investigate further. After all, one could pick no more risky a spot in the whole hemisphere, for the wreck lay in a forty-mile-square area of reefs far from any land. I was content to speculate and to dream.

Now, however, if we were to take Sea Diver to Turks island, where Verhoog believed Columbus had seen a light just prior to his discovery of San Salvador, it seemed reasonable to include a trip to the Silver shoals, only a hundred miles beyond.

By the summer of 1954 our plans were pretty well set. We would begin our expedition by searching for the Santa Maria at Cap Haitien. From there we would go to the Silver shoals, some 150 miles to the northeast. With this phase of our trip completed by early summer, we would head for Turks island and the Caicos to investigate the possible Columbus routes. We expected to spend several months in these three enterprises, varying the time spent on each according to our findings.

Ed and I found ourselves swamped with correspondence in regard to the three projects—with Mendel Peterson at the Smithsonian, with Captain Weems, the Criles, and the dozens of other candidates who hoped to join us at various times. There was an exchange of letters with officials in the Bahamas, Haiti, the Dominican Republic, and arrangements to be made for caches of fuel oil for Sea Diver and special aviation gasoline for the Widgeon, which Ed intended to have available to aid in our searches.

We corresponded with Captain Verhoog and Dr. Morison in order to clarify questions which arose as to points in their theories of Columbus's route. We were swamped with requests for information about our plans from magazines and newspapers. And in our spare time we continued to hunt out every last bit of material we could find in regard to all three subjects.

I was surprised to learn that we were going into an

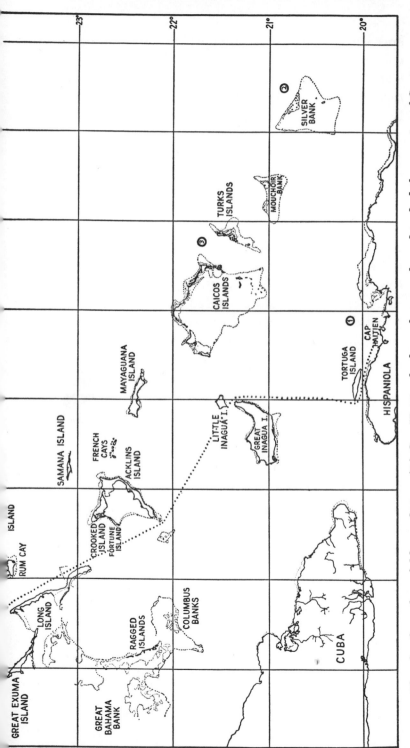

The plan for a three-fold expedition: (1) Cap Haitien harbor where we hoped to find the remains of Santa Maria; (2) the Silver shoals where Captain William Phips salvaged millions from a Spanish treasure ship; (3) the approach to Caicos islands where we had reason to think Columbus made his first landfall in the New World. (Dotted line shows intended route from Nassau to Cap Haitien.)

area where it would be impossible to provide ourselves with many of the necessities of civilization. There were many special problems which must be solved ahead of time. It would be no easy task to foresee and to equip Sea Diver with all the essentials which would be required for months away from our mechanized civilization.

For instance, it was necessary to install extra water tanks and to investigate a method of purifying our water supply for the time when we would have to refill our tanks from the questionable water sources to be found in the remote islands. We would need extra parts for engines and machinery.

Once our supply of fresh meat, eggs and vegetables was used up, we would have to depend upon less perishable foods which could be stored aboard indefinitely, for we would be far from land for weeks at a time, and only the simplest requirements would be obtainable from the small ports which we might visit in between. We must be provided with medicines and first-aid equipment to take care of any emergency, for at the Silver shoals we would not even have radio communication.

Ed felt that the newly installed radar and sonar, as well as a Bludworth depthometer which was to be installed, would be of great assistance in our navigation and search. In addition to assembling a complete set of charts of the entire area, he ordered special charts drawn up for the loran, thus making it possible to use this instrument in a section of the ocean to which it had never before been adapted.

Two large rubber life rafts with escape equipment were added to Sea Diver's gear, and the ever-faithful glass-bottomed skiff was provided with two new outboard motors. But the real addition to our boating equipment was a shallow-draft eighteen-foot cruiser which Ed designed and equipped to be used in dangerous reef waters where it was unsafe to venture with Sea Diver.

With all preliminary arrangements completed, we started out from Miami with Sea Diver in February of 1955, Ed and Vital and myself. Our three-phase expedition was not scheduled to begin until later in the spring. Now, after picking up Kemp at West End, we planned to head for the fringes of the north Bahama banks. Once more we were on the trail of brass cannon. Only this time our search was secondary to trying out the new cruiser which was carried on Sea Diver's deck, as well as checking other newly installed equipment.

Ed had really outdone himself in planning the cruiser, and he was very pleased with the result. He had redesigned a broad, stubby little plywood craft, originally planned for use with an outboard, to carry a Kermath gasoline engine which would operate the boat by means of a water jet, making it possible to steer the boat sideways and backward as well as forward. Because the boat had neither a wheel nor rudder, and the jetting pipe was only a few inches beneath its bottom, it would be practically foolproof in shallow water and dangerous reef areas.

It was designed so that the engine power could easily be transferred to an air compressor which operated two sets of diving equipment aboard, the air hoses readily accessible from revolving reels in the cockpit. Inside the small cabin, two square openings had been cut in the bottom near the bow and fitted with Plexiglas, making it possible to view the underwater while resting comfortably on the airfoam-cushioned bunks on either side. A small head and galley aft completed the equipment of the little cruiser, so that she could be used for overnight trips. She was even provided with a fathometer and a radiotelephone, so that communication could be maintained with the mother ship at sea.

Ed felt it most necessary to determine her handling characteristics before taking her to some remote part of the world where it would be difficult to make any changes. So he had decided to pursue another tale of brass cannon on the north Bahama banks, which had been told us by a Danish salvager, Willy Dahl, and, at the same time, gain some experience with the new craft.

We anchored several days later in the lee of Miss Romer cay, as far from civilization as it was possible to get on those remote northern banks, having picked up Kemp en route at West End. There, while the new cruiser bobbed prettily from the outrigger on Sea Diver's port side, she was christened Reef Diver. To complete the naming of the trio of boats, we called the hitherto-nameless glass-bottomed skiff Wee Diver. A bottle of rum from the ship's store made the christenings official.

A strong northeast wind struck at Reef Diver as we rounded the end of Miss Romer cay the next morning on the cruiser's maiden voyage. We could feel her recoil in momentary astonishment. Then, with Kemp's coaxing and a slight increase in power, she dug her broad bow into the waves and set out to cross the miles of water between us and the seaward reefs, where Ed had been told the cannon were to be found. Even at that distance we could see a fine show of rolling blue waves and white, breaking seas.

As Miss Romer cay was left behind, we bounced about in waves which became ever larger and rougher. Twice Kemp turned Reef Diver about to test her responsiveness and to see how she would handle in a following sea. She answered instantly to guidance in any direction. The water jet beneath our hull seemed completely adequate, and we continued toward the reefs with more assurance.

One thing troubled Ed. Because of the low stern, which originally had been fashioned to accommodate an outboard motor, a following sea might easily swamp the cockpit and sink the boat. He would have this remedied as soon as we reached Nassau, he declared, by having a removable cover constructed, so that the cockpit area could be enclosed when we were in rough seas.

As we drew nearer the reefs, I saw to my surprise that what had appeared to be a long single chain of coral was actually a staggered grouping of reefs almost a half mile deep. As Kemp steered a course toward them, Ed took frequent bearings on the islands behind, then scanned the water ahead, looking for a passage which led seaward between the reefs. He told us that the cannon had been seen between this passage and a low pinnacle of rock which jutted out of the water just to the west. He thought it doubtful that we would be able to discern this marker, for it was probably concealed in the foaming breakers which churned the whole outer area of reefs.

It also seemed unlikely to me that in these turbulent waters we would be able to distinguish the deep passage. I would have turned about gladly and given up the search, but neither of the men seemed to have any idea of abandoning the effort. So I stifled my fears and glued my eyes to the watery chaos ahead, full of doubts as to how far this untried craft might be trusted and more or less resigned to whatever fate might bring.

As we approached the reef area, Kemp did a wonderful job of handling Reef Diver, twisting her this way and that between half-hidden patches of brown coral an acre or two in extent and the white, curling crests of waves that formed and grew and broke as they encountered the rocky barriers.

It was bad enough heading out toward sea through these hazards, I thought. What would happen when we had to turn and make for shore, pursued by these frightful white-maned monsters? I was terrified.

"Please, Ed," I pleaded, "let's go back. It's so dangerous."

But Ed had spotted the rock we had been looking for, and he wanted to get as close to it as possible. After instructing Kemp to continue toward it, he disappeared inside the cabin to watch the bottom for signs of the guns. I stood in the cockpit, braced against the wind, exerting every bit of self-control I possessed, for I was certain we would either be capsized in these waves or swept upon a reef.

Moments passed that seemed like hours. Kemp guided Reef Diver carefully between a series of rolling combers. I wanted to shut my eyes, yet I was fascinated at the wild grandeur of the sight. We made a slow way past the pinnacle of rock which was revealed every now and then from beneath a smothering cover of white foam.

At last Ed reappeared and gave the signal to return. This was the crucial moment. Would we be able to come about without shipping quantities of water? Would it be possible to outrun the waves which formed and broke around us as they raced for shore? I braced myself for whatever might come.

With careful timing, Kemp swung Reef Diver's bow about until we were headed for distant Miss Romer cay. I waited for one of the huge waves which followed us to overtake us and burst into the cockpit. Instead, Reef Diver gallantly rode their crests and shot ahead on their surface until the speedier waves disappeared forward of us. Indeed, we discovered, we had a boat well adapted to her task. For with an ordinary craft under such circumstances, the rudder and wheel would have come out of water each time a wave rolled beneath, with consequent loss of steerageway. Reef Diver, on the other hand, sat solidly in the water, her neatly placed water jet maintaining constant control.

We were safe from the whole waves, but what of those whose crests were breaking all around us? Surely, we would be caught by one of them and swamped!

Twice, huge seas broke just as they reached our stern, and twice Kemp, anticipating them, swung Reef Diver around to face them. They burst harmlessly against our high bow. Perhaps we would survive after all.

I began to feel braver. When we were through the worst of the pursuing seas, I felt sufficiently reassured to take a turn watching the bottom through the glass panels in the cabin. There, lulled by the familiar sight of white sand bottom, green-brown grass and mottled coral formations, half veiled by murky, sand-filled water, my composure returned.

But the next morning, when Ed decided to go out to the reefs again, I was quick to offer to stay aboard Sea Diver and let Vital go in my place. Although the wind had gone down considerably, the distant reefs were still white with foam, and I had no desire to repeat the experience of the previous day. Promising to be back by lunchtime, the three men cast off Reef Diver and soon disappeared around the end of the island, which hid the reefs that were their destination from my sight.

I set about catching up with some tasks aboard, and before I knew it the morning was gone. It was not until lunchtime that I began to wonder why they did not return.

As the afternoon wore on, my imagination ran wild. Suppose Reef Diver had been swamped? Or suppose the engine had quit and they had been carried out to sea by the tide? I checked the tide tables, only to find that the tide was indeed running out. This did not help my morale.

I was alone on Sea Diver, miles from the nearest settlement. There had been no sign of a human being since we had anchored two days before. I could not launch Wee Diver alone, to say nothing of getting the outboard in place and started. And I did not know how to contact a Bahamian station by radiotelephone. Besides, I did not want to raise an alarm unless I was sure it was necessary.

I climbed the ladder up Sea Diver's mast to the cabin top. From there I was able to see across the top of the cay toward the section of reefs the men had headed for. But even with the binoculars I could not make out a sign of the little cruiser. I swung the glasses wildly back and forth, to no avail. Then, way off to the west, in the shelter of Double Breasted cay, I picked out a small dinghy. Closer inspection revealed two native fishermen—surprisingly, with an outboard. How could I attract their attention?

For the next half hour I alternated between tooting Sea Diver's horn and waving our large American flag, which I removed from the stern. At last I caught their attention, and they headed my way. I waited impatiently until they had drawn alongside Sea Diver and cut their motor. Their curiosity turned to sympathetic understanding as I explained my predicament. I asked them if they would take their boat around the end of the cay to where they could see the outside waters. If Reef Diver was in trouble, would they please go to her assistance?

I waited, nearly hysterical with fear, while they disappeared from sight, and then another long twenty minutes until I saw them coming back toward Sea Diver. To my relief they reported the cruiser was on the way in. She was close to the outer shore of the cay, and that was no doubt why I had not been able to see her.

I thanked them sheepishly, gave them some money for their trouble, and waited impatiently for the three men to return. When Reef Diver finally drew up alongside, I met them, thankful for their safe return, yet seething with all the emotions which had coursed through me during the past hours—worry and fright over their long absence, the stunned realization that alone on Sea Diver I was helpless to handle the equipment, and indignation at Ed for thoughtlessly subjecting me to long hours of fear for their safety.

I'm afraid I gave him a bad time, for when I finally broke down in tears, he gruffly commanded me not to be foolish. "It was much quieter out there today," he said, "and we had a good chance to look over the bottom. I never dreamed you would be worried."

And I'm sure he meant it, for, when Ed sets his mind on a specific objective, every other consideration fades into the background. I said no more, but this was one of the times when I wished for another woman aboard, who would have understood and sympathized with my feelings. And I'm sure it was one of the times when Ed would have been just as happy with only a male crew.

We had planned to leave for Nassau the next morning, but when we woke there was scarcely any wind, for the first time since our arrival. So we piled into Reef Diver and headed seaward. I went along because, after my experience of the previous day, I preferred to brave the hazards of the reefs than to stay alone aboard Sea Diver and fret.

This time we found that the sea within the reefs had calmed down considerably, except where the waves rolling in from the open ocean continued to break with a great white roar upon the reefs. Ed and I disappeared into the cabin to have a look at the bottom as we neared the pinnacle of rock which was our landmark. Perhaps today we would be able to sight the brass cannon.

Beneath our hull, the white sand was ridged in wide windrows, like snow after a blizzard has swept across the fields. Here and there the erratic tracks of conches marred its pristine perfection. Half hidden by a thick, greenish-brown sea growth which was swept flat by the force of the incoming tide, brown patches of coral sheltered the usual collection of bright-colored fish life.

I saw a few shapes reminiscent of cannon in the white sand, but always upon closer inspection they proved to be only coral. As I strained my eyes to examine a particularly deceiving one, it unexpectedly disappeared beneath the flapping wings of a huge, breath-takingly beautiful leopard ray. We circled the area again, but where the ray had been there was only coral. No cannon.

I suddenly became aware of the roar of breakers outside the cabin. After only one glance from the window at the breaking seas on a nearby reef, I quickly buried my head once more in the well of the glass bottom. The sea might indeed be calmer today, but there was still danger in approaching so close to those breakers.

Even Ed agreed it was too wild to attempt anchoring or diving upon the bottom. From the direction of the open sea the long waves of the Atlantic continued to assault the reefs with heavy strokes. It was no time to be searching for brass cannon.

A short time later Ed rose from the bunk opposite me. "There's no use looking any longer," he said. "We'll have to wait until summer, when the weather is more dependable, so that we can search the bottom with the metal detector."

He reluctantly gave orders to Kemp to turn back, and we headed once more for the anchorage behind Miss Romer cay, where we could safely swing Reef Diver aboard the larger boat. That afternoon we set out for Nassau, where we planned to berth Sea Diver until the start of our expedition to Haiti early in April.

*Part
Three*

*Search
for the
Santa Maria*

1

All night long Sea Diver had rolled and tossed in a heavy cross sea as she forged through the rough waters between Great Inagua and the north coast of Haiti. From the moment we had poked her nose out into the open waters beyond Northeast point, she had wallowed on a wet and uncomfortable course.

Unfortunately we had begun this portion of our trip just at sunset, and by the time I had prepared a simple supper for the crew, there was scarcely anyone left to eat it. Vital, Bill, and Clayton had quietly disappeared with their uneasy stomachs to the solace of their bunks. Only Captain Weems, Kemp, Ed and myself had stuck it out, taking our turns at wheel and galley, but happy to head for our cabins, too, as our particular duty ended.

Now it was dawn, and my turn for the watch. I ascended the ladder sleepily, battling to maintain my footing as I pushed back the stubborn hatch, and stumbled out upon the deck. In my mind lingered a vision of the Bahama islands we had known during the past few days, long, low, monotonous coastlines scarcely breaking the smooth curve of the horizon. I was totally unprepared for the sight which met my eyes.

On both sides of Sea Diver loomed brown, tumbled mountains. Recalling the chart which I had studied the night before, I realized that we were approaching the wide, deep stretch of water which separates Tortuga island, pirate stronghold of bygone days, from the mountainous north coast of Haiti. The sun was not yet up, and only a pale glow suffused the eastern sky ahead of us, barely lighting the mists which clung to the high brown shores.

As I made my way forward to the pilothouse to take over the watch from Ed, a wave of anticipation swept over me at the thought of seeking Columbus's lost Santa Maria in these strange, picturesque surroundings. Captain Weems was there also, eager to savor with us our first view of the Haitian coast. Neither of the men had any thought of retiring, for at last our track was joined with that of the Santa Maria; she had sailed these same waters only days before meeting her tragic end on a shoal off Cap Haitien. From now on it was important to check and compare our every move with both present-day charts and the word picture presented in Columbus's log.

Our bow was now cutting directly into the waves which rolled through the passage from the east, headed straight into the sunrise, and Sea Diver had at last ceased the unpleasant roll which had plagued us throughout the night. Reassured by the smoothness, Bill and Clayton soon joined us, wide-eyed at the splendor of the towering mountains on either side.

Thinking that I had better feed my crew while things were quiet and peaceful, I turned the wheel over to Captain Weems and transferred my activities to the galley. When I returned to the pilothouse some time later, we were about halfway through the channel. There was not a habitation or a sign of life to be seen on Tortuga's steep sides, smothered in a tangle of jungle growth. There were no signs of road or path, no fortifications left from pirate days; not even a boat was visible along its rocky shore. However, several miles distant, on the Haitian shore, we could see a small town nestled against a towering mountain. We identified it as the old, historic French city of Port Paix.

I picked up the binoculars and scanned the shore, comparing it with the chart spread before me, seeking various landmarks mentioned in Columbus's *Journal* of that long-ago December in 1492, when he had sailed the very same route. This was the land Columbus had called Española because it reminded him of Castile.

Nearly five centuries had passed since he had gazed upon the same steep coastline. On the morning of December sixth, Santa Maria and Niña had passed the western cape of Hispaniola and glimpsed Tortuga in the dis-

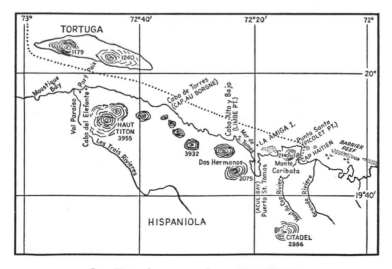

Sea Diver's approach to Cap Haitien.

tance. Pinta, the third ship of the little fleet, had deserted her sister ships more than two weeks before; and, under the command of Martin Alonso Pinzón, had set out to seek Baneque, an unknown island to the northeast, where the Indians had assured them they would find gold. There had been no further word of the Pinta.

Columbus's *Journal* of that voyage had been our constant companion since we had first conceived the idea of our own twentieth-century voyage of discovery; and I now leafed through it, seeking the parts which described his passage along these shores. My eye caught the name Isla de la Tortuga. I read, "That island seemed to be very high land, not filled with mountains, level like lovely fields. . . ." I swept the ragged cliffs of Tortuga with my glasses. Where were these Elysian fields today?

Columbus wrote that he had anchored in a protected harbor on the north shore of Hispaniola, opposite the western point of Tortuga. "He was anxious to examine the strait between these two islands in order to view the island of Española, which is the loveliest thing in the world," I read. But the two ships had contrary winds, and a whole week elapsed before they were able to continue on their way. In the meantime "he set up a great cross at the entrance of the harbor on the western side, on a very conspicuous height, as a sign, he says, that your highnesses hold this land as your own, and especially as an emblem of Jesus Christ, Our Lord, and to the honor of Christendom."

From Moustique bay, Columbus had gone only a few miles and anchored once more, this time near the mouth of a river. This appeared to be Trois Rivières, just west of Port Paix. There he had explored a beautiful valley which he called Val Paraiso, lying at the base of his Cabo del Elefante. It was easy to identify these places—Port Paix with the Elephant, which was Haut Titon, towering four thousand feet above it.

Here Columbus lingered two days, getting acquainted with the Indians and seeking information as to gold. He found the Indians very friendly, once they had overcome their shyness. He noted, "they are the best people in the world and beyond all the mildest. . . . They were all stout and valiant, and not feeble like the others whom he had previously found and with very pleasant voices."

"This land," his *Journal* recorded, "is very cool and the best that tongue can describe. It is very lofty and on the highest mountain, oxen could plough and all could be made like the plains and valleys. In all Castile there is no land which could be compared to this for beauty and fertility. . . ."

When his two ships set out once more, the wind was blowing straight at them from the east, just as we were encountering it today. But whereas we were able to forge ahead under diesel power at a steady eight knots, the two square-riggers had been forced to tack back and forth all day long without making much progress.

The sun had now risen ahead of us in blinding splendor. The strong northeast wind kept the anemometer between eighteen and twenty-five knots; and as we approached the eastern end of the channel, Sea Diver once more began to pitch and roll. I found a secure seat amidships and braced myself against the cabin top. Vital, Bill, and Clayton soon followed me on deck and stretched out on the wide stern seat, eyes closed and pained expressions upon their faces. Captain Weems and Ed were firmly planted in the pilothouse, deep in navigation problems. As the sun rose higher, the heavy mists which enveloped the mountains mingled with the clouds and rolled across the mountaintops. I gazed shoreward across the tossing waters until I could almost see the bellying sails and high poops of the ancient flagship and the slighter, more graceful caravel as they tacked across the wind toward me.

It was now past eight o'clock, and Tortuga was well behind us. As the sun gradually burned through the heavy haze, it high-lighted certain areas of the wooded mountainside, disclosing scattered huts and steep, narrow trails twisting up to the heights. The secondary ranges, pale violet shadows in the background, were revealed now and then as the swirling mists on the crests melted into the low-hung clouds, which broke up in fast-changing patterns in the winds from the ocean.

As I watched, I suddenly saw revealed in these twisting vapors of mist and cloud the shape of a cross—a large, heavy cross such as Columbus might have erected to claim these lands for his queen. It hung there in the sky for a long interval while I stared at it spellbound, scarcely daring to breathe. Then its base began to curl and fray at the edges, and it melted away into the rising mist. Soon the whole apparition had vanished.

I blinked my eyes several times and looked back at the water between Sea Diver and the shore, half expecting to see Santa Maria and Niña, sails full set, driving in our direction. But the sea was blank. I surveyed the three supine sailors on the aft deck. They still lay with closed eyes and resigned expressions. I was sure they had not looked skyward for some time.

Had I really seen the cross in the heavens?

I made my way back to the wheelhouse to see if Ed or Captain Weems had noticed it, but they were still occupied with charts and navigation instruments. They smiled a little condescendingly when I told them of my vision, as if to say, "Might as well humor the poor girl."

We spent the next three hours picking out landmarks and identifying their present names with those which Columbus had given them as he came upon them on that first voyage: Cabo de Torres, now Cap du Borgne; Cabo Alto y Bajo, now Limbe point; and Dos Hermanos, for the twin peaks we could see ahead.

By this time we had picked out Cap Haitien, which was our goal, far in the distance. It appeared just as Columbus had described it, a mountain "which juts into the sea and which from a distance, owing to a ravine which there is on the land side, seems to be an island apart. He named it Monte Caribata—it is very lovely and full of trees, a vivid green."

Ed and Captain Weems were as thrilled as I, as we traced the identical course which the Santa Maria had sailed in the last eventful days before her destruction. Because Columbus's ships were forced to sail against the wind, it took him until sunset of the second day before "he entered a harbor which was between the island of San Tomas and Cabo Caribata."

Although Sea Diver was well out at sea, in order to avoid striking any of the reefs which our chart indicated nearer shore, we could still make out Rat island, which Columbus had called La Amiga. It marked the entrance to Puerto de la Mar de San Tomas, present-day Acul bay, one of the prettiest and most protected anchorages in the world. Columbus had written a very painstaking account of how to reach it through the dangerous outer reefs. He claimed that "now this surpassed all, and in it all the ships of the world could lie and be secure, with the oldest cable on board a ship it would be held fast."

We could see only a small portion of the harbor, for it lay in the shelter of Cap Haitien. Behind it, many miles to the south, we identified the square-crested mountaintop which is the Citadel, that tremendous fortress three thousand feet in the sky, built by the black Emperor Henri Christophe early in the nineteenth century.

It was from this landlocked harbor of San Tomas,

four days after his arrival, that Columbus set out with the two ships for an Indian village on the far side of Cabo Caribata, where lived the Indian king, Guacanagari. For the four preceding days the Spaniards had been joined by Guacanagari's people in revelry and feasting. It was now the day before Christmas, and the white men planned to celebrate the holiday ashore at the Indian settlement.

"The Admiral felt secure from banks and rocks," according to the *Journal*, "because on the Sunday, when he sent the boats to that king, they had passed a full three leagues and a half to the east of the said Punta Santa, and the sailors had seen all the coast and the shoals that there are from the said Punta Santa to the east southeast for a full three leagues, and they had found where it was possible to pass; he had not done this during the whole voyage."

Before sunrise, the two ships weighed anchor with a land breeze. Although the prevailing winds along this north coast blow mainly from the northeast and east, making it most difficult for an eastbound sailing ship to make any headway, there is a short period each day in the early morning when the breeze blows from the land. It is at this time, even today, that sailing ships leave port to get clear of the shore.

So it was that early morning as Santa Maria and Niña maneuvered to clear the reefs and shoals at the mouth of Acul bay. Then, finding themselves with little wind, and that coming from the east, it took them the whole day and part of the night to reach the northeast end of Cap Haitien, which Columbus called Punta Santa.

As Sea Diver skirted the rocky hillsides of Cap Haitien, we could pick out ahead of us Punta Santa, now Picolet point. Crumbling stone fortifications from French colonial days dotted the steeps; and as we came abreast of the point itself, a lighthouse appeared halfway up the slope, looking eerily like a mechanical man standing guard over the entrance to the harbor.

It was eleven o'clock on Christmas Eve, Columbus noted in his *Journal*, that "he was distant one league" from this point. The account continued, "Our Lord willed that at midnight as they had seen the Admiral lie down and rest, and as they saw that it was a dead calm and that the sea was like a small bowl, all should lie down to sleep, and the rudder was left in the hand of that boy (a young ship's grummet), and the currents which were swift carried the ship upon one of these banks."

Thus calmly did the *Journal* announce the disaster which resulted in the loss of the Santa Maria.

From Sea Diver's position off the seaward side of Point Picolet, we tried to reconstruct what had happened. When Columbus's ships had reached this spot, they must have changed course toward Guacanagari's village, which apparently lay several miles distant close to the inner shore of the large harbor that stretched before us. We could see many breaking reefs ahead to starboard. They formed a wide semicircle which curved away toward the distant shore.

We could not understand how Columbus, in the dead of night, had had the temerity to sail into completely strange waters, knowing that there were reefs in his path. The sailors who had explored the route the previous day must have been aware of the dangerous waters they must cross. Surely they would have warned their master. And yet the Santa Maria had sailed on, with both Columbus and the master of the ship asleep and only a ship's boy to guide the boat!

Could this be the same Great Navigator who had led his ships across three thousand miles of unknown ocean to the shores of an unknown land, and then guided them with admirable judgment and ability through the intricate Bahama passages to the reef-bound shores of Cuba? How could he have been so careless as to enter a reef-strewn harbor at midnight, knowing only that on the far side he would find an anchorage near a low, sandy shore?

Had he celebrated too freely the past few days as he entertained Guacanagari and his people in quiet Acul bay? Could he and his men have been sleeping off the effects of late hours and too much liquor, that he would risk his ship in such a fashion? Ed and Captain Weems could offer no other explanation.

I proffered the lame excuse that perhaps Santa Maria was following Niña, and that only the lead ship had carried any pilots. Because she was a smaller ship with less draft, Niña had either sailed over or skirted the reef without her crew being aware of it, while Santa Maria, only a few yards to port or starboard of her course, was unlucky enough to go aground.

We ceased our speculations as Ed checked the harbor chart and then turned Sea Diver to follow the eastern shore of the peninsula into the bay, where we could just discern a white blotch at the base of high green mountains which was the city of Cap Haitien. About three hundred yards to our starboard the rocky hillside sloped steeply into the sea.

Fortunately we saw the two black buoys on our starboard bow in time. Checking with our chart, we found that they marked the western edge of Le Grand Mouton bank, a large shoal area directly in the center of the harbor entrance. How easy it would have been in the days before the shoal was buoyed, to strike it, for the terrain, with its steep banks leading down to the water's edge, promised deep water for some distance out. Had Columbus erred by striking this bank in the night, it would be understandable. But according to all accounts we had read, the Santa Maria had been headed in a more easterly direction across the harbor.

Sea Diver's captain at the Silver shoals.

Sea Diver at anchor in the Bahamas.

he Links aboard Blue Heron the winter the diving bug bit. William, Clayton, the author and Ed.

Florida Keys Photo Service, Marathon, Fla.

Barney, Jane and Pete examine coral-encrusted relics from the Looe.

The author about to make a dive.

Bill Thompson happily displays a bar found beneath cannon on ocean floor.

Florida Keys Photo Service, Marathon, Fla.

Author looking for a cannon.

Helmeted divers use jetting hose on remains of 1733 wreck.

Mark Kauffman—courtesy LIFE magazine, Copr. 1953 TIME Inc.

Mark Kauffman—courtesy LIFE magazine, Copr. 1953 TIME Inc.

Ed uses underwater detector near ballast of Spanish wreck while Pete and Art McKee follow to investigate findings.

Art McKee with pewter plates and battle axe from Spanish wreck.

At right and below: corroded pieces of eight and coral-encrusted keys from wreck.

Two photos: Mark Kauffman—courtesy LIFE magazine, Copr. 1953 TIME Inc.

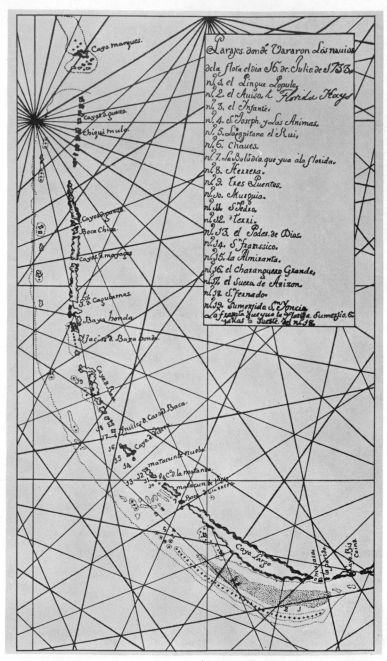

This ancient chart of the 1733 hurricane wrecks, made in 1766, differs from other Spanish documents as to the names and the number of the ships involved. It was obtained from the British Museum.

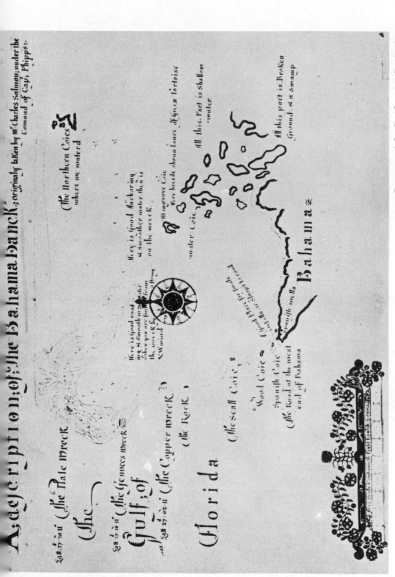

A description of the Bahama banck; originally taken by mr Charles Salmon, under the Comand of Cap. Phipps.

Lat. 27.10 n The Plate wreck

The Northern Coies where we watered

The Gulf of

Lat. 27.10 n The Gennes wreck

Lat. 27.02 n The Copper wreck

The Rock

Here is good road in a smooth to 2 fathom water when you are far from the wreck & from N windd

Here is good Anchoring & smooth water then is on the wreck

Mangrove Coie here breeds abondance of sea tortoise

under Coies

All this Part is shallow water

Florida

The scall Coies

Wool Coie

Spanish Coie

The Road of the west end of Bahama

All this part is Broken Ground & a swamp

Bahama

Courtesy of the Smithsonian Institution

Seventeenth-century chart of three wrecks located by Captain William Phips on the north Bahama banks.

Bill, the author, Clayton and Ed on aft deck of Sea Diver upon arrival at C Haitien.

Captain Weems charts Sea Diver's course as Ed pilots vessel.

Kemp guides us close to reefs in Cap Haitien harbor.

Clayton dives on two cannon at Cap Haitien.

Ed poises crowbar over ol
anchor nearly buried i
coral reef.

Ed about to salvage ol
anchor, later identified :
probably having come fro
Columbus's Santa Maria.

Two photos: Peter Stackpole—courtesy LIFE magazine, Copr. 1955 TIME Inc.

in Weems and Ed prepare to raise anchor from nineteenth-century wreck.

Captain Weems, Ed and I study evidence that we have found anchor from Santa Maria.

Prefect Sam receives anc from Ed, while U. S. A bassador Davis, Capt Weems and author look

Anchor in Port-au-Prince museum, found during eighteenth century in Grande Rivière, and said to have come from Santa Maria.

Author back aboard Reef Diver after inspecting "lone rock" which identified general location of Spanish treasure wreck. Below: Kemp and Vital rig magnetometer off Reef Diver's stern.

Peter Stackpole—courtesy LIFE magazine, Copr. 1955 TIME Inc.

View of Caicos giving impression of "many islands," as described by Columbus a place close to where we believe his first landfall in America was made.

Point of land which could easily be converted to an island fortress, and ha "no more disturbed than the water in a well," such as Columbus described; Lorimer creek, Caicos islands.

As we steered a careful course between Le Grand Mouton and shore, we could see on our port clear to the horizon the breaking white reefs which protect the inner harbor from the sea. Somewhere out there the Santa Maria had gone aground. Somewhere beneath those foaming breakers lay what was left of Columbus's ill-fated flagship. Now that we were so close to our goal, I wondered again: Could we possibly find that historic wreck after 463 years?

2

o

o

o

If Colonel Max Chassagne, chief of the Haitian Army in northern Haiti, had not given us temporary permission to explore for the Santa Maria exactly when he did that Saturday afternoon before Easter, I doubt if we would ever have found the ancient anchor, symbol of Columbus's first visit to the Antilles. And if Captain Weems, with unflagging enthusiasm, had not kept hot on the trail of the officials responsible for granting that permission, I'm sure Ed would have given up in despair and sailed on to our next objective, the Silver shoals.

We had been in the harbor at Cap Haitien since Wednesday. The day after our arrival we had moved Sea Diver from her anchorage in the open road, where we had bounced about considerably in the choppy waters, to the small inner harbor close to the sea wall which flanked the town. Here we were well sheltered from wind and sea by the municipal dock to our north and a small cay just east of us.

Several seagoing sloops from Turks island, the native

trading ships of this island area, were anchored near us. They furnished constant entertainment as the colorful families aboard them went about the business of living on a small boat—cooking their meals on deck over smoking charcoal fires, hanging their washing in the rigging, and joining in tuneful calypso as they sat about the decks in the cool of the evening.

Since the afternoon of our arrival, Captain Weems and Ed had been occupied in chasing from one office to another in a vain effort to get our search under way. Everyone they approached had been most courteous. But nothing happened.

Unfortunately for us, it was Holy Week, a week of Haitian celebration. We found the afternoon of our arrival that all public offices, both in Cap Haitien and in the capitol city of Port-au-Prince, were closed for the next two days. On Saturday morning they would open briefly, then close their doors again for the remainder of the weekend.

André LeBon, assistant U.S. consul, with an office at the Royal Netherlands Steamship Agency near the water front, had been most co-operative. He had helped Ed telegraph the American Embassy in Port-au-Prince, after several attempts to reach them by phone had failed. Captain Weems, listening to the one phone call which Ed was able to get through, counted thirty-seven "hello's" and twenty-eight "Can you hear me's?" on Ed's part. When the call was finished, Ed had still been unable to get his message across. Now he wired:

CAPT WEEMS AND MYSELF SEARCHING COLUMBUS VOY-
AGES. ALSO THINK WE COULD FIND REMAINS OF SANTA
MARIA. LAST YEAR OUR EXPEDITION WAS CLEARED FOR
THIS SEARCH AT CAP HAITIEN AND CONSUL ADVISED
THROUGH SECRETARY DULLES BUT WE WERE UNABLE
TO COME. WOULD YOU CHECK WITH AUTHORITIES TO

He received a reply the following day from Ambassador Roy T. Davis:

As we were already in close touch with André LeBon, who was as helpless as ourselves, we waited impatiently for Saturday to come. Meanwhile Ed occupied himself with a few of the many jobs aboard Sea Diver that only he could do—assembling and checking gear for searching and diving, and installing the magnetometer in Reef Diver so that it could be operated from the smaller craft.

While Ed, assisted by Vital and Kemp, labored aboard, Captain Weems escorted Bill, Clayton, and myself on many forays into Cap Haitien. Known to its inhabitants as Le Cap, this interesting town had an air of the Old World, with its narrow streets and tall, shuttered doors opening directly on the sidewalks. Seated in the doorways, ill-clad women of every degree of color, many big with child, nursed naked babies at their breasts as they watched the toddlers playing at their feet and the noisy antics of the older children who raced about the narrow streets. Within the doors we caught glimpses of newspaper-covered walls, a clutter of poor furniture and scattered clothing, in small connecting rooms, one behind the other.

Here and there, the solid, pastel-tinted fronts of the houses gave way to empty spaces, where broken foundation stones of old buildings lay almost concealed by enveloping green vines. The cobbled streets were fashioned from ballast stone, brought to Cap Haitien from all parts of the world to be replaced by cargoes of sugar and other products of the island. At the street crossings we stepped over the barrels of old cannon, now being utilized as curbstones.

It did not take us long to discover that although Cap Haitien is a city rich in history, there are few landmarks left of its early days. A brief review of the island's stormy past soon told us why.

Navidad, Columbus's first settlement in the New World, was created of necessity following the loss of the Santa Maria. It did not endure very long, for when Columbus returned from Spain the following year with ships and men to reinforce the Spanish colony, he found that the colonists he had left behind had been massacred and the town destroyed. He then selected a location farther east along the coast in what is now the Dominican Republic, nearer the region where gold was to be found. Thus the white man's occupancy in the area of Cap Haitien died a quick death.

Unbelievably, within fifteen years of the Spaniards' arrival, all but a few thousand of the three hundred thousand Indians who had inhabited the island had been enslaved and destroyed. Western Hispaniola, with its rugged mountain terrain, became a neglected land, for as soon as the quick fortunes to be obtained from gold and enslaved manpower began to dwindle, the bulk of the Spanish adventurers moved on to the riches of Mexico and South America.

It was inevitable at this time that pirates should appear in adjoining seas to harry the richly laden ships which sailed constantly for Spain. Tortuga Island, with its unapproachable shores and mountain fastnesses, became a haven for the rough characters who manned the pirate ships. Wandering to the shores of Hispaniola in search of wild cattle to be killed and smoked to supply their vessels, many of the buccaneers eventually settled there. Gradually the superior numbers of French in the area asserted themselves until, at the end of the seventeenth century, Spain yielded control of the western part of Hispaniola to France.

The French colony grew rapidly, with Cap François (now Cap Haitien) as its core. The rich lands, cultivated by the constant importation of Negro slaves, produced quantities of sugar cane, tobacco, sisal and cotton. Under the capable management of these French settlers, Saint Dominique became the richest colony in the New World.

By 1789 the French Revolution had spread to Saint Dominique. A decade of struggle followed, during which a large number of the white population were murdered and their plantations destroyed. Toussaint L'Ouverture, a former slave himself, had scarcely established order as a leader of his people, when Napoleon, who could not see his richest colony lost without a struggle, sent five thousand veteran soldiers and a vast fleet of ships to retrieve the province. There followed a series of struggles culminating in a battle just outside Cap François, in which the Negro leader, Dessalines, defeated the French and established the independence of Saint Dominique. It was renamed Haiti, the original Indian name, meaning "high land."

Once more the new Negro republic started to rebuild the capital city, and by 1820, at the death of Henri Christophe, much of it had been restored. Then Cap Haitien stagnated under a succession of poor rulers until a fateful day twenty years later, when a terrible earthquake tore great fissures in the land and at the bottom of the sea, creating a tidal wave which inundated the lower part of the city. Fire broke out among the crumbled ruins, and once again the ill-starred city was destroyed. It never recovered from this last blow, and the new town which gradually evolved was a poor one in comparison to the splendor of the earlier city.

At last Saturday morning arrived. Ed and Captain Weems hurried to the office of M. LeBon with every expectation of finding a message from Port-au-Prince, giving us permission to start out on our search with Sea Diver. They came back disappointed. Not wishing to waste any more time waiting around, Ed set out with Bill in Reef Diver for a small island in the bay where he could try out the magnetometer equipment, leaving Captain Weems to deal with problems ashore.

They had no sooner gone than a telegram arrived:

FOREIGN OFFICE STATES YOUR PRESENCE PORT AU PRINCE NECESSARY. SUGGEST YOU COME MONDAY. AMERICAN EMBASSY.

Captain Weems and I were appalled. There was no plane to Port-au-Prince until Monday afternoon. *Life* magazine was sending a photographer and a reporter the first of the week. William and Clayton must return to school the following weekend. And we were committed to leave for the Silver shoals the week after that. Furthermore, I knew Ed, never a patient man, would blow his top at this new obstacle to his plans. He would never spend three days of the coming week making a trip to the capital.

The moment was crucial. Captain Weems set out to find Colonel Chassagne, who, we were told, was the only official in the province with sufficient power to act. Our story interested the colonel to such an extent that he insisted upon returning to Sea Diver with the captain. He viewed our equipment with great interest and, before he left, agreed to let us start out the next morning with the understanding that we would return to Cap Haitien and continue our efforts to secure permission from Port-au-Prince on Monday.

3

o

o

o

We sailed from our anchorage at eight o'clock on Easter morning with high hopes and exuberant spirits. At last we were headed for the reefs in the outer harbor, where the Santa Maria was supposed to lie!

There was already a brisk wind from the northeast, and as we worked our way toward Picolet point, Sea Diver's bow rose and fell to the long ocean swells. Reef Diver followed docilely along at the end of a forty-foot towline. We were uncertain as to how much sea she would take, as this was our first experience at towing her in the open ocean, but we found that she rode easily and well.

Ed and Captain Weems had plotted the course which they thought Columbus might have taken on that far-off night before Christmas. Three miles from Picolet point they had drawn a course of 130 degrees to the western end of the Limonade barrier reef, which encloses the entire eastern section of Caracol harbor. From here the line angled to 110 degrees, tracing a course through the deep-water channel between the outer reef and the group of inner reefs, upon one of which Morison believed the Santa Maria had come to grief.

Once on the heading from Picolet point, Ed engaged the automatic pilot. Next he turned the switch on the fathometer. The white chart showed no depth indication, for the depth here was greater than the two hundred feet it would record. He left it operating, however, so that he would know the exact instant when Sea Diver reached shallower water. He could then ascertain, from the depth registered, our position in relation to the one hundred-fathom line on the chart.

I looked at the many other instruments which crowded the wheelhouse—the Sea Scanar, which would record not only the depth of water beneath us, but also, when set at an angle, all underwater obstructions within nine hundred feet in any direction; and the radar, which turned night into day by registering upon its screen every object of any size on the surface within a radius of twenty-five miles, besides giving an accurate measurement of the distance between Sea Diver and these objects. There was the loran, which would fix our position electronically far at sea, when no land was to be seen; the radio compass, which could be tuned to locate the direction of radio stations within a long range; and the radiotelephone, with which we could call for help in case of trouble.

And I thought of Columbus, starting out from Spain with his three small sailing ships across unknown seas. For his guidance he had had only a crude free-swinging needle compass which oscillated so constantly that he could only guess his exact direction, a sounding lead, and perhaps an astrolabe to measure the angle of sun and stars, although it is uncertain whether he was able to use this instrument successfully until his later voyages.

Perhaps most important of all to our safety, Sea Diver was equipped with a powerful diesel engine with which we could maneuver out of tight situations; whereas Columbus, in the same close quarters, would have had to cope with unco-operative winds and square-rigged sails, giving him little chance to run away from trouble.

We had almost reached the outer barrier reef before the fathometer began to register depths within its scope. We altered our course at this point and glided slowly along behind the outer reef, which foamed and broke for miles. Somewhere among the scattered inner reefs to our starboard must lie the remains of the Santa Maria, if Morison's prognostications were correct.

Ahead of us rose the lovely pavilion shape of Monte Cristi and a whole chain of mountain peaks leading inland, while behind us was bold and beautiful Cap Haitien, with the old city nestled at its base. To our south stretched the low inner shore of the harbor, edged sometimes with mangrove, sometimes with white sand beach, backed by the fertile plains of the Vega Real, extending for miles to the distant mountains.

As we passed behind the barrier reef, the rolling ocean swells diminished. I inspected with interest the three reefs to our starboard, distinctly marked by the white breakers which charged upon them. These were the reefs we expected to search. It was high tide, and the brown patches of coral were underwater except for a scattering of knobby heads. Floating lengths of bamboo attached to hemp lines marked the locations of fish traps placed by the local fishermen.

We continued to the end of the third reef before making a wide circle to starboard, and then dropped anchor behind the middle reef. Here we found the sea much quieter, with two lines of coral between us and the ocean. The wind was blowing more and more strongly from the northeast, however, and we realized it would soon be too rough to search in the vicinity of the reefs.

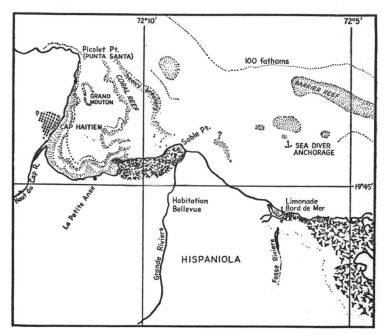

Harbor at Cap Haitien showing Sea Diver's anchorage behind
reef where Santa Maria was thought to have been destroyed.

Reef Diver was pulled hurriedly alongside, and in a
matter of moments Ed, Captain Weems and Bill, with
Kemp at the wheel, had started off to make a quick survey
of the area which they had selected as having the best
possibilities.

I picked up Columbus's *Journal* and leafed through
the pages, seeking to refresh my memory as to the events
of the shipwreck.

> The ship went upon it [the reef] so gently
> that it was hardly noticed. The boy who felt the
> rudder ground, and heard the sound of the sea,
> shouted, and at his cries, the Admiral came out
> and was so quick that no one had yet realized that
> they were aground. Immediately the master of the

ship, whose watch it was, came out and the Admiral told him and the others to launch the boat which they carried at the stern, and they took an anchor and threw it astern, and he with many others jumped into the boat, and the Admiral thought that they had done that which he had ordered them to do.

Juan de la Cosa had not obeyed the admiral, however, but had jumped into the small boat and set out for the caravel Niña, which was lying half a league away.

The caravel would not take them aboard, therein acting rightly, and on this account they returned to the ship, but the boat of the caravel reached her first. When the Admiral saw that they were running away and that it was his crew, and that the water was growing shallower and that the ship was now lying broadside to the sea, as he saw no other remedy, he ordered the mast to be cut and the ship to be lightened as far as possible, in order to discover if they could draw her off. And as the water became shallower still, he was unable to save her, and she lay on her side, broadside on to the sea, although there was little or no sea running, and then the hatches came open, but the ship remained whole.

The Admiral went to the caravel, in order to place the crew of the ship on the caravel, and as a light breeze was now blowing from land, and there also still remained much of the night and they did not know how far the banks extended, he hung off until it was day and then went to the ship from within the line of the bank.

When morning came, Columbus sent a boat ashore to find his friend Guacanagari:

who had his town inland, about a league and a half from the said bank. When he heard the news, they say that he wept and sent all his people from the town with very large canoes and many of them to take off everything that was in the ship. This was done and everything was taken from the decks in a very short space of time. So great was the great haste and diligence which that king showed! And he in person, with his brothers and relatives, were active both on the ship and in guarding that which was brought to land, so that everything might be very safely kept.

From time to time Guacanagari

sent one of his relatives to the weeping Admiral, to console him, telling him that he must not be troubled or annoyed, that he would give him whatever he possessed. . . . He commanded everything to be placed near the houses, while some houses which he wished to give were emptied, that there everything could be placed and guarded. He ordered armed men to be set around everything to keep watch all night. He and all the people with him wept.

Columbus must have been truly moved by all this kindness, for he wrote:

They are a people so full of love and without greed, and suitable for every purpose, so that I assure your highnesses that I believe that in the world there is no better race or better land. They love their neighbors as themselves, and they have the sweetest voices in the world, and soft, and always they are smiling.

Well might the Indians have wept with Columbus. Not only for the calamity that had befallen him, but for themselves—sweet-natured, innocent, defenseless people, welcoming the white men into their midst as brothers, sharing with them their homes and substance. Had they realized that in a few years' time scarcely any of them would survive, would they still have come so generously and lovingly to the aid of these strangers?

The kindly Arawaks, having set aside some houses for the homeless crew, spent the next few days ferrying the Spaniards back and forth between the stranded Santa Maria and shore, to salvage everything that would be of use to them. Then the white men and their helpers removed as many of the ship's timbers as possible, to build a fort and a tower as Columbus ordered, for a good portion of the crew must now stay behind when he returned to Spain. These men were not unhappy, however, for they looked forward to spending the intervening time until Columbus's return the following year in accumulating a rich hoard to take back to Spain.

The admiral, with only one ship left, desired only to reach home safely, to report his discoveries and to return with more ships and colonizers. He would carry enough gold and other evidences of the wealth of this new world to convince Queen Isabella that another expedition would be worth her while.

The two groups worked amicably together during the succeeding days as Columbus prepared the Niña for her journey, loading her with firewood and water and available foods. He planned to explore the coastline to the east as he went along, so that he could make a full report as to the size and geography of the island to his queen. It was during this time that some itinerant Indians brought word that the missing Pinta had been seen at anchor in a river mouth far to the east.

Two days before Niña was to sail, Columbus demonstrated the power of the guns he was leaving with his men. A lombard was loaded and fired into the side of the stranded Santa Maria where she lay in the harbor. The ball passed through her hull and on across the water for some distance. Then the Spaniards, in full armor, staged a combat on the beach. Although the admiral explained to Guacanagari that the artillery would be useful against his Carib enemies to the south, he intended it as a warning that the men he was leaving behind would be well able to look after themselves.

When Columbus sailed, he left thirty-nine men in the fortress which had been built, along with "all the merchandise which the sovereigns commanded to be brought for purposes of barter, and this was much, in order that they might deal and exchange it for gold, with all that had been brought from the ship. He left them also bread, biscuit for a year and wine and much artillery, and the boat of the ship. . . . He left them also some seeds to sow, and his officials, the escribano and the alguacil, and with them a ship's carpenter and a caulker and a good gunner who well understood machines, and a cooper, and a doctor, and a tailor, and all, as he says, seamen."

The little settlement was called La Villa de Navidad, because the events leading to its founding had occurred on Christmas Eve.

This, then, was the story of what was probably the most famous and important shipwreck in history, for it resulted in the founding of the first European settlement in the New World, and thus established Spain's rights with the Holy See to this part of the earth for several centuries to come. Had Columbus returned to Spain without leaving this seed of colonization, it seems very possible that Portugal or England, which were already planning similar expeditions into the unknown, might well have established their claims first.

Reef Diver's high-pitched whine as she coursed up and down near the reef slowly penetrated my consciousness and brought me back to the fact that it was Easter, 1955, and that I was sitting on Sea Diver's aft deck with a book in my hand. From our anchorage I could just see the spire of the church at Limonade Bord de Mer, several miles away on the barren, sandy shore. It was this little fishing village which Morison had picked as being close to the original site of Navidad. Others believed, however, that Columbus's settlement had been part of an Indian village inland, probably on the banks of one of the rivers which emptied into the harbor. The shore was too far away to make out any details, but I resolved to investigate it more closely before we had completed our search for Santa Maria.

Reef Diver had by now returned from her preliminary survey. As she came alongside, Bill climbed aboard, and Clayton and I quickly dropped from the rail into the smaller boat. We wasted no time, but headed once more toward the reefs, for the sea was becoming constantly rougher.

Ed and Captain Weems had tired of staring through the glass bottom, so Clayton and I took over the watching posts in the cabin, stretching ourselves upon our stomachs on the airfoam bunks to gaze down through the glass panels in the bow. I found that the sea bottom on these north Haitian reefs had a character all its own. The clean white sand to which we had become accustomed in the Florida keys and the Bahamas was missing. In its place was a hard-looking composition, almost covered with clumps of kelp and grass. I saw large clumps of stag coral towering from the lowest depths, tangles of finer coral forming hiding places for brilliant small fish which darted in and out, and the usual yellow and purple sea fans and Gorgonia. There were no big fish, which surprised me, and only a few small grouper and blue parrot fish. Clayton caught a glimpse of a leopard ray and a small barracuda, just before he turned over his watching post to Captain Weems.

That morning, on our way from Cap Haitien, we had reviewed what we might find of Santa Maria's remains by means of this surface scanning. Long ago the ship's timbers must have disappeared, eaten by teredo worms, loosened and washed away in rough seas, or possibly covered with sand. There could have been little metal on this early ship—a few cannon; cannon balls, if they had not been removed by the survivors; possibly an anchor or two; and a limited number of fastenings and spikes, which would have held the key timbers together. The only other indication which might be visible from the surface would be the ballast stone which the Santa Maria must have carried.

And then Captain Weems and I thought we saw them! A scattering of irregular-shaped rocks! We were past them before we could be sure, so we asked Kemp to turn back over the spot once more. Yes, it was ballast stone, according to Ed, who came in from the cockpit to verify our find. The stones were scattered over a wide area, and only in one place, where the bottom coral seemed to be broken away, could they be seen in any quantity. I also saw some coral-covered shapes at the edge of this break, which, it was easy to conjecture, might be the stock of an anchor or metal fittings from the ship. From the look of the coral at this spot, Ed surmised it must be a very old wreck.

At this point he returned to the cockpit to ascertain our exact location on the reef. He found that we were on the northwest side of the first reef, a most logical place for a vessel to strike, coming in from the open sea in the dead of night as Columbus had. A later check showed it to be almost exactly on one of the spots selected by Dr. Morison as a likely place for the Santa Maria to have gone down.

Our hopes were high, that Easter Sunday noon, that we had found the historic flagship. Earlier, in making our plans, we had acknowledged that we were apt to find the remains of several wrecks in this area, and that our problem might be to ascertain which was that of the Santa Maria. Surprisingly, this was the only bit of wreckage we had sighted in our combing of the reefs. It would require much investigation and checking to verify whether it was indeed the right ship.

First of all, before anything was disturbed, we planned to photograph the whole area. Then Ed would go over the bottom with the underwater detector, seeking the pattern of the wreckage beneath the coral. Captain Weems or one of the boys would follow him, marking with bricks any spots that indicated the presence of metal. Later they would investigate these locations and remove whatever might be there, hidden in the coral. It might be necessary to dynamite lightly to break up certain coral formations which otherwise refused to reveal their secrets. But dynamite is destructive, and must be employed very carefully. We would use it only after everything else had failed.

We headed back toward Sea Diver for lunch and to secure the necessary equipment to dive upon the ballast. By the time we had eaten, the wind was blowing out of the northeast at twenty-five knots, preventing us from exploring the reef that afternoon. Before the end of the day it had reached thirty-two. The high wind also forced us to change our plan of returning to Cap Haitien for the night, for we were doubtful as to how Reef Diver would make out, trailing along behind us in the heavy following seas which had built up in the ocean.

So we spent the rest of the afternoon and evening in dreaming and talking of the possibilities ahead of us. If we had indeed come upon the Santa Maria, never had we had such luck in locating the object of our search with so little difficulty.

4

o

o

o

We dropped our hook in Cap Haitien harbor about seven o'clock on Monday morning. We had risen at dawn and set out from our anchorage behind the reefs so that we would waste no time in obtaining final permission from the Haitian government to carry on our search. Since our discovery of the ballast, we could hardly wait to get overboard with our diving equipment to explore for the Santa Maria, which we had convinced ourselves must be there. We resented the waste of even another day.

Scarcely was our anchor down when we were hailed from the shore. A Haitian voice informed us that the Captain of the Port wished to see Mr. Link immediately. Ed went ashore to be met with a storm of disapproving words from the port officer, but because the latter spoke in the native tongue, Ed had to wait for an interpreter to inform him exactly how he had displeased the captain. Why had we exceeded our permission to go out on the reefs on Sunday by staying overnight? he was asked. Officialdom was pacified when Ed explained that we had been afraid to risk towing Reef Diver back in the heavy seas.

Ed then headed for the cable office and wired the American Embassy in Port-au-Prince, in answer to their message requesting his presence there:

IMPOSSIBLE TO COME TO PORT AU PRINCE AS I HAVE ONLY THIS WEEK LEFT FOR SEARCH AND TRIP WILL CONSUME MOST OF THE TIME LEFT. I HAVE NOTHING TO GAIN PERSONALLY BUT HAITI HAS MUCH IF SANTA MARIA CAN BE FOUND. LIFE MAGAZINE REPORTERS ARRIVE TODAY AND WILL GIVE HAITI MUCH VALUABLE PUBLICITY BUT IF WE CANNOT START TODAY ALL WILL BE LOST. PLEASE EXPLAIN THIS TO HAITIAN AUTHORITIES AND ADVISE. E. A. LINK

The morning and afternoon passed with no word from Port-au-Prince. Then Kurt Beck came to our rescue. M. Beck, German born but a Haitian citizen, was the proprietor of a small hotel perched on the mountainside overlooking the harbor. Hearing of our plans to search for the Santa Maria through the newspapers, he had written us before the start of our trip, offering any aid which he might give. From the moment we introduced ourselves, he and his wife and son exerted themselves to make our stay pleasant and to help us.

That afternoon M. Beck took Captain Weems in his car in search of Colonel Chassagne. When they could not locate him, Beck suggested that they call on Prefect Guillaume Sam, governor of the province. They returned to Sea Diver with the news that after much persuasion, Prefect Sam had agreed to give us temporary permission to search, starting the following day, until we should receive a definite yes or no from Port-au-Prince. We would have liked to leave for the reefs immediately, but it was already late in the afternoon and we realized the ocean would be too rough to risk towing Reef Diver. We planned instead to leave at daybreak the next morning.

To celebrate our apparent success, Captain Weems

took us to dinner at the Hotel de Roi Christophe, one of the historic places of the town, a walk of only a few blocks from the harbor. We had downed some luscious crawfish Thermidor and were attacking a delicious beef filet, when M. Beck arrived to tell us that Prefect Sam had changed his mind. The governor did not want to assume the responsibility of letting us search without sanction from Port-au-Prince.

Our spirits hit bottom once more. Ed said quietly, but with grim finality in his tone, "If we can't get permission tonight so that we can go out tomorrow morning, I'm through." And we knew he meant it.

Captain Weems volunteered to make one last attempt to locate Colonel Chassagne, who had been unreachable all day. He and M. Beck departed, the steak dinner forgotten. Ed, Bill, Clayton and I disconsolately ate our dessert, drank our small cups of black Haitian coffee and started back to Sea Diver.

But our bad luck had only begun. As we headed across the harbor toward Sea Diver, a strong wind caught Reef Diver and carried us into the shallow water close to the sea wall. In full skirts and high heels for the first time since my arrival, I was standing on the engine box when the cruiser came to a violent stop, and I was catapulted unexpectedly to the deck between the cabin and the engine box. In the darkness we had struck the arm of an old anchor which lay on the bottom and had punctured a hole in our starboard bow. Fortunately the damage was above the waterline and could be easily repaired.

I did not fare so well, however, for as I picked myself up, I was aware of a very painful area high in my right side, where I had struck against the dashboard, and there was a sickish feeling in the pit of my stomach. I could hardly wait to get aboard Sea Diver and head for my bunk.

It was nearly midnight before Captain Weems returned with the welcome news that the colonel was sending us a permit at four thirty the next morning, so that we could set out early for the reefs. He told us how, after leaving us at dinner, he and M. Beck had again visited both the prefect and the colonel, but to no avail. He had then phoned the ambassador in Port-au-Prince and learned that the Haitian authorities had promised to send a telegram to Army headquarters in Cap Haitien, granting us permission. He and M. Beck had then returned to the colonel's office, to find that the telegram had been received and filed unbeknown to the colonel.

The few hours of the night that were left passed very quickly in spite of my discomfort. Before it seemed possible, we were awakened by a car horn and shouts from the shore. Ed hurried on deck, telling me to stay in bed until we had reached the reefs.

When I finally came on deck after a painful struggle to get into my clothes, Sea Diver was just being anchored behind the middle reef in a position that would put her as close as possible to the ballast, where we expected to be working. By nine o'clock we had finished breakfast and were gathered on deck, ready to embark on Reef Diver and start our search. We looked toward the reefs, expecting to pick out the location of the ballast without any difficulty.

Captain Weems and I pointed to a spot on the reef just to our starboard and said, "That's the place." After careful scrutiny, Kemp selected the far end of the reef to our port. Ed sided with him, knowing Kemp's faculty for recognizing almost any spot on the ocean bottom he had seen before. It was decided to search the latter.

The wind was blowing hard by this time, and, when we approached the reefs, we found the seas were already breaking over them. For more than an hour we searched without seeing a thing. Perhaps we were searching the wrong reef after all. Why not try the other one? We carefully combed the waters in front of it.

All this time the sea was becoming rougher. The tide was coming in, and great rollers were breaking on the coral, making it more and more impossible to approach very near. Kemp insisted that the ballast was close in on the other reef, but so close that he dared not guide the boat near it for fear of being caught in the breakers. We headed in that direction, and Ed and Captain Weems took a turn at watching the bottom.

Suddenly there were excited shouts from inside the cabin. Captain Weems and Ed had spotted something. Kemp maneuvered the boat back over the spot as I hurried into the cabin to see what they were looking at.

"Two cannon," they exulted. We cruised back and forth while they examined them from above.

"They're not old enough to be from the Santa Maria," Ed said. "Must be another wreck."

That was disappointing, for if we were near the ballast which we had spotted on Sunday, then it and these cannon could have come from the same wreck. In that case it was probably not the Santa Maria's ballast we had seen previously. We would never know until we located the pile of rocks. By this time it had become too rough to anchor and dive on the cannon, so Kemp marked the location with a yellow buoy and we headed back to Sea Diver.

Bill and Clayton were waiting at the rail to greet us, but neither appeared very happy. The ship performed a slow rock and roll the rest of the day, the wind building up to thirty knots from the east. Over Cap Haitien the skies became black and stormy. We reluctantly concluded that once more we would have to spend the night behind the reefs. The boys retired to their cabins, not the least interested in preparation for dinner.

It was apparent that if we were to have sufficiently calm water to work around the reefs, we would have to make an earlier start in the morning. High winds were evidently customary in this part of the world during the spring months.

We were up at five the next morning, and were on the reefs at six thirty, planning to dive on the spot where the cannon had been buoyed. A light, early-morning breeze from shore had replaced the steady onslaught of the prevailing easterly, and Sea Diver rode quietly at anchor. Inspired by the temporary calm and the promise of some underwater activity, Bill and Clayton were in the best of spirits.

Captain Weems, certain that he could find the missing ballast, set out with Vital and Clayton in Wee Diver. They planned to search both reefs while the water was calm enough to get in close to them. The rest of the party boarded Reef Diver and headed for the buoy which marked the cannon. Although the sun was still low, we found that there was sufficient light to be able to see the bottom clearly.

As soon as we were anchored over the cannon, Ed and Bill went overboard with the air hoses. I floated on the surface, watching the divers as they inspected the cannon, which lay side by side below. I could see no other signs of wreckage, and when Ed came to the surface, he confirmed this.

"They are old French sakers," he said. "There's nothing else around. Perhaps they were thrown overboard to lighten some ship so that it could be gotten off the reef."

His remark reminded me of that time when this same harbor had been a regular port of call for the commerce of the world. Here once had lain at anchor Napoleon's mighty fleet of conquest. There must have been many times when anchors had dragged or ships had been forced upon the reefs in adverse winds and tides. Some of them must have ended disastrously on the bottom of this now-deserted harbor.

We were just climbing back aboard when we saw a launch approaching Sea Diver from the direction of town. It was the *Life* magazine team we had been expecting for several days. We pulled up our anchor and went to greet them—Peter Stackpole, world-renowned photographer, particularly keen on underwater picture-taking; and Kay Hampton, reporter.

There was an envious look on the faces of our two sons as they watched the launch cast off to depart for town, for by now the early-morning calm had retired in favor of the usual strong wind and rolling seas, and they were both seasick again.

Despite the roughness of the water, Peter and Kay pleaded to be taken out to the reefs to see the cannon. So Ed, pleased to demonstrate our little Reef Diver, set out to introduce them to our place of operations. They were back in no time, Kay making a brave attempt to overcome the queasiness she had felt while looking at the bottom as Reef Diver pitched and tossed. The wind by now had risen to forty knots, and any further exploration that day was out of the question.

There was a general exodus to quarters. Only the hardy ones remained on deck to watch as Peter set up his cameras and enclosed them in the six gleaming black-and-crystal lucite cases which he had made for their use underwater.

We were again up at five the next morning, and by sunup were on the reefs with both boats. As on the previous morning, there was a slight land breeze and the water was fairly calm. Ed dove on two likely spots which he had buoyed previously, only to find that what had appeared to be stone ballast was boulder-shaped coral.

We combed the area thoroughly that morning, searching close to the temporarily docile reefs, but we were unable to find the pile of ballast which we thought we had seen on Easter Sunday. We could only conclude that we had been deceived by a scattering of coral rocks on one of the sites which Ed had later examined and rejected.

We returned to Cap Haitien that afternoon, as Bill and Clayton had to be in Port-au-Prince the following day to board the airliner for home. Never were sailors happier to get back to port! By then the entire Link family had succumbed to "Haitian tummy." Clayton was running a temperature. Bill was a mass of sunburn, and I was sure I had at least one broken rib. To everyone's relief, Ed decided to keep Sea Diver in port the next day. The whole crew was weary from the constant beating we had taken, and there were many chores on board that needed doing. Sea Diver would not set out again until Sunday.

5

o

o

o

When Sea Diver returned to her labors two days later, her crew very much refreshed, I did not accompany them. I had visited a doctor in Port-au-Prince after putting the boys on their plane. He had advised that I should stay quietly ashore for a few days. I did not have any broken ribs, as I had feared, but the tendons were badly strained, and I was tightly bandaged. So I spent the time at the Becks' hotel, very much irritated at my enforced idleness.

Sea Diver's crew, meanwhile, had abandoned their search of the three reefs which had originally occupied us and moved on to a bank of reefs just west of them. There now seemed only one thing to do, to proceed from reef to reef, wherever they figured the Santa Maria might have sailed, and carefully explore each one. It promised to be a long and grueling task.

There was one chance of shortening the search. Morison had chosen the reefs we had examined after first convincing himself that Navidad had been located on the shore in the approximate vicinity of Limonade Bord de Mer. He had then applied the *Journal's* account of the salvaging of the Santa Maria and figured that the flagship must have struck upon one of these reefs.

But there was no proof of where Navidad had actually stood. Moreau de St.-Méry, the French historian who lived in Hispaniola for a time at the end of the eighteenth century, claimed that the fort was erected inland on the banks of the Fosse River, which in Columbus's time probably emptied into the sea near Limonade Bord de Mer. Yet he also recorded the discovery of one of the Santa Maria's anchors in the muddy bottom of the Grande Rivière, a mile from its mouth and some two miles west of that fishing village.

Was Navidad on the shore, or was it located on the bank of one of these two rivers? If Navidad was in the vicinity of the Grande Rivière, it would be logical to look for the remains of the Santa Maria to the west of where we had been searching, on a line east of Punta Santa to the mouth of the river. Several times, when Sea Diver had remained at anchor overnight behind the reefs, I had watched the native fishing boats as they sailed forth at dawn from the anchorage in front of Limonade Bord de Mer, some three miles from us. I felt that a visit to this area might provide the answer to some of the questions that were puzzling us.

Meanwhile I reviewed what had happened to Navidad and its thirty-nine settlers between the time Columbus left them to sail back to Spain and his return the following fall with men and supplies to strengthen the colony.

He found Navidad burned and not one of the settlers still alive. Columbus must have counted much upon the existence of that first colony. He had no doubt looked forward to the accumulation of a vast treasure of gold in his absence, as well as shelter and fresh food, for his sea-weary men. For on this second voyage, he had arrived with seventeen vessels carrying more than twelve hundred seamen, colonists and soldiers, his mission to establish a permanent colony close to the source of gold, which was to augment Spain's wealth and power.

This fleet, having just arrived, was standing on and off outside the reefs a league from shore on the evening of November twenty-eighth, "where the Christians had been left. The Admiral ordered two lombards to be fired in order to see if the Christians who had been left with Gaucanagari would answer, since lombards had been left with them." There was no reply.

Columbus, already alarmed at the discovery of the decomposed bodies of two bearded white men on the shore close to his last anchorage, now felt sure that his colony had met catastrophe. A short time later his ship was approached by Indian messengers in a canoe. They informed him that their chief, Guacanagari, was now living in a village some distance away, as there had been a battle with two other Indian kings and the village had been burned. They admitted that some of the Spaniards whom Columbus had left "had died of grief and others as a result of quarrels that had arisen between them." But they also indicated that still others were alive and well.

"Next day they [the fleet] expected Guacanagari in the morning, but he never came, and after a while some landed by order of the Admiral and went to the place where Guacanagari usually was. They found it burned, and a hut, strengthened with a palisade, where the Christians had lived and kept their property, was likewise burned and destroyed."

After further investigation, Columbus pieced together what had happened. Scarcely had he sailed for Spain with the Niña than the Castilians who were left behind had aroused the anger of the friendly Indians of the village by their lust for gold and their pursuit of the women of the tribe. A band of the Spaniards who were roaming the countryside and terrorizing the inhabitants were at last set upon and killed by order of the Indian chiefs Caonaboa and Mariema. The warriors had then attacked the Indian village to ferret out the rest of the Spaniards and had slaughtered them.

Guacanagari, evidently feeling obligated to his friend Columbus in spite of the despicable way the Castilians had behaved, had tried to defend them, thus bringing disaster upon his own people. Now Guacanagari had retired to the main Indian village to the east, supposedly to recuperate from a leg wound he had received in the fighting.

As there was no longer any reason to settle at the site of Navidad, Columbus sent exploring parties in both directions in a vain search for a likely site for the new settlement he proposed to establish. He finally determined to return along the coast to the east and build a town nearer the area where gold had been found.

So, early in December, almost a year after the wreck of the Santa Maria, the fleet departed, leaving as evidence of white occupancy only a broken ship on a coral reef, the burned ruins of Spain's first settlement, and a scattering of European belongings which had found their way into the huts of the Indians who had salvaged them. It would be many years before the white man would return to make over this part of Hispaniola to his design.

I spent the next two days quietly at the Beck hostelry while each morning Sea Diver and her crew set out to continue their exploration of the reefs. They came upon no signs of a ship as old as the Santa Maria, but they returned at the end of the second day to report the discovery of a most intriguing wreck. The watchers in Reef Diver's hull had first spotted a large anchor pointing shoreward. When Ed and Captain Weems went skin diving upon the area, they came upon the remains of a large ship, including two more anchors, a coral-crusted, boxlike object and much standing rigging, jutting out of coral formations which undoubtedly concealed many other things.

But what had excited their curiosity most was a square pile of blackened, sediment-encrusted bars, the same size and shape as the silver bars which had come from the Cay Gorda wreck. Skin diving on them had failed to reveal their composition, and it was too late in the day to bring Sea Diver close enough to use the salvage equipment.

So they had set out early the next morning in great excitement to investigate their find, leaving me thoroughly disgusted at having to remain behind. But even though I was not yet in condition to join the searchers on Sea Diver, I thought that perhaps I could accomplish something ashore.

I was sitting at the breakfast table, mulling over the possibility of tracing the Santa Maria's wreck site by somehow establishing the location of Navidad, when M. Beck happened along. I asked him how I could get to Limonade Bord de Mer, the site of Navidad, according to Dr. Morison. He had never been there and said he was not even sure it could be reached by road, but he promised to make inquiries for me.

I was elated when he returned to tell me that it was possible to drive within a short distance of the village and then to follow a footpath the remainder of the way. He offered to take me there in his station wagon, along with his wife and son. This was my opportunity. I stifled some thoughts as to whether the trip would be too strenuous for me, and what Ed would have to say about my going, and told him I would be delighted. So after lunch we started out.

Taking a road from town which led through Quartier Marin, a tiny farming village, we crossed a bridge over a wide river bed and turned north along a narrow dirt road leading along the river. It was known locally as the Parois, the Becks told me in their halting English, but it was really the Grande Rivière. What luck that I would have an opportunity to inspect this stream, in which the Columbus anchor had been found, as well as the lay of the land behind Limonade Bord de Mer.

Although there was not much water flowing over the rocky bottom at that time of year, I could see from the height of the banks on either side that the wide bed was used to carrying quantities of mountain water. It was lined on either side by great shade trees, some as much as five feet in diameter, the silvery-gray, thorny trunks of the sablier and the rich shining green of the mango mingling with the coarse-patterned leaves of the breadfruit. Clumps of yellow-green bamboo and stubby palms grew at their feet.

Wherever the river made a turn, creating dry, rocky spaces on the inside of each curve, small groups of women from the countryside were on their knees at the water's edge, doing their laundry. None of them wore clothes above the waist. They splashed and chatted happily as they scrubbed, festooning the shrubbery along the shore with the freshly washed clothes.

The road became rougher and narrower, and M. Beck was forced to shift into low in order to negotiate many of the rutty places. Branches slapped against the car as we passed. Soon we left the river and drove through woods and fields until we came to a clearing. Here were a few small houses, the ruins of a very old French Colonial brick-and-stone wall, and at a distance from the road in the direction of the river, the moldering walls of an old sugar mill.

This was Habitation Bellevue, formerly the location of one of the many wealthy plantations which had dotted this fertile plain. It was near here, in the bed of the river, that the Columbus-type anchor now in Port-au-Prince had been found nearly two hundred years before.

M. Beck stopped before one of the thatched cottages to make inquiries of an old man who volunteered to show us the rest of the way to Limonade Bord de Mer. He crowded into the front seat with the two Beck men, and we left the clearing to enter a thicket of lacy logwood trees, their feet buried in flat, claylike soil.

Emerging from these woods, we were confronted by a wide channel of water cutting directly across the road. Here we had to leave the car and set out on foot, crossing the shallow water by means of some logs which lay at one side of the road. It was evident from the ebbing flow of the water that this was an arm of the sea reaching back into the interior.

We followed the path across a wide stretch of saline flats and then into a tangle of mesquite. The ground became softer and swampier, and the path meandered into a large patch of mangrove, its edges splashed with colorful sea grape. Here strong sea breezes sweeping across the low bushes cooled our heated bodies.

A group of ragged Haitians passed us, carrying water on their heads in a variety of containers, their feet splashing through the salty mud of the path. We had taken to the more solid ground alongside, but soon found that if we would continue to the beach, we would have to wade through the muck also. Fortunately, an obliging native with a machete came along just then and solved our problem by cutting enough mangrove branches to make a dry path across the ooze.

At last we came out on the narrow beach. The coarse brown sand was littered with debris from the sea. A few crude fishing boats, obviously carpentered by hand from a variety of woods, and calked with black tar, were drawn up on the beach. Three others strained at their moorings just offshore in the choppy waves kicked up by the afternoon's prevailing east wind.

We walked the remaining quarter mile to Limonade Bord de Mer through loose, deep sand, our heads bent into the wind as we struggled along. My side pained me and I was breathing hard. I wondered why I had ever set out on such a trip, when the doctor had warned me against going out on Sea Diver because it would be too exhausting.

The village proved to be a scattering of poor, thatched huts around the nucleus of the old French Colonial church, whose steeple had been the focal point of many of the bearings we had taken from Sea Diver while out on the reefs. It was a desolate spot—no grass, no trees, only a low, shrubby growth in the vicinity of the houses, and no fertile land for garden patches. We found that there was only brackish water in the wells behind the church, and that fresh water had to be carried from the Grande Rivière, more than a mile away. All day long the village was exposed to the hot, tropical sun as well as to the full fury of frequent stormy winds and seas.

Unless this stretch of beach had differed vastly in Columbus's time, I could not believe he would have picked such a location for Navidad. Yet Morison was convinced that Navidad had stood along this seacoast, within a half mile of the little church. On the other hand, St.-Méry, who knew the area well in the decade before the black revolution, believed that Navidad was located more than a league up the Fosse River.

It seemed improbable to me that the Indians would have chosen this barren shore for a permanent village. Wasn't it more likely that they would have selected higher

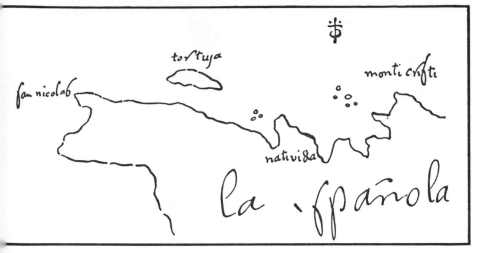

Only surviving chart made by Columbus upon his return to Navidad in 1493. It is impossible to determine the actual location of Navidad from this crude drawing.

Early charts of first settlement in New World.

Las Casas's chart of section of Hispaniola showing location of Navidad and Isabela, the settlement which replaced it. The two indentations in the coastline in the vicinity of Navidad make it appear that Navidad was located near the Grande Rivière, the other river being Haut du Cap near the present city of Cap Haitien.

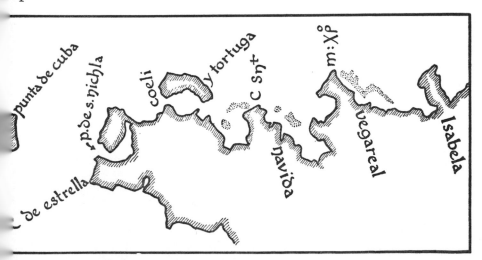

ground, with fertile land for their crops, a nearby supply of fresh water, and a quiet landing place for their canoes? I remembered that Las Casas, the historian who had visited the site of Navidad during Columbus's lifetime, had described it as being "overgrown with so many and such great trees." Perhaps like those I had seen along the banks of the Grande Rivière before we had reached the barren shore lands.

Also, I recalled, the morning after the Santa Maria was wrecked, Columbus had found it necessary to send a messenger to inform Guacanagari, "who had his town inland about a league and a half from the said bank." I had read other passages which indicated that Navidad was inland, doubtless up a river. But which river? The Fosse today was a dried-up river bed with no outlet to the sea, while the Grande Rivière was a wide, deep river bed, carrying a quantity of water even at this dry season.

According to all accounts, the mouth of the Grande Rivière had been built out into the sea with silt both before and since the time of St.-Méry. A map of the area in St.-Méry's time had shown a deep indentation at the mouth, while today the shore line extended some distance into the harbor. So the anchor which was found at Habitation Bellevue, a long way from the sea, might in Columbus's time have lain much closer to the outlet.

As I returned with the Becks that afternoon to Cap Haitien, I examined the Grande Rivière with new interest. It seemed very probable that somewhere along its shores the Indian village and Navidad had once existed. I wished that it were possible to explore its lower reaches where it entered the sea, for the extent of this delta land might be a clue as to where the Santa Maria had found its last resting place. Perhaps Ed and I could visit it later with Reef Diver, from the direction of the sea.

I learned at dinner that the "silver" bars in the tempting pile had turned out to be only iron ballast. Ed said that the wreck was that of an early paddle-wheel steamer with sails. The square, boxlike object had turned out to be the boiler. Because of the large amount of brass and copper to be seen, he figured the ship must have been British, these finer metals being a well-known characteristic of English shipbuilding.

Captain Weems was much intrigued by a copper object which he had tentatively identified as a strange kind of depth finder. Using a small charge of dynamite to free it, he had emerged with what appeared to be a lead sounding weight and a cluster of copper rods, each two feet long, and hooked, so that they folded back and forth upon each other. His interest was aroused more than ever when he found that there were sixty-six of these rods, measuring an exact twenty-two fathoms. He could scarcely wait to get it back to Annapolis to seek help in identifying the depth finder.

There was no doubt from their eager conversation that Sea Diver's crew had had a most satisfactory afternoon, although their morning search of the reefs had still failed to produce any signs of the Santa Maria.

Peter Stackpole urged that they return to the wreck the next day, for he wanted to get some underwater-camera shots of the divers in action. How about raising one of the anchors? he suggested. M. Beck thought this would be a fine idea, for the prefect had already expressed a desire for an old anchor to decorate the park by the sea wall.

I listened to their talk enviously, for although we had been in Haiti for two weeks at this point, I had not yet been underwater. I wondered if my bandaged side would allow me to make a dive the next day; then desperately determined to make the attempt.

So we rose at four thirty the next morning and drove through the silent pre-dawn streets to the dockside. Sea Diver was soon under way. When we arrived in the vicinity of the wreck, she was eased into position, close enough to one of the old anchors so that her lifting equipment could be used in raising it.

As soon as there was light enough to see clearly beneath the surface, we went overboard—Captain Weems, Ed, and I with the air hoses, and Peter and Kay with tanks strapped to their backs. It was good to be on the bottom again. I enjoyed myself immensely, swimming about the wreckage and scanning the coral formations in hopes of discovering some object which the others might have overlooked the previous day. As long as I did not use my right arm I found that my ribs did not hurt too badly, but I dared not exert myself.

In the meantime Ed and Captain Weems had succeeded in prying loose an anchor from the coral and sand. While Peter maneuvered about the men with his camera, they secured a heavy chain about its shank and then signaled to Vital and Kemp on deck to start the winch. By the time the anchor had been dragged across the bottom to a spot just below the lifting gear, the water had become so murky it was hard to see anything.

I swam clumsily toward Sea Diver's bow to look for the large anchor which had been the first sign of the wreck, thinking the water would be clearer in that direction. It was then I discovered that my air hose, floating free near the surface, had become entangled with a mess of other lines and hoses stemming from the same section of Sea Diver's deck. I swam an intricate pattern to extricate myself from them, and then headed again toward the bow, carefully scanning the coral bottom for signs of wreckage.

I was about thirty feet beyond the boat when I became sharply aware that there was no more air coming into my mask. I took quick stock of the situation. Should I head back to the ladder some sixty feet away? Should I swim to the surface, trusting that I could keep myself afloat in spite of the lead belt around my waist, until someone discovered my predicament? Or should I struggle with the fastening of the belt in the hope of getting it off before attempting to surface? I knew that the latter was the proper procedure, but I doubted if I could pull the buckle free with the handicap of my bandaged side.

But as these thoughts flashed through my mind, I was already making a quick leap in the direction of the ladder. The water there was so murky I could see only vague shadows. Just as I thought I could not go without air a second longer, I realized that I was once more breathing.

I gratefully inhaled a gulp of air as I seized the bottom rung of the ladder and pulled myself up, to find Ed freeing my hose from one of the metal legs, where it had become entangled. It had evidently floated to the surface when I was maneuvering to get clear of the anchor tackle, and as I swam toward the bow, had caught on the ladder and kinked. Ed had often assured me that he kept an eye on me when I was underwater. Now I knew that he meant it.

A short time later we had the nine-foot anchor lashed to Sea Diver's rail. We were removing our diving gear when a launch drew up alongside with the prefect, the colonel and the Becks aboard. As Ed hurried down the deck in his bare feet to greet them, he kicked a corner of the freezer box. Feeling a quick stab of pain, he examined his right foot to find the fourth toe bent straight back on itself. He wrenched it back into place, hoping it was only out of joint, and continued aft to help our guests aboard.

We headed back to Cap Haitien that noon and deposited the anchor on the municipal dock, where it was put in charge of the Port Captain until a permanent place could be arranged for it. Then M. Beck drove Ed off to a doctor. They returned an hour later with the disturbing news that the toe was broken. It would take at least a month to heal, even if he were very careful of it.

6

o

o

o

"I saw that Spanish cross in my dreams again last night," I said, as we ate our breakfast aboard Sea Diver the next morning, preparatory to starting the day's search. "It looked exactly like the one I saw in the clouds over the mountains the day we arrived."

Ed stared at me absent-mindedly. "Did you?" he said.

I could tell his mind was not on this evidence of the supernatural's interest in our expedition. He was wondering why the Nordberg diesel was spitting oil and had suddenly become so cussed to start, for he immediately said: "Vital, when you get the time, take the head off that diesel. I'd like to see what's wrong with it."

But Kay, who was dawdling with her cereal, for her appetite was never very good at this early hour, turned to me in excitement. "Marion, isn't that fascinating? It's the second time you've seen that cross. Do you suppose it really has some significance?" We both felt a little thrill of superstitious awe at the thought.

The men proceeded to talk over plans for the day. At

any moment we were expecting Charlie Martin, pilot of the harbor launch, who had promised to take us to an anchor which, he said, was known throughout the port as the Santa Maria's anchor.

After searching almost every likely spot for nearly two weeks, we had received this information with skepticism; particularly as it was evidently in a section of the harbor where it seemed dubious Columbus had ever taken the Santa Maria. In spite of our doubt, however, we could not afford to pass up the possibility that this local legend might have some truth in it.

Charlie arrived just as we finished breakfast. He suggested that we take Sea Diver as far as possible, transferring to the small boats when we reached shallow water. So we set out, towing Reef Diver, and heading a little south of east. We anchored about two miles from town in four fathoms of water. From here Ed piloted Reef Diver while Kemp manned the outboard. The rest of us distributed ourselves between the two boats.

We had gone only a short distance when the bottom climbed steeply to a flat, spreading shoal of cobblestones and grass. Near its edge, jutting from the water, was a reddish-brown curved object which at first glance might have been a fisherman's marker or the dead branch of a tree. Instead, to our amazement, Charlie pointed it out as the arm of an old anchor, which lay well buried in the bottom.

Captain Weems, who was in the Wee Diver with Kemp and me, climbed overboard to investigate, and I soon followed. It was low tide, and we were in water just above our knees. We found that the protruding arm of the anchor had lost its fluke, and the other arm was completely buried. The shank extended for nine feet under the surface of the water, but the ring was gone.

Captain Weems, who had started poking about with

a glass-bottomed bucket, soon discovered an anchor ring a short distance away. He shouted that he had found the missing part, but then found that it was the top of a second anchor, completely embedded in the shoal. More scouting revealed a third anchor within the same area. They were all of similar design and period, which Ed informed us was eighteenth-century French. None of them, by a long shot, could qualify as having come from the Santa Maria, but they must have lain there nearly two hundred years, since Haiti was a French possession.

Our guide then directed us toward the nearby mangrove shore. There, close to the narrow, sandy beach, which was uncovered only at low tide, were the arms of three more anchors jutting from the water, the remainder of them entirely concealed in the sand. We gazed curiously at them.

Charlie told us that in the past this narrow strip of beach had been a loading place for ships coming in for the products of the countryside. This, then, explained the presence of the quantities of small, round boulders in the water. They were ballast which had been discharged overboard when the ships had taken on cargo. Probably the three anchors on the first shoal had served as moorings for the same purpose.

Regretfully Ed told Charlie that while these anchors were very interesting, none of them was at all the kind we were seeking. Did he know of any other very old anchors?

Charlie reminded him that he had already told us of one near the black-can buoy, coming into the harbor from Point Picolet. He did not know whether it was very old. He could only say it was a "different-looking" anchor.

Ed said without enthusiasm. "Well, we might as well take a look at it."

We returned to Sea Diver and got her under way, heading north toward the mouth of the harbor. We found from the chart that we were on our way to Le Grand Mouton reef, that shoal in the very center of the harbor entrance which had challenged our attention when we first entered Cap Haitien harbor. Coming up behind it, we anchored Sea Diver in deep water and pulled Reef Diver alongside. This time the search boat carried Kay, Peter, Captain Weems, Ed, Kemp, Charlie and myself—a full crew, to say the least.

Charlie, standing on the bow, guided us toward the reef, now and then signaling Kemp to zig or zag as he hunted the location of the "different-looking" anchor through the clear water. At last he indicated that we had reached the spot.

Kay and Captain Weems, who were watching the bottom from inside the cabin, exclaimed at the anchor, which could be glimpsed below. It was impossible to see it clearly, for the glass had become very scummy from the water of the inner harbor, so Captain Weems volunteered to dive on it to see if it were worth further investigation. He reported other wreckage scattered about as he swam toward the bow. It all looked very modern, he said.

After diving several times on the anchor, which lay just ahead of our bow, he finally reported that it was a very odd shape, but that he did not think it was very old, as it had only a thin covering of coral. He wished someone else would examine it.

As Ed did not want to wet the bandage on his broken toe unless necessary, I offered to take a look at the anchor from the surface. I studied it a few moments. Like Captain Weems, I was confused, for I could not make out the shape clearly. Ed then decided to examine it himself. While I waited for him to get into his Desco equipment, I swam around, looking over the other wreckage scattered about. It was evident that the ship had broken up not too many years ago. We had apparently drawn another dud.

Then, about a hundred feet from Reef Diver, I saw

another anchor! It was much smaller than the one Charlie had brought us to see. It was heavily encrusted with coral, its simple lines unbroken by flukes. The ring and a part of the shank were missing. This was much more the type for which we had been searching.

I called to Ed, "There's another anchor over here. Better have a look at it, too, when you get into the water."

I really didn't give it much thought. I was pretty well surfeited with anchors after the number we had seen that morning. Besides, we were quite a ways from the area where the Santa Maria was supposed to have gone down.

Finally arrayed in his underwater gear, Ed climbed clumsily over the side of Reef Diver. He headed in my direction, and I led him to the spot where the ringless anchor lay. I watched from the surface as he dove to make his inspection. The anchor was in about twelve feet of water. He looked it over carefully, making crude estimates of its length and breadth with his outstretched arms. Then, instead of swimming over to the larger anchor which had puzzled Captain Weems and me, he swam toward the boarding ladder on Reef Diver.

I followed him on the surface, arriving just in time to hear him say, "I think perhaps we've got it."

There was an excited interchange of data. It was the right shape and size; it was heavily encrusted with coral; its ring and flukes were missing.

Immediately there was a general scramble overboard as all those in swimming gear made a beeline for the spot where my discovery lay. While the swimmers hovered over it and dove upon it, Ed investigated the first anchor which had excited our curiosity. He dismissed it with scarcely a glance. Back on Reef Diver he told us that it was a modern patent anchor with a stock which folded back on the shank when not in use. Coral had grown over it in grotesque hunks to give it its strange appearance.

Kemp dropped a yellow buoy on the spot, and we

hurried back to Sea Diver for additional equipment. Vital joined the others when they returned to raise our find while Kay and I remained on the larger boat. We were most excited. Strange to have found it in such a location, but it surely had the look of the anchor we were seeking. We waited eagerly for Reef Diver to return.

At last we heard the boat's high-pitched hum. We hurried to the rail. We could sense excitement in the men's voices and their smiles as they approached Sea Diver. The anchor was lashed to the iron superstructure of the little cruiser, the broken end dragging in the water.

"This looks like the real McCoy," Ed called.

They were indeed pleased with their find, for this anchor might very well have come from the Santa Maria. It was photographed like a prima donna; first as it hung from the stern of Reef Diver and, later, reclining upon a tarpaulin on the aft deck of Sea Diver.

Careful measuring showed it to be seventy-eight inches long without the missing ring end. The arms were irregular in length, probably because of the missing flukes. The distance from the end of one arm to the other was fifty-five inches. Ed made detailed and accurate measurements of each section as Captain Weems noted them on paper.

Then Ed took a hammer and chisel and carefully set to work, where the shank and arms joined, to remove enough of the coral covering to reach the original iron. It was quite a job, for the encrustation was an inch and a quarter thick, and he did not want to damage the anchor. As he had expected, there was evidence of crude welding of the two parts, and a hand-wrought look to the iron. Only very early anchors were made in this fashion; later they were cast, he said.

Further testing at the end of one of the arms showed a narrow channel in the metal where the fluke had originally been forged to the arm. A third test spot at the severed end of the shank showed it to be roughly broken, the soft condition of the corroded metal in its core testifying to an invasion of salt water sometime in the past, when the fracture had occurred.

Ed had seen enough to feel very certain that we had a Columbus-period anchor. But would we ever know whether it had indeed come from the Santa Maria?

Strangely, he had discovered, when he went to loosen it from the bottom, so that it could be raised, that it was already lying free. Most assuredly, an anchor nearly five hundred years old and as thickly covered with coral as this one would have been cemented so securely to the spot where it lay that nothing less than a charge of dynamite could remove it. Unless it had been buried in sand. How, then, did it get to the location where we had found it, on a hard-coral bottom?

Then I recalled the numerous woven-cane fish traps of the natives, which we had seen on almost every reef, weighted to the bottom with large rocks or whatever heavy objects could be secured for the purpose. I remembered watching that first day on the reefs as a sturdy fisherman dove over the side of his crude sailing craft to inspect a fish trap near Sea Diver's anchorage. He had come up with two conch shells from a fathometer-measured depth of forty-five feet. Was it not possible that sometime in the past another fisherman had snagged and transported this broken anchor to the spot where we had found it?

This led to further speculation. Perhaps the anchor had lain in sand with only its ring and upper part cemented in the coral. Then, after hundreds of years of corrosive action, a strong pull from the surface on its lower part had caused the shank to break under the strain. Ed had already remarked that the coral which covered the anchor was a sand-formed encrustation.

Granting that such a thing might have occurred, and

that this was an anchor from the Santa Maria, we seemed to be just as far from our objective. We still did not know where the Santa Maria had gone down. We could only guess that in the coral of one of the reefs in the harbor might lie the ring and upper end of the anchor. If we could find that spot, we might also find other indications of the Santa Maria's last resting place.

We had eliminated the possibility that the Santa Maria might actually have sunk on Le Grand Mouton because of Columbus's statement that he was a league distant from Punta Santa an hour before he struck the reef.

Unfortunately, unless we could somehow find the remains of the Santa Maria, we could never say positively, "Here is an anchor from Columbus's flagship, first to visit the New World and first to go to its grave upon the reefs of Hispaniola." We could only say, "Here is an anchor that may have come from the Santa Maria. It is of that era, of the proper size, design and workmanship."

In any case we had found one of the oldest anchors ever discovered in the New World. Only the one in the museum at Port-au-Prince could lay claim to being as old. We were more curious than ever to see that historic anchor and to compare it with our find.

7

o

o

o

The morning following the finding of the ancient anchor, we got Sea Diver under way and began to search the western end of the ten-mile barrier reef at the outer edge of the harbor, which we had avoided until now. With only two days left before Captain Weems and the *Life* team would be leaving, we had decided to concentrate on any likely areas we had so far missed.

We had eyed the long coral bank each time we had passed it on our way to the inner reefs, questioning the possibility that the Santa Maria might have gone on it in the darkness of that Christmas Eve. But always the large ocean waves which burst mightily upon it made it look very hazardous to approach in any of our boats.

Fortunately we had chosen a quiet morning. We anchored well inside the barrier, with enough room for Sea Diver to swing in any direction. Although the sea was calmer than we had yet seen it, there were already breakers upon the reef. Ed had mapped out a plan of search covering about two miles of its western extremity, for he thought that if the Santa Maria had grounded here, it could only have been at this end. Captain Weems and Vital were to follow the inside of the reef in Wee Diver, while the rest of us, in Reef Diver, would investigate the outer edge, as close to the reef as the rolling sea would allow.

We found the water very rough, and as the wind came up and slack tide changed to a rising one, our project became increasingly hazardous. The waves reached the outer edge of the reef in large swells and charged across it in foaming white crests. Ed steered as close as he dared, but was forced to keep Reef Diver at a distance of nearly forty feet. Kemp was perched on the bow, where he could watch the bottom with his "X-ray" eyes, and the rest of us took turns at the viewing glass in the cabin.

Now and then we caught glimpses of Wee Diver on the inner side of the reef, working past us in the opposite direction. She looked very small and helpless as she appeared and disappeared behind the breaking seas. Still, she was on the safe side of the breakers, where a stalled outboard would only result in her occupants' being carried away from the reef in the direction of shore. I tried not to imagine what would happen to us if the engine of Reef Diver should suddenly stop. It demanded all the power that Ed could muster to keep us at a safe distance, with wind, waves and tide all conspiring to carry us on the reef.

I spent an unproductive half hour looking through the glass in the cabin. When I returned to the cockpit, we had just passed Wee Diver on the other side of the barrier reef, only a few hundred yards from us. I could see only Vital at the outboard. Captain Weems undoubtedly was sprawled in the bottom of the boat, his eyes glued to the passing scene below; for he, like myself, was so intrigued with this means of exploring the ocean floor that the rest of the world was blotted out whenever he had a chance to search.

Just then Vital must have seen a break in the foaming barrier and recklessly decided to join us on the outside, for unexpectedly I saw him turn the little boat and head into the breakers. It did not seem possible that he could make it.

Wee Diver was almost through, white crests forming and breaking on either side, when a large sea made up directly in front of her. The wave struck the little boat with sufficient force to broach her, while water poured in over the side and drowned the outboard motor. It was fortunate that Captain Weems was lying in the bottom at that moment, or Wee Diver undoubtedly would have filled and sunk. As it was, quick-witted Vital grabbed an oar and, using it as a paddle, maneuvered the boat so that its bow was again headed into the sea. He held it there while the wet and startled captain scrambled to a sitting position and started to bail.

Meanwhile Ed headed Reef Diver toward them, and Kemp, on our bow, prepared to heave a line as soon as we should be near enough. Vital paddled madly to keep from capsizing. With skillful handling, Ed maneuvered Reef Diver to a position in front of the toiling men. He then turned her bow into the seas and, reversing the power, backed the little cruiser slowly in toward the breakers. We were within fifteen feet of Wee Diver before Kemp was able to cast a line in her direction. Then Ed put the power ahead and we towed her slowly seaward until they had cleared the rocks on either side. We then turned and, paralleling the reef, headed west with Wee Diver still in tow. We were all relieved after the narrow escape.

I returned to the cabin at this point so as not to miss any more of our search than necessary. Once I poked my head outside to see how the small boat was making out, for Reef Diver was bouncing about a great deal in the big seas.

Vital was sitting in Wee Diver's stern, holding his oar like a paddle, guiding the little boat through the tremendous waves which chased us astern. On his face was the rapt look I had seen him wear when shooting rapids in a canoe in his native Canada, while the boat coursed from side to side like an aquaplane. I marveled at this French-Canadian, who, until a few years before, had never been out of the northern bush. How quickly he had made the transition from forest to sea, accustoming himself to life on a heaving deck, and mastering the mechanics of the intricate equipment aboard Sea Diver. He was indispensable to the success of our voyage.

Captain Weems was not to be seen. He was evidently on his stomach again, looking through the glass, determined not to miss a square inch of bottom.

By the time we had rounded the end of the reef and returned to Sea Diver, the sea was too rough to risk working the outer reef any more that day. Back in port, Ed and Vital set out in Reef Diver to make further tests with the magnetometer, which they hoped to use on Le Grand Mouton reef the next day. Captain Weems and I, escorted by M. Beck, hunted up the Dominican consul in order to secure papers for our eventual arrival in Puerto Plata, for we planned to leave the following week for the Silver shoals.

We returned from this errand just in time to welcome aboard Ambassador Davis, who, with his wife and party, was making an official visit to Cap Haitien that weekend. The ambassador had heard about our discovery of the Columbus-type anchor and evidently wanted to see it. That night we had dinner with the Davises and their group.

We started out the next morning on our final day of search. It was our last opportunity to locate the Santa Maria before leaving for the Silver shoals. Since we had found the ancient anchor on Le Grand Mouton reef, we figured we should return there and examine the bottom more thoroughly. After all, the missing ring end might be somewhere on the shoal, imbedded in the coral, with the remainder of the Santa Maria lying near it.

We did not realize until after we had anchored behind the bank that we might have difficulty in relocating the spot. We had made two errors. The men had removed the yellow buoy which marked the location after raising the anchor, and we had not thought to bring Charlie along on this second trip to show us the way. We combed the area thoroughly all morning but never came upon the spot where the ancient anchor had lain.

We would still have enlisted Charlie's help had we been able to bring him back from town that afternoon, but by noon the sea had become too rough for us to continue. Once more it was brought home to us how difficult it is to locate a definite spot on the ocean bottom, even with the best of bearings.

Our time had run out, and we had not found Columbus's flagship. The following day we would officially present the ancient anchor to the city of Cap Haitien, replenish our water and supplies, and make ready to leave for the Silver shoals. But Ed was resolved that when his stint there was ended, he would return to Cap Haitien and continue the search for the Santa Maria.

We were up at dawn the next morning to ready ship for the ceremony, which was to take place on the municipal docks at noon. We scrubbed and polished Sea Diver until she shone, broke out all her flags from the masthead, and arranged our choicest relics, pieces of eight and gold doubloons, for display.

Then, when we had moved Sea Diver from her mooring to the dock, the men rigged the anchor from the small boom so that it could be swung ashore easily. Sea Diver and the ancient relic suspended above her deck immediately became such a center of attraction that the Port Captain found it necessary to mount a guard on our aft deck in order to prevent an increasing number of sightseers from coming aboard.

As the noon hour approached, the dock swarmed with people and cars. We welcomed aboard Prefect Sam and his wife, who had arranged a gala dinner in our honor that night; Mme. Magloire, sister of Haiti's president; and Colonel Chassagne, who invited us to his home for champagne after the ceremony. Soon after, Ambassador Davis and his party arrived.

The anchor hung from the rigging above the deck, slim and white in its coating of ancient coral, awaiting the signal to be swung ashore into the truck which would carry it to Army headquarters. Sea Diver was crowded and so was the dock.

When the moment arrived, Prefect Sam, Ambassador Davis, Ed, Captain Weems and I lined up on the dock near the anchor. Ed made the presentation to the prefect, who then accepted it for the city to the cheers of the crowd, while the anchor was eased into the back of the truck. Then it seemed that everyone on the dock flocked aboard Sea Diver. For a while we were very busy greeting our guests.

This was indeed a contrast to the first week we had spent near this same dock, indifferently received and completely frustrated in our efforts. We could now appreciate that most of the delay had occurred because we had arrived in the midst of Holy Week and a national holiday. Certainly no one could be warmer and friendlier than these same people, now that we had come to know them. They were as pleased as ourselves that we had found this evidence of Columbus's first visit to Hispaniola.

Colonel Chassagne assured us the relic would be carefully guarded at Army headquarters until a suitable place could be prepared for it. He urged us to hurry back and continue our search for the flagship. Ed, disappointed at having to leave at this time, promised a swift return. He had already cabled Mendel Peterson of our find and looked forward to his joining Sea Diver for the following weeks. Pete would then come back to Haiti with Ed to make a more positive identification of the anchor.

Some five weeks later, after an adventurous interval at the Silver shoals and their vicinity, Sea Diver was anchored once more in Cap Haitien harbor. Among her crew was Mendel Peterson, who had come aboard during a stopover at Turks island.

No sooner had the party completed formalities with the customs than they headed for Army headquarters, where the anchor still reposed. In the clear sunlight of the drill yard, Pete subjected the ancient relic to a minute inspection, as he wielded calipers and chisel and tape.

It unquestionably dated back to the time of Columbus and could very well have come from the admiral's flagship, he said. He noted that the crescent shape of the arms placed it before the seventeenth century, when V-shaped anchors were first made.

The anchor was almost completely oxidized, he pointed out, with only an eighth inch of sound metal left at the core of the three-inch cross section. It must have lain in salt water a very long time to form a coating of calcerous matter an inch and a quarter thick. For comparison he cited the anchor from the Looe, which had gone down in the Florida keys in the eighteenth century, yet had less than a quarter inch of coating when found.

Of course, Pete said, our anchor could have been lost by one of the ships which accompanied the admiral on his second voyage to Hispaniola in 1493. There was no way of knowing. If the anchor in the Port-au-Prince museum should prove to be similar, however, it would be a strong indication that the two had come from the same sunken ship.

It would not be surprising for two similar anchors to turn up, he explained, for it was customary in those days for ships to carry several anchors. When a ship was helpless off a lee shore, her anchors were often the only thing to stand between her and shipwreck. A ship like the Santa Maria normally would have carried two large anchors on deck at the bow and one or two astern. There would have been additional anchors in the hold, for it was not uncommon to lose anchors at sea. He said the Santa Maria probably carried an even larger number on this voyage, as no seaman of Columbus's ability would have set out without several spares.

The following day Pete and Ed flew to Port-au-Prince to inspect the famous anchor which had been found in the muddy bottom of the Grande Rivière in the eighteenth century. One of Haiti's most prized possessions, it was housed in the National Museum.

At first glance it presented a completely different appearance from the one we had found on the ocean floor. It stood more than three feet taller and was crowned with a large, hand-wrought-iron ring. At its base the curved arms ended in sharply pointed flukes, which were missing on our find. But the greatest difference was in the look of the structure itself, for it was long and slim and dark in color, while the one from the bottom of the sea was thick and heavy with coral.

It was hard to believe that the two anchors had anything at all in common. But after examining it long and carefully, Pete finally delivered his opinion. "The similarity would be striking," he said, "if the anchor at Cap Haitien were not broken and corroded."

He explained the difference in corrosion: the Port-au-Prince anchor had lain in alluvial river soil, where it was seldom, if ever, exposed to salt; while our anchor had been exposed constantly to the electrolytic action of sea water for nearly five centuries. Very little corrosion takes place in fresh water or mud, he said.

The two anchors were of the same type of construction, Pete found. The arms and shank were of the same approximate weight and cross-sectional size. The Port-au-Prince anchor measured sixty inches from fluke to fluke, while our anchor—minus the flukes, which had completely corroded away—measured fifty-five inches. The complete anchor was 117½ inches long, while the broken one measured 78 inches. The missing section of shank and ring would easily make up this difference. The two anchors originally could have been duplicates.

"I believe these anchors definitely came from a shipwreck," Pete declared, "for it is most unlikely that a ship would otherwise lose its two main anchors in the same harbor. As the Santa Maria was probably the only ship of that period to go down in Cap Haitien harbor, it seems very logical that both anchors came from her."

He later took samples of the metal from both relics to be tested by the U.S. Bureau of Standards. Their reports confirmed that the two anchors were fashioned from iron of the same type and period.

It was Ed's intention to continue his search for the Santa Maria during this second visit to Cap Haitien. But he had not reckoned on the weather. This time, instead of high winds and rough seas, he found that the rainy season had commenced, and that swollen rivers and streams were dumping quantities of mud into the harbor. The water, which had been clear in the spring, was so fouled that it was impossible to see an object three feet away. Any underwater exploration was out of the question.

Disappointed, he was forced to give up any further attempt to locate the Santa Maria. Instead, he took Reef Diver to examine the coast between Limonade Bord de Mer and the mouth of the Grande Rivière. Somewhere on this shore, he was sure, Columbus had unloaded the salvage from the Santa Maria, for it was the only section of coast where mangrove did not grow right to the water's edge.

He made two landings, one at the town and one just east of the delta at the mouth of the river. Each time, he found that the bank shelved so steeply that it was possible to drop the bow anchor a hundred feet offshore and then ease Reef Diver back on the line until another anchor could be carried ashore and sunk in the sand. There were native fishing boats secured in similar fashion in both places.

Upon going ashore he found that the Grande Rivière was deep enough to be navigable except for the delta at the mouth, which could be crossed in a shallow-draft boat only at high tide. The low, muddy ground which was formed by the river's deposit extended for perhaps a quarter to a half mile inland before a change in the character of trees and vegetation indicated solid ground.

It was up this river that St.-Méry had recorded the finding of the anchor now at Port-au-Prince. Could it have been the same anchor which Dr. Chanca, Columbus's physician on his second voyage, had reported seeing near a cluster of rude Indian shacks on the shore as he accompanied Columbus from the burned and destroyed Navidad? ". . . an anchor belonging to the ship which the Admiral had lost here on the previous voyage," he had written. St.-Méry had conjectured that the anchor which

Dr. Chanca had seen on the shore had not been moved, but that the mouth of the river had gradually built out into the sea beyond it, because of "the frequent high waters of this river and the immense quantity of earth and of sand which was carried from the mountains to the sea."

Ed found the delta and the muddy flats near the mouth of the Grande Rivière, through which he waded, an indication of its constantly changing contours, for on St.-Méry's map of this area, made in 1796, had appeared a deep indentation in the shore line, where, today, the land jutted into the sea. If Navidad were located on solid ground up the Grande Rivière, it must necessarily have been some distance inland.

Ed returned to Cap Haitien very little wiser as to the actual location of Navidad, but with some new ideas. He explained these to me when next I joined him at the Caicos islands late in June.

Following Morison's theories as to the location of the wreck, Ed pointed out, we had searched all of the reefs which the Santa Maria might have struck on a course from Picolet point to Limonade Bord de Mer if she had sailed between the barrier reef and the inner line of reefs. But if Columbus were heading for Guacanagari's village, and it was in the vicinity of the Grande Rivière, he would have taken the more open and accessible passage between the inner line of reefs and shore. In this case he might have gone aground on a shoal lying less than a mile from the sandy shore just east of Cape Sable and directly in the path of such a course. There is a wide expanse of deep water both on the outer side of the shoal and between it and the shore.

A study of an air photograph of this area indicated that the shoal consisted more of sand than coral. We felt sure that our anchor had lain for many centuries on a sandy bottom while its thick coating of sand coral was formed.

In clear water the anchor could easily have been spotted from the surface and picked up by a fisherman as a weight for his fishing trap, then brought to the reefs we had searched, which were hard coral rising from a hard bottom with scarcely a trace of sand. This shoal nearer shore, on the other hand, while it might contain coral rock, was largely composed of sand and mud from the river mouth.

We continued to study all the material we could get our hands on. It seemed more and more plausible that what was left of the Santa Maria might be buried in this shoal which we had failed to investigate. Of one thing we were convinced: the ship had not gone down on any of the reefs we had originally explored.

It seemed a shame that this possible solution had not occurred to us sooner. But that is the way with any kind of research. It is only by eliminating the false assumptions and carefully following every new clue that progress is made. We looked forward eagerly to investigating this new lead when we once again returned to Cap Haitien, for our finding of the anchor had convinced us that some-day the remains of the Santa Maria would also be found.

Part
Four

The
Silver
Shoals

1

o

o

o

At last Ed and I were on our way to the Silver shoals, mecca of every treasure hunter for the past three hundred years. The greatest treasure hunt of our lives had begun.

Silver shoals! The very name was enough to send thrills of excitement up and down the spines of everyone aboard Sea Diver.

Ever since our first diving expedition to the Florida keys five years before, when we had heard of the Silver shoals during night-long bull sessions with the other divers, Ed and I had read and talked about these far-off reefs, where, more than three centuries ago, a Spanish galleon had gone down with millions in gold, silver and precious jewels. We had speculated constantly on our chances of seeking and finding the remains of this fortune, for there is not a chart in existence which correctly portrays the extent of these banks and the exact locations of the thousands of dangerous reef formations which are scattered over them.

Barney and Jane Crile were with us in those first sessions, leaders in the plans we made, discarded, and made again to visit these shoals one day. Now they were with us once again, as we set out from Cap Haitien on April twenty-fifth, to make our dream come true—a dream of exploring these fabulous reefs, of diving in the depths of these mysterious waters, and of succeeding, where countless others had failed, in locating the remains of this famous treasure wreck.

Also aboard Sea Diver was Glenn Krause, a civilian employee of the hydrographic department of the United States Air Force in Germany. He had joined us that morning, just before we sailed. Glenn had always led an adventurous life, numbering among his experiences a part in one of the Navy's expeditions to the South Pole. He was a map maker, a photographer, and a seaman—a long, thin, very bald man in his forties, with the nonchalant air of the adventurer.

Glenn had come as an emissary for Alexander Korganoff, that White Russian historian and researcher from Paris who had visited the Silver shoals as part of an expedition a few years earlier. The expedition had ended abruptly with a mutiny of the native crew, which he had assembled in the Dominican Republic. Nothing daunted, Korganoff had returned to the shoals a short time later in a small sailing boat. There he claimed he had located the site of the galleon wreck, spotted an anchor, and, he was convinced, had seen the coral-covered hulk of part of the ship.

Ed and Korganoff had been in communication with each other for more than a year, as the Russian was arranging a second trip to the shoals at about the same time we had planned to go. They had agreed to combine forces and to meet in that area soon after the middle of April.

Our other plans, to search for the Santa Maria off Cap Haitien and, later in the summer, to trace the course of

Columbus through the Bahamas, had all been made around this date with the French group, and Ed had recruited his volunteer crews for the entire cruise with this in mind. Consequently, when Korganoff was unable to organize his part in the venture in time to reach the shoals as planned, we were forced to carry through our plans for the trip as scheduled. It was finally arranged that Glenn Krause would accompany our party as Korganoff's representative. If we found anything of consequence, Korganoff was to be notified so that he could join us.

We left Cap Haitien in the early afternoon, and soon had Point Picolet abeam. From there Ed charted a course toward the Silver banks, 160 miles away.

Our course skirted the outer edge of Monte Cristi shoals and the low sandy islands known as the Seven Brothers, which extend in toward Monte Cristi itself, that famous pavilion-shaped mountain at the eastern end of Cap Haitien bay which Columbus noted in his *Journal* as he coasted along the northern shores of Hispaniola.

By dark we were well out at sea, knowing that we had had our last glimpse of land until our adventure at the Silver shoals should be ended. For there is no land near these dangerous banks, only ocean for scores of miles in all directions, and the brown look of coral just beneath the surface, marked here and there by foaming white breakers.

It was here, in the seventeenth century, that a Spanish galleon, heavily laden with the wealth of the New World and badly crippled by a hurricane, had foundered as it sought to reach the Spanish harbor in Puerto Rico for repairs.

Many are the tales which have come down through the years about this lost treasure ship. Stories emanating from Jamaica, from Puerto Plata, from New England and even from England tell of a whole silver fleet going aground in 1644 on the Ambrosian banks, as the Silver shoals were known at that time. One of the ships, said to be the flagship of the fleet, was found and salvaged in 1687 by a New England sea captain, William Phips. Phips took from the wreck more than a million and a half English pounds' value in treasure. The other ships of the silver fleet were never located, although the reefs were searched exhaustively by the hundreds of boats which flocked to this area after word got out of Phips's success.

Korganoff, after many years of research in the archives of Spain, had a different version of the story of the wreck. Of course he has had access to records which were completely unavailable to the rest of the world in the seventeenth century, when Spain and the other European powers were at each others' throats.

The story that he unearthed in the Spanish archives was that of the Nuestra Señora de la Concepcion, the flagship of a fleet of thirty ships which sailed from Havana for Spain on September 13, 1659. The galleon was in no condition to put to sea. The protests of her admiral that certain repairs must be made before setting out on such a journey were overruled by the General of the Fleet, who ordered him to prepare to sail immediately.

The admiral of the Nuestra Señora was also disturbed because the general had concentrated the bulk of the huge treasure which the fleet was carrying on the admiral's ship and his own. Both ships were old and rotten. Their hulls had not been cared for since they had left Spain, more than a year before. The admiral had insisted to no avail that the valuable cargo should be distributed more equally among the many ships of the fleet.

The silver fleet had been at sea only a day and part of the night when the Nuestra Señora began to leak so badly that even the impatient general conceded she would have to return to Havana for repair. Upon the fleet's arrival there, divers were sent down to examine the Nuestra Señora's hull and to patch the rotten timbers. Twenty-four hours later the convoy got under way once more.

This time it had just reached the narrowest part of the Bahama canal, between Florida and the Bahama islands, when it was set upon by a hurricane. The Nuestra Señora was tossed and beaten about by the huge waves. Her sails were torn away in the violent winds, and the crew hastened to cut down the tall masts, which threatened to overturn the galleon. The dozy timbers of her leaky hull, wrenched apart by the violence of the seas, let in such quantities of water that in spite of desperate work at the pumps, the ship was in constant danger of foundering.

However, when the storm was over, the Nuestra Señora was still afloat, but separated from the other ships, and well north of the spot where the hurricane had first struck. The admiral, after surveying the damage, decided it would be necessary to head for the nearest Spanish base at Puerto Rico for repairs before continuing the voyage across the ocean. But first he ordered the ship hove to for several days while masts were jury-rigged and emergency sails prepared. The pumps were operated continuously in an attempt to lower the level of the water in the holds, and wherever it was possible, repairs were made to the leaky hull from the inside.

At last the ship was able to get underway once more, although sadly handicapped by her makeshift sails. Her course carried her east until the ship's pilots declared they had gone far enough to clear the last outposts of the Bahama islands. Then the Nuestra Señora was headed south.

The admiral protested that they had not gone far enough to the east, and that if they changed course at this point, it would bring them into dangerous waters along the eastern shores of the Bahamas. The pilots refused to concede that he was right. Knowing that he must accept their pronouncements because of Spanish naval law, the admiral assembled the ship's passengers and crew on deck and publicly washed his hands in a basin of water, a symbolic protest that he would not be responsible for the consequences of the pilots' decision.

About a week later, in the dark of night, the admiral was suddenly awakened by a shout from the watch. A frightened ship's boy reported to him that there were reefs in all directions. He hurried on deck and gave quick orders to haul down the sails and cast over the anchors. Before the galleon's speed could be checked, however, she was in the midst of the reefs; and before she could lose momentum, the sharp coral was grating and tearing at her sides.

There was pandemonium on board as both passengers and crew rushed topsides. The anchors had caught by now, and the Nuestra Señora hung poised, her starboard side bumping and scraping against the rocks as the ocean waves rolled in from the sea. Otherwise she lay quiet. The admiral surveyed the situation in despair, hoping that the anchor lines would hold until daybreak, when it would be possible to see the surroundings and determine what should be done.

But the sea gave them no peace. One by one the heavy hawsers which held the anchors snapped as they sawed against the rough coral on the bottom. The longboats were put overboard and manned to hold the ship off the rocks. At dawn the admiral directed the oarsmen to tow the galleon along a path of open water which showed ahead through the reefs. Unfortunately, when the crew attempted to raise the anchors which still held the ship, they discovered that they were caught fast in the coral on the bottom. The admiral gave orders to cut the cables which held the anchors and to abandon them.

As the ship moved slowly among the reefs in the wake

of the longboats which towed her, she was carried side-
wards by the tide, first into one rocky head and then another. Several of the twenty bronze cannon with which
she was armed were sacrificed as anchors to hold her from
drifting into these menacing obstacles. Each time, they
caught in the rugged coral on the bottom, and had to be
cut loose in order to allow the galleon to continue. By
nightfall only a few hundred yards had been gained, and
there were still reefs on every side. The admiral gave orders to put more of the bronze cannon overboard as anchors
to hold the ship fast until daylight.

Perhaps the ship still would have survived. But in the
middle of the night a wind sprang up, causing the heavy
galleon to tug powerfully against her moorings. The anchor
lines, which had been straining for hours against the knife-
like coral on the bottom, suddenly began snapping one
after the other.

The Nuestra Señora was aroused from her restless
slumbers, and, with a slight tremor through her planking,
slowly drifted toward the reefs. She picked up speed as
the wind caught the high stern, and when she reached the
rocks, she carried upon them sideways with such force as
to rip great holes in her hull.

The galleon hung there awhile. Then, as a particularly
large sea rolled in, she freed herself momentarily while
the stern drifted around, and grounded again, this time for
good, caught in the narrow valley between two reefs.

Needless to say, a fortune such as was carried by the
Nuestra Señora could not be lost to the world for long
without efforts being made to find and salvage it. The wonder is that the Spanish did not return immediately to the
wreck, led by some of the survivors who had managed to
reach Hispaniola. But it was a difficult time for Spanish
shipping, for the rich traffic between Spain and her colo-

nies was constantly threatened by pirates and the daring privateers sent out from England and France to harry it.

The waters surrounding the West Indies in the seventeenth century were a constant battleground for desperadoes of every nation, intent on seizing for themselves a part of the wealth which flowed so freely from the New World to the Old. Spain's prestige and power, established by reason of her being first to discover and exploit this part of the world, was gradually giving ground before the onslaughts of her enemies, led by men like the English Morgan and Drake.

France was by now well established in western Hispaniola, in the wake of the "pirate colony" on Tortuga island, a motley crew representative of all the seafaring nations, which had finally come under French leadership. And England possessed colonies in the Bahamas, Barbados, Bermuda and Jamaica as well as on the North American continent. English sea power was in the ascendancy, a powerful weapon which she would use to mold the world to her pattern for centuries to come, while Spain, with the destruction of the Spanish Armada, was already on the downward path.

During the years between the sinking of the Spanish galleon and its eventual discovery by William Phips, there are on record attempts by the ships of many nations to seek its resting place. In 1683, Charles II of England commissioned two ships, the Bonetta and the Faulcon, under Captain George Churchill and Captain Edward Stanley, to discover and salvage the Hispaniola treasure, as it was then called. The two ships spent nearly three years in the vicinity of the silver banks, "ever scanning the sea for a lone rock rising high above the water." This lone rock was mentioned many times in early accounts of unsuccessful searches.

It was during this time that a sailor, Thomas Smith,

told the English sea captains that he had seen the Spanish wreck on the Ambrosian banks. He described the location as near a rock which rose up nearly fifty feet, while the rest of the reefs barely cleared the water. The hull lay about forty feet away, wedged between the rocks, and on the surface of the rock he said he had seen "sows and pigs of silver heaped high." He claimed that the owner of his ship had refused to attempt the salvage of the treasure because a gale had come up and he was afraid of losing his ship on the reefs, as he did not have sufficient cable and anchors.

The English captains engaged Smith to guide them to the spot, but after extracting all the information they could from him, Captain Stanley was so sure they would be able to find the location that they sailed secretly from Puerto Plata one night, leaving Smith behind. The result was that they never came upon the treasure ship. During the search, one of the ships struck a reef. While trying to free it, they lost all their anchors on the sharp coral and had to return to port to replace them. They were recalled to England before they could make another attempt.

Meanwhile, in New England, a young sea captain, William Phips, with adventure in his blood and a desire for quick wealth whetted by tales of lost treasure ships, had just returned from a partially successful trip in search of three valuable wrecks on the north Bahama banks. While on this voyage he had garnered tales of the Spanish treasure ship said to be lying beneath the water on the banks north of Hispaniola. What he learned inspired him to set out for England to enlist the aid of the Crown in providing men and equipment to salvage the wrecks on the Bahama banks and search for the Spanish galleon.

He must have been most convincing, for he succeeded in obtaining from King Charles II a commission to captain the Rose Algier, a small ship of eighteen guns and ninety-five men, on a voyage to the West Indies to look for the treasure.

He was gone almost two years, during which time he scoured the Ambrosian banks and the waters north of Hispaniola in vain. The rough, unsavory characters who first comprised his crew soon became discouraged with this unrewarding search for treasure and demanded that Phips turn pirate with the Rose Algier. He refused, outwitting them in two separate attempts at mutiny. He then hastened to Jamaica, where he discharged the dissenters and signed on new hands to continue his search.

This time he headed for Puerto Plata, the port on the north shore of Hispaniola nearest the banks on which the wreck was said to be. After scouting about the town for several days, he had the good fortune to strike up an acquaintance with an old sailor who was a survivor from the shipwrecked galleon. He is said to have given Phips very careful directions as to the location of the wreck. Phips headed back to the Ambrosian banks and continued the search, but was finally forced to give up, as his supplies were running low. He returned to England without success.

Although Phips still felt sure that he could locate the wreck, he found that the Crown was no longer interested to the extent of paying the cost of a freshly equipped expedition. But again fortune was with him. He succeeded in enlisting the interest and financial support of the Duke of Albemarle and a few wealthy friends who were willing to speculate on the venture. They obtained a patent from the Crown, granting them an exclusive right to the wrecks that might be discovered, provided the king received a tenth of their gain.

Some time later Phips set sail for his old hunting grounds on the Ambrosian banks, this time with two ships: the James and Mary, a two-hundred-ton ship carrying twenty-two guns, and the Henry of London, a small frigate of fifty tons with ten guns. Phips commanded the James and Mary. He placed the frigate under the command of Francis Rogers, who had been his second mate on the Rose. The two ships had good salvaging equipment for their day, and they carried a stock of goods for trade in the West Indies ports, in case the quest for the treasure ship should fail.

Arriving at Puerto Plata, Phips lingered nearly a month, preparing his equipment, putting aboard supplies and trading with the inhabitants. During this time he and his men constructed a periagua from a cottonwood tree, so large that the finished boat would carry eight to ten oarsmen. This craft, he figured, could be taken in close to the reefs, where it would be too hazardous to risk his sailing ships.

On January 13, 1687, he sent Captain Rogers with the Henry to search for the wreck on the banks some twenty leagues to the north of Puerto Plata. The frigate was gone nearly a month. Rogers returned to report in seeming dejection that they had failed once more to find their objective. But this was only his strange idea of humor. That night, while he and Phips were sitting around the table, he produced from beneath it a sow of silver worth two or three hundred pounds.

In reply to Phips's joyful questioning, he told of days of fruitless searching with the small boats in the vicinity of the "boylers" on the north bank of reefs. The Henry, meanwhile, was anchored about a mile and a half to the south of the reefs in the deeper water of the banks.

One wonders what they used for search in those days. Did they have anything similar to the glass-bottomed bucket which the Bahamian natives use today in hunting for crawfish? If so, the crude glass of that day must have made it difficult to see very clearly. Or did they send swimmers out to dive on likely places, straining their eyes to penetrate the depths of water to the bottom? We can be sure that at least one person was stationed on the highest part of the boat, his eyes glued to the water, even as Kemp, with his "X-ray" eyes, studies the bottom today.

Came their last day of search before returning to Puerto Plata. Rogers was in one small boat with a diver and oarsmen. The periagua carried two other divers with its crew. Deeply discouraged at having failed to sight any evidence of the wreck on this, their last attempt, they were returning to the Henry at the end of the afternoon when one of the divers saw an unusually beautiful sea feather in the clear water below. He went overboard to retrieve it and take back to the ship as a curio.

He returned with the purple feather and the exciting news that he had seen several cannon lying on the bottom. As he handed the Gorgonia over the side of the boat, a blackened coin was seen clinging to its base. At last they had found the wreck!

Rogers sent the diver down again, and this time he returned with a "sow." Before buoying the spot and returning to the Henry for the night, they picked up "two sows, 51 pieces-of-eight, a bar and a champeen and some broken plate."

Three days later, when a blackening sky and strong northwest winds threatened a coming storm and caused Rogers's men to halt their salvaging and head for Puerto Plata, they carried with them a quantity of sows and "dowboys" of silver and nearly three thousand silver coins.

Upon hearing news of the discovery, Phips hurriedly completed his trading in the port. After taking on supplies of food and water, the two ships set out for the banks on the night of February sixteenth. Six days later they anchored near the wreck, "the reef making like to a half moon."

"By Mr. Covell's observations we hoisted our pinnace. Mr. Covell and Mr. Strong and two of our divers went in to the wreck and just as day began to shut in they came on board bringing with them out of the wreck 89 whole dollars, 51 half dollars." So read the entry in Captain Phips's log of the James and Mary on that historic day.

They did not attempt to sail either of the ships near the reefs where the wreck was located, but went back and forth each day with the pinnace, the periagua and the ships' boats. For nearly two months they worked the wreck day after day, with the exception of Sundays, which Phips insisted they should observe as a day of rest. At the end of each day, Phips recorded in the ship's log fresh figures of treasure removed from the wreck and stored aboard the James and Mary.

They had been on the spot less than a week when they were astonished to see sails approaching. They were soon joined by two smaller vessels, one under the command of William Davis of Bermuda and the other under Abram Atherley of Jamaica. Phips had become acquainted with both men on his previous voyage, when he was searching the wrecks on the Bahama banks. He soon made a deal with them to work on half shares in return for the use of their boats and divers.

Several weeks later, Davis's sloop damaged a rudder on one of the reefs and was forced to head for Jamaica for repairs. Her captain promised to keep the discovery of the treasure a secret and to return as speedily as possible.

When the sloop did not return at the expected time, Phips became worried that she might have been captured by French pirates, who were known to be haunting the waters in the vicinity of the island of Tortuga. He lived in constant fear that word of their find might have leaked out, and that pirates might suddenly descend upon them and rob them of the treasure.

At last he could bear the suspense no longer, and he set sail for Turks island in the James and Mary, accompanied by the Henry. He left his divers and salvage equipment behind on Atherley's shallop, with instructions to continue working the wreck for the next week, while awaiting the return of the missing sloop. If it had not showed up by the end of that time, the shallop was to bring what had been salvaged in the meantime and join him at Turks island.

When Atherley later appeared at Turks island, he had seen nothing of the sloop which was expected from Jamaica. During the additional week he had remained on the banks, however, he had salvaged more than a ton of silver to add to that already stored aboard the James and Mary. Phips paid Atherley and his men for their share in the enterprise, and then the two British ships set sail for England, where they arrived on June sixth and were received with great acclaim.

Phips delivered over to the Duke of Albemarle, his other backers, and to the Crown a fortune in gold and silver, in addition to jewels and the bronze cannon which had been hauled from the bottom near the wreck. He related the circumstances of his abrupt departure to them and urged an immediate return to secure the balance of the treasure before it could be salvaged by others, now that the news of its discovery was out.

This time he had no trouble in obtaining support for another voyage. Five months later, three heavily armed ships were equipped and ready to set out. One, the Foresight, was furnished by King James himself, under the command of Sir John Narborough. These were to be joined on the banks by two guard ships, both fourth rates, the Assistance and the Faulcon.

Phips and his escorts arrived back at the Ambrosias early in December. As they approached the vicinity of the wreck, they were astonished to see that the waters thereabouts were dotted with ships. Like vultures they had gathered from every port around to snatch what they could of the treasure feast so lavishly spread on the ocean floor. There were ships from Jamaica, Barbados, Bermuda, the Bahamas and even faraway New England.

When the armed vessels of the English appeared, many of these boats left precipitately. The captains of those which stayed promised to turn over what they had secured on shares, and to continue working with Captain Phips in return for a portion of the finds. However, the small divisions they were promised did not prove sufficient to keep them at the arduous task, and one by one they cut their cables in the night and sailed away.

This time the wreck proved very disappointing to the searchers. Phips's divers had already skimmed the cream on his previous visit, and the scores of small boats which had scoured the spot while Phips was gone had removed whatever else was easily come by. Now it was necessary to break up the coral that had grown over the wreckage and hoist great chunks of the rock to the decks of the boats, where they were pounded apart to uncover the valuables within. It was slow and difficult labor, and it taxed the strength and ingenuity of the salvagers to the limit.

During their search, the divers reported to Phips the discovery of a large section of the ship lying on the bottom, so heavily encrusted in coral that it was impossible to break into it with their pikes and other equipment. They were sure that it contained a large portion of the gold and silver which the ship had carried, but their heaviest assaults failed to penetrate it, and they were finally forced to give up.

The English ships stayed on the banks and worked the wreck until May eighth, then headed back to England by way of Turks island. They arrived there on August twelfth, carrying nine tons of silver and very little gold, a relatively small reward for their efforts when one considered the high hopes with which they had set out.

The small sailing craft which were frightened away by Phips's return undoubtedly made a killing while he was in England preparing for the final expedition. Phips must have known when he allowed the sloop to return to Jamaica for repair on that previous voyage that word of his discovery would soon leak out. And of course, when the James and Mary and the Henry stopped over at Turks island on their way back to England, there is no doubt that the news must have spread from his sailors and divers to the crews of other ships sailing in and out of the port.

It was a hard decision Phips was called upon to make during that first salvage attempt—whether to continue working the wreck and securing more treasure at the risk of being raided and losing all, or to take his winnings and go back to England while there was yet time. He no doubt made the wise decision.

In addition to allotting Phips twelve thousand English pounds for his part in the expeditions, King James made him a knight. Furthermore, soon after Sir William Phips returned to his patiently waiting wife in Boston, he was named Governor of the Colony of Massachusetts. Phips was undoubtedly the luckiest and the most successful treasure hunter the world has ever known.

It was ever thus. Rogers did the searching and found the wreck. Yet to this day Captain Phips is given all the credit, and he received the lion's share of the spoils which were recovered.

For many years thereafter, these dangerous and out-of-the-way Ambrosian banks, which now became known as the Silver banks, were the scene of continual searching by sailing ships from all of Europe and America. It was generally believed that only a part of the treasure had been raised from the galleon which Sir William Phips had found. There was also much speculation as to whether only one ship from the silver fleet had gone down, or whether other ships from the same fleet had foundered somewhere on this forty-mile stretch of reefs.

Fantastic stories were told wherever seamen gathered, in the course of which more and more galleons sank beneath the waves, carrying ever-greater quantities of gold, silver and jewels to the bottom.

Even in our own century, Captain Phips is still the hero of many treasure tales. The story of his expeditions has been recorded with fair accuracy, but the treasure hunter of today can only guess at the facts of the loss of the Spanish treasure. Was only one ship sunk? Or did a whole fleet disappear? Did the ship which Phips salvaged sail from Havana in 1644 or 1659? Did Phips and the other salvagers who followed him get all the treasure, or did they leave on the bottom, as some believe, an impenetrable section of the hull containing millions more in gold and silver?

If the remains of this treasure still lay on the bottom, would it be possible for us to find and raise it with the aid of modern diving equipment and underwater explosives?

On board Sea Diver we probably had the most complete diving and salvage equipment available in the world today for exploring waters such as those to be found on the Silver banks. With our small glass-bottomed boats we could search the entire area of reefs. With our magnetometer and metal detectors we would surely be able to find indications of any metals covered by sand or coral. With our up-to-date diving equipment we could reach any spot underwater. And with our salvaging tools and equipment it would be possible to uncover and raise whatever we might discover.

We had finally convinced ourselves that this was the time and that, logically, we were the ones to make this one more attempt to locate the long-lost treasure ship.

Subsequent research revealed that little was actually known of the Silver shoals. We read several accounts of adventurous voyages to these waters—each writer seemingly intent on outdoing the other in the extravagance of his descriptions of the wild seas, the treacherous reefs, and the dangerous sharks, barracuda, octopi, and other sea life that were said to inhabit these waters in great numbers.

We also read descriptions of the wreck itself, standing on the ocean floor as it had gone down centuries ago, its decks littered with wreckage and its holds filled with bars and treasure chests. Always it was so armored in coral or so guarded by ferocious underwater monsters that it had proved impossible for divers to approach or penetrate the hull, except in one case where the writer described having been unexpectedly precipitated through the rotting deck of the ancient wreck into its dark, terrifying hold.

We had discounted most of these stories. From their descriptions we were more than doubtful that the writers had ever come upon the actual location. We well knew that it is impossible for a wooden ship to remain on the bottom for any number of years in waters such as these without the timbers breaking up or being destroyed by the ever-present teredo worms. We knew that all telltale cannon had been removed, and that the ship had sacrificed its anchors in other areas to hold it off the reefs. There would be very little evidence left to identify it.

There were other possible hazards. We did not know just how dangerous to our own boat these reef-strewn waters would be, or if we would be able to find a safe place to anchor in case of storm. We also wondered if, there on the Silver shoals, we would encounter some of those legendary deep-sea monsters which we were always reading about but so far had never seen.

We were well aware that what we were about to attempt would require more real seamanship, careful navigation, and painstaking planning than anything we had ever done before. There would be no margin for error on the Silver shoals. We would be completely on our own, no other ships within reach, and no shore stations within range of our radio transmitter.

To find a secure anchorage would be a real problem. When it came to searching the reefs with the small boats, we would be in serious danger at times from the suction of the boilers. When we went underwater, we could expect to find a most perilous bottom with great jagged ridges and pinnacles of coral reaching upward eight to twelve fathoms. We would doubtless encounter fierce sharks from the ocean deeps and schools of barracuda which used the reefs as their feeding grounds.

Small wonder that we approached the Silver banks with trepidation as well as expectation.

2

o

o

o

The hydrographic charts depict the Silver banks as a forty-mile-square area located in the open waters of the Atlantic Ocean between the eastern end of Hispaniola and the easternmost islands of the Bahamas. The northern edge extends in a northwest-southeast direction, marked almost its entire length by a heavy concentration of coral reefs, nearly a mile wide in places. The southern line of the bank is about two thirds the length of the northern. The water on the banks varies in depth from six fathoms to twenty. In addition to the almost solid line of reefs on the northern side, the charts show a thin scattering of reefs on the other three sides.

The nearest harbor is Puerto Plata in the Dominican Republic, more than eighty miles away. A hundred miles to the northwest is Turks island, the first land to be encountered in that direction. Elsewhere there is only ocean and more ocean, much of it nearly two miles in depth.

According to some of the accounts we had read, there was one small exception—a lone monument of coral, rising out of the water even at the highest tide. This was said to be close to the spot where the galleon had foundered. No longer was it fifty feet high, as the sailor Smith had described it to Stanley before that long-ago seventeenth-century search; according to Korganoff, it now stood a scant two feet above the water.

Ed did not expect to find the lone rock and the location of the wreck too easily. He was frankly skeptical that it was the only dry rock in that vast extent of reefs. He was still disappointed that the day he had flown a distance of nearly six hundred miles from Nassau to take air photographs of these reefs and to reconnoiter them, he had encountered such heavy clouds and rain in the vicinity of Turks island and south of there that he was unable to reach the Silver shoals. How much simpler our task would be if we had such an aerial picture to augment the crude chart, left from the time of William Phips, for it was very puzzling to try to visualize the pattern of a bank of reefs from the deck of a small boat or even from the masthead. Without the aid of such a picture, it would be very difficult to locate the spot where the galleon had foundered.

That evening, as Sea Diver plowed along under the guidance of the automatic pilot, Barney, Jane, Glenn Krause, Ed and I gathered around the table in the main cabin to go over the material we had accumulated among us and to talk over a method of locating the wreck we were seeking.

The Criles had arrived with a portfolio of papers and charts which they had secured from an "armchair" treasure hunter in Texas who had made it his hobby to figure out the location of the Silver shoals treasure, but who had no means of testing his conclusions. We also had the seventeenth-century chart and the log from Phip's ship, the James and Mary. The hydrographic charts of the area were of little use, for, though they indicated the total extent of the banks, with the relative depths, the reefs themselves had never been accurately charted.

However, we were overjoyed to find that Glenn had brought an air photograph of the reefs on the northern banks, which he had secured from Navy sources, giving a very accurate picture of their arrangement. This, with a pen drawing which Korganoff had sent of the spot he had investigated previously, gave us a fairly clear idea of the area we were looking for.

As nearly as we could tell, all these sources agreed that the galleon was located near the center of a thick cluster of reefs which formed an inverted triangle on the northern edge of the banks. The group of reefs lay some distance in from the east end of the bank, and was bordered on the west by a wide channel to the open water north of the banks. To the east of this area, it could be seen that the southern edge of the reefs formed two long half moons. I recalled that Captain Phips's log had recorded anchoring the James and Mary near the wreck, "the reef making like to a half moon."

Our procedure, then, was to maintain Sea Diver's course in deep water until daylight, then pick up the south edge of the banks and cross them in a northeasterly direction until we came to the line of reefs which formed the north edge of the banks. We would hope to strike this northern edge somewhere to the east of the center of the forty-mile-long area. It would then be up to us whether we should turn east or west along it, to find the nest of reefs with the lone dry rock which we were seeking.

As it was late in the evening and we knew that the next day would be a strenuous one, Ed checked Sea Diver's course and the log, assigned the watches for the remainder of the night, and the rest of us turned in.

When Ed came on watch at daybreak, he discovered that the automatic pilot had slipped slightly in the night, and Sea Diver had carried us several degrees south of the intended course. A check of those on duty during the night revealed that no one knew when our course had changed or how long the ship had been heading in the new direction.

That is one of the difficulties of sailing with amateur crews. They do not function with the clocklike precision of trained personnel. Fortunately, in this instance, there was no danger, as we had been in deep water all night long. It was still impossible to pick up any indication of bottom with the fathometer.

Ed corrected the course a few degrees to the northeast and continued to take soundings until, at about nine o'clock, the fathometer picked up depths of a hundred feet. We steered this same course for another hour and a half and then changed our heading to straight north, thinking thus to intercept the northern line of reefs we were seeking.

We were making a very unorthodox approach. Had we headed for the Silver banks from Puerto Plata, as we had originally intended, we could have made use of the bearings given by Captain Phips in his log for reaching the site of the wreck, as well as those of Korganoff and others; but, coming from Cap Haitien as we did, we had to figure it out for ourselves.

It was not long before we began to see isolated coral heads around us, and soon we were forced to shift course frequently to avoid them. Kemp took his station on the pulpit, where he could keep an eye on the water depths and the location of the heads, and Barney climbed the mast to the crow's-nest, where he could view miles of startlingly clear blue-green water. The occasional coral head appeared as a pale, lime-green blotch against it. Glenn, Jane and I watched in mounting excitement and anxiety as the formations of coral grew thicker and Ed disengaged the automatic pilot and took over the wheel to steer a devious course between them.

A short time later Barney called from the masthead. "Breakers on the starboard bow."

Ed turned Sea Diver in the direction indicated, but found that he was forced continuously to the southeast by intervening coral heads. Suspense lay heavy on us all. We knew from past experience that we could hunt for days, even weeks, for the spot we were seeking. We had no bearings to go by, no present-day accurate charting of these rocks, and, because of our inaccurate course the night before, a very hazy idea of what part of the bank we were on at the moment. We only knew that if we could find a small dry rock just sticking its head above water, we might be able to find the spot.

We were very lucky. For as we moved slowly along in soundings of ten to fifteen fathoms, there was a hail from the crow's-nest. "Over there to the left, just off the bow! I see a rock sticking up!" Barney was pointing with his whole arm extended and shouting like a madman.

Down on the deck we had to use the binoculars, and even then it was some time before we could spot the rock, as Ed continued to edge the boat in its direction. Glenn brought out the little sketch that Korganoff had given him.

As we drew closer, we could make out a narrow channel leading to the almost solid line of reefs ahead of us. The dry rock was now plainly visible, sticking up from a flat reef to our port.

The day was calm, and Kemp, on the pulpit, could spot any dangerous heads well in advance. The moderate sea was breaking gently over the reefs, leaving a slight tracing of white to mark their location. Beyond the dry rock we could now make out a circular area of deep water, encircled by reefs except for the narrow channel just ahead. The men debated whether we should follow it in and anchor Sea Diver in the quiet water within, or drop our hook in the more open water outside.

"Let's go on in," Ed said. "Kemp, keep a sharp lookout for heads. I think there's plenty of room."

Kemp guided us carefully between the reefs, which rose on both sides, close to the surface. Once inside, after carefully reconnoitering our position, we dropped anchor in almost the exact center of the haven. It was just noon.

Glenn, in the meantime, had been up the mast with Korganoff's sketch, checking our position. He came back with the incredible news that we had stumbled upon the very spot which was our goal. From the air photograph, Phips's ancient chart and Korganoff's drawing, the men judged the boat's approximate position in relation to the reefs and discussed which was the most logical area to search.

We had a quick lunch and then launched Wee Diver. We were all anticipating our first glimpse of the bottom on these famous banks. I'm sure I thought that it would be only a matter of moments before the searchers would signal back to Sea Diver that they had discovered wreckage on the bottom.

It was decided that Barney and Jane should start out first, with Kemp at the outboard. After they had given the reefs a quick once-over, Kemp was to return for Ed and me. I watched them depart in mounting excitement. They headed for the reefs to the west of the dry rock, where Korganoff had indicated the wreck might lie, and Wee Diver started patiently circling them, Kemp running the motor, Jane and Barney lying prone in the bottom of the boat as they gazed through the glass bottom. I stood on the pulpit watching their every move.

Soon I saw Barney go overboard, then Jane. While Kemp continued to police the reefs, watching from the surface as he went, Barney and Jane started off in different directions on exploring trips of their own. They were swimming farther and farther away from Wee Diver, and Kemp, in the boat, was working farther away from them all the time.

I was truly frightened. Didn't they know that these were the Silver shoals? How dared they swim so far away from the boat and from each other? These waters were certain to be full of dangerous sharks and barracuda! Here on these sixteen hundred square miles of banks and rocks was a perfect haven for the fish life of the entire Atlantic!

I stormed inwardly at Barney and Jane. Why didn't they stay together? Why hadn't they told Kemp to keep near them? I railed at Kemp. Why didn't he keep his boat within calling distance?

Then Barney disappeared from my sight completely. The last I had seen of him, he was swimming in the direction of the dry rock. By this time I had communicated my fears to Ed and Glenn. We got out the glasses and took turns searching the waters for Barney. At last Glenn picked out his bobbing head a quarter mile from Wee Diver. He was swimming slowly in the direction of the boat. Jane was now near enough to Wee Diver to signal Kemp. After he had picked her up, they headed in Barney's direction and he, too, climbed into the boat.

They returned nonchalantly to Sea Diver, completely unaware of the fright they had given me. They were enthusiastic over the beauty of the bottom and urged Ed and me to hurry on to see it. They had not spotted anything of importance during their quick survey. They hadn't even seen any big fish, so all my fears had been needless, and in any case they were soon forgotten in my eagerness to get started. I could hardly wait for Kemp to refuel the outboard, but at last we were on our way.

I was overwhelmed at what I saw through the glass bottom of the boat—great towering coral cliffs, honeycombed with caves, rising from a white-sand floor, topped by pinnacles bizarrely fashioned like something from the Arabian nights. There were vast outcroppings of every kind of coral—tangled jungles of branch coral like berry bushes in a pasture, solid beds of lettuce coral, waving Gorgonia and sea fans, and topping all, the lovely yellow-brown stag coral, forming shady parasols for the teeming, colorful small fish beneath it. Not only were the reefs a tumbled mass of coral, but the whole ocean floor was scattered with these formations, some close to the bottom but many towering thirty and forty feet.

It was in bottom such as this that we discovered that Sea Diver's anchor and chain had become ensnared, as we cruised over them on our return, after a solid hour of unsuccessful search. No amount of pulling or hauling would ever free them. Ed, the only deep-water diver in the party, would have to go down, unwind the chain from the coral with which it was entangled and clear the anchor.

But because it was already late in the day and the weather seemed good, he decided we should stay in the little reef harbor overnight. It would take some time for us to find a good anchorage on the banks outside, and the sun was already getting low.

That evening Kemp prepared a delicious fish chowder for our supper from a kingfish and half a tuna he had caught on his trolling line in the morning as we crossed the banks. Half a tuna because, before he discovered that he had a fish on his line, the rear half of the tuna had been gobbled by a passing barracuda.

While the chowder was cooking and we were sitting around the table in the deck cabin enjoying a drink, we heard a shout from Vital on the aft deck. He was dancing up and down in his excitement as he hauled with all his strength on the heavy fishing line he had just put overboard, baited with the entrails from Kemp's fish. We arrived in time to see him pull alongside a shark about eight feet long.

This was an occasion to be celebrated, for ever since Vital had first joined us in Marathon five years before, he had been angling for a shark. Night after night he had made his preparations, fastening a large hook to a length of strong chain and then to a heavy line which he strung out behind the boat, well baited with whatever choice bit he thought might attract a shark. Sometimes the bait was gone in the morning. Twice the hook and chain had both disappeared, leaving the frayed end of the heavy line. But never had he pulled in his line with a shark on the other end. This time, when he finally had the shark safely on the deck, we had a drink of Barbincourt with him in celebration.

Early the next morning Vital caught a nearly fifty-pound barracuda on his line. We began to think that we were indeed in the center of an area of big fish, even though we had not seen any in our searching the previous afternoon.

I could feel the goose pimples rise as I watched Vital pull the creature over the side and still its powerful thrashing with a few blows from an iron bar, and I glanced aloft to the top of the deckhouse, where the shark's head was impaled with its wide-open mouth and sharp, gleaming teeth. Vital was preserving it as a souvenir to take back to his home town of Maniwaki, Quebec. I could see him upon his return, displaying it with a carefully cultivated unconcern to his woodsmen friends, who thought a big fish was an eighteen-pound lake trout or pike.

We hadn't spent a very comfortable night there in that harbor surrounded by reefs. The mental hazard was probably the worst, for we realized that it was a dangerous place to be caught in any kind of storm. We also knew that once darkness had set in, it would be impossible to leave our anchorage until morning no matter what might occur, for we would never be able to find our way out of that maze of reefs in the night. In any case we were bound to the bottom as long as our anchor and chain remained entangled in the coral, unless in desperation we sawed through the heavy links of the anchor chain and left it, as had many sailing ships in the past when faced with disaster.

Ed and I sat on the rail of the aft deck that night after everyone had gone to bed, gazing at the white circlet of breakers that surrounded us. To our starboard were the broad, flat reefs, almost touching the suface at low tide, near which we thought the Nuestra Señora had gone down. We speculated. How could a ship of its size, carrying over five hundred people and a solid cargo of gold and silver, have disappeared so completely? There just had to be some evidence beneath these waters that she had been there, even though all visible signs had been removed three centuries before. Surely we would be able to find some traces, for even if the remains were completely encased in coral, we had our metal detectors and the magnctometer to seek them out.

It was a beautiful spring night. The water inside the reefs was almost still. The soft air was like a caress, and a new moon shone softly on the waves outside the reefs, which broke gently along the edges of the coral with scarcely a sound.

What must it have been like on that night so long ago? I grieved for those poor souls who, having survived a hurricane and nearly two months at sea on a mangled and badly leaking ship, had suddenly found themselves shipwrecked on these very reefs which surrounded us. I could picture their panic as the galleon broke loose from its moorings and struck upon these rocks, gouging great holes in its hull, and then slowly settled toward the bottom as its frightened passengers crowded to the upper decks.

There must have been an insane dash for the few small boats which had already been launched. There was violence, no doubt, as passengers and crew fought to secure places in them.

Meanwhile, the admiral, knowing he had failed in his last efforts to save his ship, must have puzzled how to preserve what he could of the treasure in his charge.

In the end, when the ship finally foundered, its prow sinking to the sandy bottom eight fathoms below, carrying with it many of the doomed passengers as well as a large share of the gold and silver stored in its hold, its stern wedged between two of the flat reefs, assuming a crazy angle against the sky, it was said the admiral had given orders for some of the most valuable chests and plate, which had been stored in his own quarters, to be placed on the flat surfaces of the nearby reefs, in hopes that they could be salvaged later.

As daylight appeared, some of the survivors set about fashioning rafts and floats from what materials they could salvage. Standing up to their waists, even to their necks, in water, they labored, for there was little room left on the slanting decks, littered with wreckage where the poop deck protruded from the surface.

What a holocaust! One by one the boats and rafts had taken off, the lucky ones aboard beating off the clutching hands of those in the water who had no other means of rescue. They headed south, most of these makeshift rafts, so heavily laden it was doubtful if any of them could survive in the open sea. No one knew exactly where the Nuestra Señora had gone aground. The pilots insisted they were on the reefs of Anegada, between Puerto Rico and Hispaniola, but the admiral declared they were still north of Hispaniola, on the Ambrosian banks. The admiral was, of course, correct.

Foolishly, many of the survivors attempted to carry their valuables with them. Some of the rafts carried bars of gold and silver instead of food and water. A few of the makeshift craft eventually landed at various spots on the north coast of Hispaniola. A later reckoning showed that, of the 514 aboard, only 190 lived to tell the tale. The others either went to their death in these very waters or were lost on the open sea as they tried to make their escape.

When Ed and I finally went below, haunted with thoughts of that long-ago tragedy, the night was peaceful enough. But before morning, the wind came up. The breakers' gentle song on the reefs around us changed to a threatening roar, and to our uneasy ears it sounded as if Sea Diver were only a few feet from them. None of the crew had slept very much, we learned later. Toward morning a thunderstorm added to our mental tortures. With the change of wind that accompanied the storm, Sea Diver swung around on her anchor, her chain jerking and tugging at the coral heads which held her against her will.

We resolved never to stay overnight in that hemmed-in prison again. We would find ourselves a good anchorage outside upon the banks that very afternoon, we hoped in the vicinity of that half moon where Captain Phips had found secure anchorage nearly three hundred years before. Then, Ed said, we would also fix ourselves a permanent daytime mooring in the reef harbor, where we planned to search, so that we would have a quick means of picking up and freeing our anchor each day, retiring to the relative safety of the open banks for the night.

So that morning, while Jane and Barney searched the

reefs with Wee Diver, the remainder of those aboard helped Ed to free the tangled anchor chain from the bottom coral and to place a permanent mooring in almost the same spot. Until then none of us had realized that our anchor lay in twelve fathoms of water.

I floated on the surface as I watched Ed disappear down the anchor chain, hand over hand. On deck Vital and Glenn stood ready to tend the air hose and to winch in the anchor chain when it should be freed. I was to keep a lookout from the surface for Ed's signals and then relay them to the men on deck. Everything went like clockwork.

As Ed loosened the chain from the coral pinnacles with a crowbar, sometimes breaking off great arms in the process, the slack was winched in. Ed looked like a pixie in the clear, deep water below. His mission accomplished, he ascended, hanging on to the anchor chain, his feet resting on the stock while the winch slowly reeled in the anchor.

One more job remained to be done, that of placing a permanent mooring cable on the bottom. After looking over the situation, Ed chose, as a resting place for the anchor, the top of a large coral head, which was about twenty feet nearer the surface than the sea bottom itself. By placing the anchor thus, the chain would not become entangled so easily with the bottom coral as the boat shifted position in wind and tide.

We took our stations again. An anchor was lowered on a fresh length of chain while Ed swam downward to sink it securely in the top of the coral head. When he returned, he said he was sure nothing would ever budge it from above; he really wondered whether he would be able to dive it out again when the time came.

Now, we thought, very pleased with ourselves, we were prepared for any emergency that might come while we were within the reef harbor!

All the time I was watching Ed from the surface of the water, I was conscious of a large barracuda hanging around. It never came very close, but hovered nearby, watching every move we made. I wondered if it might be the mate of the one Vital had caught from the deck earlier that morning. If so, was it out to avenge its mate's untimely death? Needless to say, I was not very comfortable while it was there.

We spent the rest of the morning launching Reef Diver, for on the Silver shoals, if anywhere, we would require the services of that little shallow-draft, rudderless, wheel-less craft in order to use our compression-fed diving equipment close to the reefs, as well as to scout the depths through its glass bottom.

From time to time we caught glimpses of Jane and Barney as they cruised over the coral with Wee Diver. There were long intervals when the little boat was anchored and they were over the side, making a closer investigation of things that had caught their interest through the glass bottom. I had ceased to worry over them, for now that I had been in the water myself and had seen the reefs through the bottom of the boat, I had lost most of my concern in regard to the big fish. I now knew for a certainty that there were sharks and barracuda around us, but I also knew that they were no more prevalent than off Cap Haitien or in the Bahamas, where we had dived so often before.

I was beginning to find for myself what Ed and the Criles had discovered long before, that imagination plays a powerful part in creating a climate of fear, but that when one is concerned with the job in hand or full of interest and enthusiasm for one's surroundings, fear soon takes a back seat.

Many times when I have been alone on the bottom, I have been assailed with a creepy feeling that behind my back or just out of range of the narrow field of vision within my mask lurks some dreadful creature. I have swung around to find nothing in sight more frightening than a pair of beautiful blue-and-gold angelfish or a school of curious jacks. Or perhaps nothing. At times, even then, the feeling has persisted, not fading into the background until my interest has been caught by the ever-engrossing and exciting environment of the underwater. Now it has become almost automatic, if such a feeling nudges me, to take a quick look around, brush off my forebodings, and return to what is occupying me. There is too much to see and do in this underwater world to waste time worrying over things that might happen but seldom do.

When Jane and Barney returned to Sea Diver for lunch, they brought with them two round ballast stones they had dived up from the outside of the reef which lay between the one marked by the dry rock and the one which we had selected for special searching because of Korganoff's chart. Here was concrete evidence of the presence of a wrecked ship.

We could hardly wait to explore the location further, but by the time we had eaten, the wind had come up and it was too rough on the outside of the reefs for us to venture there. Instead we spent the afternoon in following the inside edges of the reefs to the north of us with both the smaller boats.

We returned to Sea Diver about the middle of the afternoon and, with Reef Diver in tow, started out toward the banks to seek a better anchorage for the night. There was quite a sea running and we did not look forward to spending the night tossing and rolling, as we were almost certain would be the case. But there, at least, we would have sea room in case of storm. We also looked forward to finding some clean bottom where we could drop our hook without getting it fouled in coral.

Our hopes were soon dashed. What with the poorer

visibility of late afternoon and the breaking seas, it was difficult even to spot the coral heads which were scattered here and there around us. Ed was finally forced to pick the most open spot in sight for an anchorage, and we dropped our hook, knowing full well we would have a struggle to recover it in the morning. Tomorrow, he said, we would leave the reef harbor still earlier in the afternoon and make a point of seeking a permanent mooring for our nights on the bank.

As I went aft that night on my way to bed, I was suddenly overwhelmed by the loneliness of our position. The cold crescent of the new moon just above the western horizon and a thick scattering of tropical stars barely lighted the crests of the rolling seas and the white froth of the reefs, which lay less than a half mile to our stern. The prevailing wind from the southeast blew strongly down Sea Diver's deck and whipped my hair across my face.

I was conscious as never before of the vast expanse of water surrounding us, a flood of water which somehow served to touch off in me a feeling of kinship with that wild and terrible period in the earth's history when all life lay deep in primordial seas. I shivered, although the wind that assailed me contained only an enveloping warmth. Never, even during those winter nights of cold and violence when Ed and I had braved the Gulf Stream gales alone in our little yawl, had I sensed as now that vast loneliness which the sea sometimes engenders.

Here we were in the heart of the Silver banks, completely on our own. There were no passing ships, for no captain would knowingly risk his vessel in these dangerous waters. The curling white foam on the north horizon off our stern carried a menacing threat, and in the dark waters around us coral heads hid their tops just beneath the surface.

We must be very sure that in spite of wind or storm

our anchor and chain did not fail, or we would find ourselves dashed against these same reefs which had claimed the Nuestra Señora so many centuries before.

The night passed quietly enough. In fact the wind went down toward morning, but we found ourselves hard put to it to stay in our bunks as Sea Diver rolled steeply from side to side in a cross tide. We were up early. After breakfast Ed and Kemp embarked in Wee Diver to assess the problem of raising the anchor.

They found it caught in a coral head on the bottom as they had feared, the chain twisted and turned around nearby heads. This time it was in fourteen fathoms of water, and again it was necessary for Ed to dive to this depth to free it. But now it was much more difficult, for the rough open sea caused Sea Diver to jerk and pull on the chain, and he had to time his movements while loosening it to the brief intervals when there was a little slack. He was exhausted from the struggle when he came back on board.

We were rewarded for the efforts of the previous day, however, when we approached the reef harbor, where a yellow-flag buoy floated, marking the permanent mooring we had laid. We found our way in through the surrounding reefs and heads, coasted up to the buoy, which Kemp caught with the boat hook, and secured Sea Diver quickly and safely.

It was late in the morning when we had finished eating breakfast and completed the chores on board. By the time Reef Diver was loaded with the necessary diving equipment and the two small boats were finally on their way to the reefs, the wind had come up again. Although it was fairly quiet within the reef harbor, the seas outside were kicking up quite a fuss.

We had hoped to anchor over the spot where Barney and Jane had picked up the two ballast stones, but the buoy they had placed to mark the spot was tossing about in the breakers on the outer side of the reef, and it appeared extremely hazardous to take Reef Diver there in the breaking seas.

Instead, we anchored the two boats as close as possible to the spot, but on the inside of the reef. Barney thought that by wearing a mask with the air hose connecting him to the compressor on Reef Diver, he might be able to reach this location with the metal detector to see if he could pick up any signs of wreckage, for once beneath the surface he would be relatively free of turbulence.

He started out across the reef, Jane following him on the surface, guarding his air hose to keep it from getting entangled in the bladelike millepores coral which came almost to the top in many places. This broad, flat reef could very well be the one on which the survivors of the galleon's shipwreck had placed the chests of valuables for the admiral; the very one to which they had clung as they fabricated the crude rafts which were to carry some of them to safety.

Disappointment came when Barney and the metal detector were brought up short just a few feet from the goal. He had come to the end of his air hose. This is one of the handicaps of using a compressor and connecting line. However, he had chosen it in this instance in preference to the clumsy air tanks of the self-contained equipment because he could maneuver the metal detector and himself more easily around the uneven coral formations close to the surface.

The wind continued to blow harder, and it now became impossible to accomplish anything around the reefs. We went back to Sea Diver and, after a late lunch, decided that we would try to locate the half moon where Captain Phips had mentioned anchoring his ship, the James and Mary. If we could find it, it might provide the perfect anchorage for Sea Diver. This was not the time to do so, however, for once outside the shelter of the reef harbor we found the water so churned up that it was impossible to make out either the pattern of the reefs or the look of the bottom.

As we cruised along, dodging the numerous rocky heads, Ed pondered the necessity of dropping the main anchor and chain with every prospect of having to dive them up again the next morning. It was then Kemp suggested we pick one of the coral heads near the surface of the water, but deep enough for Sea Diver's bottom to clear it safely, and plant our anchor in its top, much as we had done in the reef harbor. By attaching one end of a smaller chain to the anchor and the other end to a buoy at the surface, where it could be joined to Sea Diver with a hawser, we would have a permanent mooring.

So, with Kemp in the pulpit to pick out a likely coral head, Ed, at the wheel, guided Sea Diver in search of a promising place. Kemp finally spotted one with the proper qualifications and we steered toward it. Now it became a game of skill for Ed to bring the bow of Sea Diver into the right position and to hold it there while Kemp and Glenn, on the bow, maneuvered to place the anchor on top of the coral head, ten feet below. Jane and I wrestled with pike poles to fend Reef Diver off the stern, where it was being towed, as Sea Diver was shifted from forward to reverse and back again.

After three tries the job was done. Barney dived overboard and returned to report that the anchor was firmly set, deep in the heart of the head. We were secure —that is, if the sixty-foot length of chain could be trusted to hold. I felt very uneasy about that chain, for the reefs were only a quarter of a mile astern.

Again Sea Diver rolled and tossed all night long, as the wind whistled a tune through the radar antennae. At dinner there was talk of setting an anchor watch, but nothing was done about it. We all went to bed vaguely worried.

Barney and Jane, in the forward cabin, found it impossible to sleep because of the din made by the rattle of the rudder chains and the jerking of the boat against the anchor line. They finally sought refuge on the wide seat of the afterdeck, where they slept until dawn brought the usual thunderstorm, which drove them below decks once more. There was a splendid display of pyrotechnics from the blackened sky. The galelike winds drove the rain in sheets across the decks, and Sea Diver reeled drunkenly in the disturbed seas. Then, suddenly, it was over; the wind went down and the sea immediately calmed.

Two hours later, when we effortlessly released our line from the buoy and set out for the reef harbor, where we tied up, equally without effort, to the buoy we had left there, we congratulated ourselves that we had at last solved our anchorage problems.

The next day was most satisfying. That morning I lay face down on one of the bunks in Reef Diver, Glenn on the other, gazing through the glass bottom at the reefs below as we searched for further evidence of the ship whose ballast we had found. Kemp, with his keen Bahamian eyes, perched on top of the cabin, scanning through the water to the bottom, while Ed expertly guided the boat around the edges and then across the surface of the reefs wherever the water was sufficiently deep, for today there was not a ripple. The sea was heavenly calm.

Suddenly I glimpsed an anchor. But we were past it before I could shout, "Stop, stop!" Glenn, too, had briefly seen its ring from his side of the boat. Ed threw Reef Diver into reverse, and we were over it.

It lay on a flat shelf of the reef about thirty feet

below us, coral-encrusted, perfect, truly a thrilling find. We threw our own anchor over the side and Reef Diver hung poised above it. Ed put on his Scott mask and tank and went overboard to investigate. He measured the anchor—first its length, arms outstretched, one full reach and half again, nine feet long; then the distance from one fluke to the other, another full reach, six feet from point to point. It had cloverleaf-shaped flukes, sharply pointed arms and a large ring, no stock. It was a very old one, probably seventeenth century. It might well have come from the Nuestra Señora, or perhaps from one of Phips's salvage ships.

We searched the whole area, surface swimming, crossing the deep valley between this reef and the one containing the ballast, while Ed swam the depths below us. We skirted the outside of the ballast reef, too, carefully observing everything below.

Beneath the glassy, calm, blue-green water spread fantastic formations of wild and beautiful coral, while overhead a serene, cloudless sky lulled us into a feeling of complete security. Brilliant blue and neonlike, multicolored parrot fish swam in schools or darted in and out of the coral caves, while seventy feet below, Ed, in his Scott, searched the lower depths for signs of shipwreck, a small figure in the vast blue.

Finding no other indications of a sunken ship, we placed a buoy to mark the anchor find and went back to Sea Diver for lunch, puzzled, but also elated, for we now had two indications of the presence of a wreck somewhere in the vicinity. We decided to return and search the inside of the same reef that afternoon.

Once more we searched by boat. This time Kemp spotted more of the small round ballast stones on the inside of the reef, just in line with the spot where Barney and Jane had found the first two pieces. There were several "pebbles" in sight, with indications that more might be buried under the coral. We all went overboard once more, and spread out to cover as much bottom as possible while gazing down from the surface. We found more ballast.

I also spotted a peculiar-shaped object, flat and oblong, with two curves along one edge like bites. When Barney attempted to dive it up, it broke apart where it was cemented to the rock, and he came up with only a section, about eight inches long and five wide. It was blackened metal, heavily corroded. He placed it in Wee Diver and went back to his search.

In the meantime Ed had set out to investigate an unusual coral formation which he had observed on the sandy floor just inside the reef. It had the appearance of part of a ship, with curving ribs sticking upright from it toward the surface. We thought this might possibly be what Korganoff had considered as the coral-encrusted part of the galleon which Captain Phips had failed to penetrate in his search for the remainder of the treasure.

I watched Ed from the surface as he swam around the coral structure, which certainly bore a haunting resemblance to part of the hull of an old ship. He scanned it closely, then approached one of the protruding ribs and gave it a sharp snap. As it broke, a fine powder of white coral dissipated in the water around. Even from my distance I could see that the pure white of the inside of the arm extended clear through. There was no decayed wood here. He repeated the experiment on other extensions with similar results.

As I swam back to the reef where the rest of the party was searching, I wondered how many years it had taken this coral to develop and reach the surface. Would it be possible in, say, forty years, for an object as large as a whole section of a wrecked ship to become so encrusted that Captain Phips's divers would be unable to penetrate it? I doubted it. In nearly five hundred years the anchor of Columbus's time had been covered with only an inch and a quarter of calcerous growth. Under the most salutary conditions it was doubtful if any more coral than that could have been produced from the time the galleon sank until Phips attempted to reclaim its cargo within the same century.

There was a striking irregularity in this reef directly beneath me. The more or less solid coral rock which formed the body of the reef was transfigured by burgeoning coral growths of many types, these in turn masquerading behind creeping sponge formations in wonderful reds and yellows, and lush Gorgonias and sea fans. The whole colorful pattern stood forth against a background of deep, rich yellow-brown, the underwater look of the minute coral animals which, crowding the surface of the dead rock, reach hungry mouths into the waters around them.

In my mind I tried to compare these Silver shoal reefs with those I had become familiar with along the Florida keys and in sections of the Bahama islands. I concluded that in these crystal-clear ocean waters, a more prolific growth had produced a junglelike entanglement of corals of much greater size, as each separate colony of polyps struggled toward the sunlit surface waters.

The result was these steep, distorted, grotesquely beautiful rock castles which thrust almost vertically upward from the ocean floor, creating there on the white sand bottom such topheavy pinnacles it was hard to believe the narrow bases could support the riotous top structures.

It is the nature of coral to grow upon itself, the live polyps fastening themselves to the deserted shells of their dead ancestors, gradually building layer upon layer as they labor to create that one particular design to which a Greater Being has assigned them. There has always been great speculation as to how fast coral grows. No one knows exactly, for the rate of growth varies greatly according to location, temperature, the clarity and movement of the water, and the type of coral. It is believed that the coral of the Great Barrier reefs formed at a rate of three feet per thousand years.

It seemed, therefore, that before a sufficient coating of calcerous growth could form on any part of the wooden ship which we were seeking, unless that part were solid metal, the structure necessarily would have broken up. If what remained of the wreckage were not washed away by the action of the seas, and if it lay upon or very near the reefs, it no doubt could have been gradually enveloped by these persistently building corals. On the other hand, if it had become buried in the sand and thus protected from coral or worms, there was every possibility that it might survive the centuries. However, there seemed little likelihood of this, for the coral was too closely spaced upon the bottom, and the sand was too thin to cover much of anything.

I wondered if perhaps broken sections of the galleon lay imprisoned even now in the coral rock beneath me. For, as the staghorns and more solid types of brain corals had attained their growth in centuries past, heavy storms or earthquakes would have caused them to break from their foundations and collapse into the reef to add their bulk, thus speeding up the process of concealment.

Even though such a thing might have happened, I doubted that in the number of years which elapsed between the sinking and Phips's discovery of the wreck, any large section of the ship could have become completely enveloped and inaccessible. Surely, if this part of the galleon had been there, Phips's divers would have found a way to break into it.

After Ed returned to the anchored boats on the reef, he and Barney decided to take the metal detector below and go over the spot where the scattered ballast stone had been found. The instrument picked up indications of metal in several places, but particularly around one large yellow brain-coral formation. In spite of its size, the men reasoned that the huge coral boulder must have grown over whatever metal lay beneath it, and that they would have to dynamite it to discover what it concealed.

Ed made a quick trip to Sea Diver with the little boat and returned with the necessary explosives. He wrapped the wire expertly around a stick of dynamite and the detonator and was soon overboard with Barney to plant it beneath the coral. As soon as they had surfaced and climbed aboard Reef Diver, we moved the boat to a safe distance. Ed took the cells from a flashlight and touched the two ends of wire which led beneath the water to the two terminals of the batteries. There was a sharp, muffled sound, and a vibration which jolted the bottom of the boat. Seconds later the calm surface water boiled up and outward in ever-widening circles in the vicinity of the explosion. Soon after, the coral-roiled water was dotted with the bodies of small, dark-blue parrot fish, edged with a brighter blue, for the blast had caught a school as it was passing by.

A half hour later, when the underwater dust cloud had settled, Barney went overboard to reconnoiter. He came back to report that the explosion had shattered coral for fifteen feet around. He had been unable to locate the spot where the large brain coral had stood. He was a little discouraged, for he said the bottom was now covered with a thick coating of broken coral, and they would have to use the metal detector all over again to ascertain where to dig for the objects which it had previously indicated. He and Ed donned the air equipment and went back to work.

They emerged some time later with some broken hunks of coral which showed indications of containing metal, a badly deteriorated section of a gun barrel, and some small pieces of metal which looked as if they might be the oxidized remains of silver coins.

Now we knew that we were indeed on the site of a wreck! Whether it was the remains of the Spanish galleon or some other unfortunate ship would remain to be seen. Although none of us came right out and said so, I am sure we all felt that now, after nearly three hundred years, we were on the brink of unraveling the long-lost secret of the Silver shoals.

That evening we examined the objects which Barney and Ed had retrieved from the sea. We beat the large chunks of coral apart with an iron mallet, only to find that the metal within was so badly corroded that there was nothing left but a black, crumbling powder. The wreck must be very old indeed. The gun barrel was so deteriorated it was impossible to identify it.

Next Barney picked up the section from the odd-shaped piece which I had pointed out to him that afternoon. It responded to the metal detector, which indicates either iron or silver, but would not respond to a magnet, which affects only iron. My heart leaped! Could this be a very-much-corroded piece of silver? Because of the size and shape of the original piece, I could only guess that it might have been part of the silver stand of some ornamental altarpiece which had gone down with the Spanish galleon. The others were excited, too.

There was one more test, which would tell the tale.

By immersing a bit of the metal in acetic acid, we would be able to determine whether this was silver or merely a piece of iron so badly decomposed that it no longer responded to the pull of the magnetic field.

Slowly and ceremoniously Ed chiseled off a bit of the metal and dropped it into a small cup of the acid. It boiled madly and the metal disappeared. My dreams of silver altarpieces also vanished. It was iron.

When Ed repeated this test on the small coinlike objects that had been uncovered by the dynamiting, there was no reaction. These were indeed what was left of badly disintegrated silver coins. My disappointment fled, and I was hopeful once more. Where there were a few coins, there must be others. Perhaps we would be lucky enough to find some in good enough condition to distinguish their origin. These bits of metal could have dribbled from the corroded chests of the Spanish galleon as Phips's divers labored to raise them.

I was reminded of a very graphic account of the salvaging of the treasure, written by John Taylor, a captain's clerk on H.M.S. Faulcon, the guard ship which had been sent from Jamaica in 1688 to assist Phips on his third expedition.

> . . . At first when Sir William Phips discovered the wreck, the guns and pigs of silver and wrought plate lay uppermost, so that in his first voyage he took up 13 copper guns and one half of his plate was pigs of metal, dishes and other wrought silver which his divers went down and fastened ropes to it, and so they hoisted it in with their tackles. And so the dollars they hoisted in by whole chests of 2000 dollars together, for although the chests were rotted off and consumed, yet the dollars, with rust, were so grown together that they hung together as one lump—although the middlemost of the chest was bright and

sound—and not many of them was much wasted by the water.

Taylor also wrote that the sloops which were at work on the wreck when Phips and Narborough arrived had brought Indian divers "from Florida, New England Indians, Musceto Indians and Negro divers, many of which would stay four minutes under water." In all, he estimated, about three hundred Indians dove on the wreck, and of that number only five lost their lives.

He described the diving tubs which the divers had used to obtain air without coming to the surface each time. They were

> . . . made in the form of a bell about ten feet diameter at the open end and three feet at the closed end and six feet high. These tubs they sank with weights to the bottom, and then kept it about three feet from the bottom by ropes, so that the divers, when they wanted air and breath, would go under the diving tub and so refresh themselves, and out to work again.
>
> By this invention, the divers could stay under water at least half an hour and work in the removing of timbers and rocks; and so when they wanted breath retreat into the diving tub, which would yield them relief until the pent up air in the tub by their breath, was become warm, and then they could stay under water no longer, but they dived up and the tub was hauled up to refresh it.

Taylor completed his account with this story.

> Of such excellent use were these tubs that I have seen an Indian dive down with a bottle of brandy and so he that was underwater could, within the tub, take a dram, and they talk together at pleasure; and this I have seen frequently done on the wreck.

The Silver Shoals   277

His description of the condition of the wreck after only two score years beneath the sea interested us greatly by reason of its contrast to wrecks which Ed and I had examined after they had been centuries underwater. Taylor said that on Phips's third expedition, when the treasure was not so plentiful or so easy to come by:

> . . . with pickaxes, the divers tore up the timbers and coral rocks and cleared all live timbers and ballast from the stern to the step of the mainmast; but the stern part of the ship was so overgrown with coral rocks that they could find no inventions to clear it, but by blowing it up, which here they wanted engines to perform. But they dived into it under the rocks as into the caves, but by reason of the darkness and the rock they there got but little.
>
> Now all those rocks and timbers which they cleared were hoisted up and carried on board Sir John, where, with iron mauls they beat the coral rocks to pieces, and within the body of those growing stones found many thousand dollars. I saw a coral rock hoisted up about one ton, about which could be seen nothing like plate, but, being broken to pieces, there was found in it 7,600 dollars, and these dollars were very bright and not damnified at all by the water. I have seen several china chocolate cups taken up on this wreck unbroken and not damnified by the water, and many of the ribs and timbers of the ship that were taken up were very strong and sound, and the very hay or grass which was put between the silver dishes I have seen not rotten. The plate indeed looked very black by reason of the indigo and other colors which were in this galleon when lost.

Solid timbers and shining silver and whole pieces of china and glassware were almost nonexistent on any of the wrecks we had explored. Of course we were aware that

Taylor had viewed these objects within a half century of the disaster which overtook the galleon, whereas our previous explorations had been confined to ships which had been underwater from one to four centuries.

Here in Taylor's account we were provided with first-hand information as to the action of these waters in the vicinity of the Silver banks on foreign substances, and the rate of coral growth to be expected over a fairly exact period of time. The missing part of the puzzle was the exact number of years which elapsed between the time of the galleon's sinking and its salvaging by Phips. It might be forty-three years, as Taylor claimed, or a matter of twenty-eight years, if Korganoff was right in his research.

In either case, if coral could succeed in covering wreckage to such an extent in that very limited time, was it not possible that today, after several centuries of coral growth, the wreckage would be completely hidden from human eyes?

Mindful as we were of the different pressures at various levels below the surface and their effect on the diver, according to the depth of his dive and the length of time he spends below, John Taylor's comment on how Phips's Indian divers met the situation fascinated us. He wrote:

> And I observed that the Indian divers, when they rise up out of the water, as soon as they put their heads above the same, would in an instant duck their head under water and there keep it about a quarter of a minute, and then rise up and recover the boat; for they said if they should at first receive too much of the land air it would destroy them, but by the concoction of the first received air they got strength to enable them to receive the benefits of the air fully like others which dived not.

Taylor's observation that after "they rise up out of the water," they "in an instant duck their head under water and there keep it about a quarter of a minute," was probably one of the first records of an attempt to find a method to compensate for sudden changes of pressure on the human body.

A night of wind and storm followed our discovery of the tantalizing bits of ship's wreckage. Sea Diver rolled and bucked at her mooring, threatening to wrench herself free from the coral-head anchorage on the banks. Her unrest finally led Ed to set a watch for the remainder of the night. Those of us who stayed in bed struggled to keep from being tossed out and slept but fitfully. When morning finally came, the seas were still rolling in great waves, while the wind blew out of the northeast at twenty-five knots. We decided it would be useless to try to prepare breakfast, to say nothing of attempting to eat it, until we had moved into the shelter of the reef harbor.

While we were freeing the heavy hawser which held Sea Diver to the mooring buoy, there was a sudden exclamation from Glenn. He held up a section of the mooring line. Two badly frayed places within a few feet of each other revealed near tragedy. Upon closer inspection we found that in both spots only one strand still held. Although the length of chain had protected our anchor line from the coral, the constant sharp tugs of the heavy boat in the rolling seas had almost severed the thick rope which joined the chain to Sea Diver.

As we headed toward our reef anchorage, where the turbulent seas could be seen breaking clear over the protecting reefs, and the usual blue-green waters were transformed to a steely blue-gray under the overcast skies, we were very sober. The discovery of the damaged hawser brought home to us anew what a close game we were playing with the same fate that had carried the Spanish

galleon to its death. I was much relieved when, at lunchtime, the men decided to try a new solution to our problem. This time they planned to double-moor Sea Diver
right where she was within the reefs, so that she would
not be exposed to such seas as we had experienced the
previous night.

We were now agreed that with secure anchorage we
would be safer in the more sheltered reef harbor than on
the open banks.

By the time we had placed the second mooring inside the reef harbor and secured Sea Diver between the
two, the weather had cleared and the sea was flattening
out. We now had two anchors below, attached to chains
which in turn were attached to floating buoys, connected
to the bow of the ship with heavy line. If the wind blew
from one direction, Sea Diver would pull on only one
mooring, the other lying slack. If wind or tide shifted, the
other mooring would take the pull. If for any reason one
set of tackle failed, we would not be suddenly and un-
suspectingly carried upon the reefs, but would be held
by the second cable.

With our minds temporarily freed from worry, we
went back to the wreck site that afternoon. Ed and Barney
had spent the morning digging at the rubble on the bottom and examining it with the metal detector.

Now, as they speculated over the advisability of further dynamiting, Glenn, who had been searching in the
small boat with Vital, arrived to tell us he had spotted
another anchor on the ocean floor behind the "wreck" reef,
in line with our original yellow-flag buoy.

Ed swam down in the Scott to examine it. He found
a very old anchor, so deeply imbedded in coral it would
be impossible to move it intact. It measured six feet in
length, with an arm spread of three feet. While it might

have come from the Spanish galleon, he thought it too small to have been part of her equipment. More likely, he said, it had come from a later ship which might have been searching for the galleon. Perhaps it had come from the wrecked ship we were investigating. This was a discouraging possibility, for it would mean that the wreck we had found was a smaller ship than the galleon.

That night was quiet and peaceful. Sea Diver rode calmly at her two moorings. The wind did not come up, and the sea stayed quiet. A star-sprinkled sky lighted the nearby reefs, where just a murmur of lapping waters could be heard. The crew of Sea Diver slept soundly and well. We awoke to a Sunday morning so still and beautiful, to a sea so quiescent, so clear, that in its blue depths could be seen the finest details of coral head and fish far below. It was a day to enjoy, to relax all tensions. It turned into a morning for picture-taking.

With both Reef Diver and Wee Diver anchored on the wreck site, the air compressor operating for several divers, and two extra Scott outfits for the rest of them, the quiet spot became a beehive of activity. With as many as four divers below at the same time, and the other swimmers assisting from the surface, cameras clicked and buzzed. There was a constant exchange of diving and photographic equipment. The startled fish hung around at first and then disappeared to quiet retreats under the coral ledges. The water in the vicinity of the wreck area became cloudy with powdery coral from the stirred-up debris on the bottom.

When the orgy of picture-taking was over, the men decided to dynamite once more, close to the site of the previous explosion, where they had picked up further indications of metal in the coral. Using the metal detector, they marked two locations, laced them with a half stick of dynamite each and set them off. This time we did not wait for the water to clear, but went on with our surface explorations from Reef Diver in another area.

When Ed and Barney returned that afternoon, the water had cleared and they could look down on the destruction their explosion had wrought. Another large section of the reef had been completely flattened of rampant coral growth, leaving a large white patch on its surface. Almost in the center of the patch they could see a deep hole which had been opened up by the blast. They descended eagerly upon it.

Ed said it looked for all the world as if they might have blasted into the open hull of a coral-covered ship. They poked and prodded and examined the spot, peering down into its depths hopefully, but could discover no signs of anything man-made. Evidently the explosion had blown an opening into one of the concealed coral caves of the reef.

Once more applying the metal detector to the debris, they dug forth several pailfuls of bits and pieces from the wreck and dumped them on the deck of Reef Diver. We examined them eagerly. There was the lower part of a very old, hand-blown, square, green-glass bottle, and some small, badly corroded bits of ship's rigging, including a ringed spike with some tarred rope still attached. The hunks of coral which had showed metal indications yielded nothing worth while, only completely disintegrated metal dust which failed to give us a clue as to the original shape or purpose.

After examining everything closely, Ed reached the sad conclusion that the ship upon which we were diving was not the Spanish galleon we were seeking. He said it was probably the wreckage of a much smaller boat, which might have sunk there within the same century that the Spanish flagship vanished. There was not a single indication that a ship the size of the Nuestra Señora could have disappeared on this spot. He suggested that we give up working this location for a while and continue our search of the other reefs. Crestfallen, we returned to Sea diver.

After the many wakeful nights which had begun to wear on our nerves, we were now favored with a series of calm and beautiful days. We employed them to the utmost in making a thorough search of all the reefs in the area from the two smaller boats. Wherever there seemed to be the possibility of a wreck being concealed in coral or sand, we anchored the boats and dove overboard to inspect the spot at closer range. But in spite of the carefulness of our searches, we failed to come across any further indications.

One morning we rose to find the sea like glass. There was not a cloud in the sky. Not a breath of wind stirred. Over all hung such a stillness, it almost hurt the ears. Yet Sea Diver rose and fell to the motion of giant swells, which, in slow and silent rhythm, swept across the sea without disturbing its mirrorlike surface. Around us the reefs at low tide were plainly visible, their dry rocks jutting above the surface. No waves broke upon them; yet, as the swells raised and lowered the surface of the sea, water poured in upon them equally from all directions, as over the sides of a cup.

At breakfast we talked about leaving for Puerto Plata the next afternoon, for our time was nearly up. Kemp thought that the giant ocean swells which had appeared might indicate the presence of a distant storm at sea, which would be apt to bring high winds the next day.

We finally decided that morning to take Reef Diver to some reefs a couple miles to the west which had not yet been searched, and complete other explorations in Wee Diver nearby. We would then put Reef Diver aboard, late in the afternoon, preparatory to leaving with Sea Diver the following morning. If the weather held good the next day, we would cruise the length of the reef to the east, a distance of about fifteen miles, before starting for Puerto Plata. It was necessary to time our going so that we would arrive at our destination in daylight. We also had to figure on getting away from the reefs when the sun was still high enough for us to pick our way among the coral heads which dotted the banks.

I went along in Reef Diver. I had been in her bow two long hours, my eyes nearly popping out of my head from the strain of staring through the glass bottom, when I was conscious of unusual sounds on deck. At the same moment, the boat forged ahead under a sudden access of power, marked by the increased pitch of the jet, and I noted that our course over the ocean bottom made a sharp change.

Then Glenn poked his head through the doorway and said, "We can't work this reef from the outside. Those swells almost sucked us onto the rocks. We're going around on the inside."

I went on deck to see what was happening and found that the swells were indeed tremendous. As they reached the reefs, they seemed to envelop them, rising up about ten feet to inundate them, then suddenly subsiding. They thus created vicious-looking boilers which completely encircled the rocks. I looked at the sky, which was still unclouded, and noticed a slightly hazy, purplish cast to the southeast. There was something about the day that filled me with foreboding.

The others, too, were uneasy. We completed our search without finding anything of interest. We were just as happy. The reefs were wild in this area, the bottom rough and distorted, and the coral growth so lush, the sides of the rocks so abrupt, with ragged cliffs and caves between, that it would have been a most difficult place in which to dive.

Once, as we skirted a reef, I caught a glimpse of a large shark passing directly beneath the boat. This was the only shark any of us had seen the whole time we were on the shoals, except the one Vital had caught the first day.

Toward noon we returned to Sea Diver, where Ed was working on her ever-demanding machinery. We found that he, too, was concerned about the weather. None of us had any desire to be caught either at this anchorage in the center of the reefs or on the open banks outside, should there indeed be a storm brewing. And the look of the boilers which now sucked at the reefs all around us was a constant warning that these Silver shoals were no place to be caught in bad weather.

We put Reef Diver aboard and ate our lunch. Then Jane, Barney, Ed and I made one last pilgrimage to the site of the wreck. This time we swam from Sea Diver across the deep waters between, haunted by the thought that the Spanish galleon must lie somewhere within our range, and by our failure to find it.

We reached the reef and swam about, once more scanning the ballast and the spots which we had dynamited, white patches of broken coral in the surrounding magnificence. Schools of blue parrot fish paraded in bold beauty from golden pinnacle to burgeoning staghorn. Tiny jeweled creatures darted in and out of coral caves, and far below, half concealed beneath a coral ledge, a tremendous grouper with an ugly and ill-tempered face viewed the world about him with a jaundiced eye.

What joy to be part of this seabound, underwater domain, to be allowed to share even a small part of it.

Here on these Silver shoals, eighty miles from the nearest land, constantly swept by the endless waters of the Atlantic, we had found another world, of such beauty as to confound any attempt to describe it.

Where were the schools of threatening sharks and evil barracudas with hunger in their eyes? Where was the giant octopus which waited to wind itself about its victim as he approached the black, cavernous depths which contained the wreck?

True, the lone barracuda which had disturbed me that first day in the reef harbor was still around. I now looked upon him as a friend. Frequently, when we were in the water near Sea Diver or in the vicinity of the wreck reef, we had seen him lingering on the fringes of our shortened underwater field of vision. He never came very close.

It is only natural for man to fear the unknown, and we had had our share of qualms both before leaving for the Silver shoals and after our arrival. Fortunately, familiarity has a way of dealing with most fears. And that, tempered with a cautious and careful approach to each problem as it appeared, had saved us from any unfortunate experiences. First we had ascertained and solved the problems of safeguarding our boats in the midst of these reefs. Then we had coped with the hazards of diving and maintaining diving equipment among the rough, dangerous coral formations. For nine days we had worked our crew and our equipment to the full without a single mishap or the slightest damage to either. We felt justifiably proud that we had been able not only to survive, but to enjoy every moment, although the history of the Silver shoals is one of death and destruction.

As I thought of the accounts of other expeditions to the Silver shoals, I was impressed with the fact that this adventure of ours was one of the few in which the leaders did not have to deal with mutiny before they were through.

As far back as the time of William Phips, his crew of desperadoes had twice tried to seize the ship from his command and turn to piracy. They had sailed the waters around the Ambrosias in search of the treasure ships as long as they could take it, faced as they were with the constant dangers of reefs and storms, the monotony of stale food and water, and dreary days of unrewarding search. Then they had rebelled.

On Alexander Korganoff's visit to the Silver shoals in 1951, his expedition had come to an abrupt end when the Dominican crew which had been recruited in Puerto Plata refused to remain in the vicinity of the reefs. In addition to their natural fears of being caught there in a storm, their superstitious minds rebelled at this attempt to disturb the ghosts of long-dead shipwreck victims. When they attempted to take over the boat, Korganoff and his colleagues held them off by threatening them with dynamite caps. They headed back for Puerto Plata, arriving there just in time, for the mutineers finally set fire to the boat.

And, just before leaving Cap Haitien, we had heard of a schooner from England visiting the shoals in search of the treasure. On board, in addition to the English owner, was a "diviner," who promised to detect the presence of gold or silver with his wand, wherever it might be concealed. There were also two French divers, who were to dive up the treasure once it was located. There were rumors of quarrels and disagreements, of knives being wielded, of money disappearing on board as the unruly divers forced the owner to put in at Turks island and set them ashore. The remainder of the schooner's crew arrived at Cap Haitien completely broke, their dreams shattered, desperately seeking a means of replenishing their finances.

Later, when Ed arrived at Turks island after leaving the Criles and myself at Puerto Plata, he was greeted with another tale of trouble. This time a group of men, including Roscoe Thompson, our diving friend from Nassau, had set out to search the Mouchoir banks for the treasure ship. These banks lie just west of the Silver banks and are similar in composition. Upon their arrival the men spent only one night on the banks, and this in spite of the stormy protests of the captain, from whom they had chartered the boat. The next morning the captain headed the boat back toward Nassau, refusing to have any part in risking himself or his craft in such dangerous waters. The men were helpless to change his mind. Back in Nassau they brought suit against him, claiming that he had contracted to make the trip and that they had lost both time and money by making the voyage to the spot and then being deprived of the opportunity to search there.

It was easy for us aboard Sea Diver to understand these incidents, for we, too, had lived under the tension which comes from constant threats of danger, lack of sleep night after night, and imaginations enlivened by the many tales of unknown perils with which we had been so well fortified at the start of the voyage. The wonder was that we had come through it all so well.

Perhaps the fact that our group was so congenial, that there was no division among the crew, that we ate together and worked together and shared our experiences as one, with the same enthusiasm for a common objective, made the difference. At any rate, we arrived in Puerto Plata with a greater feeling of mutual esteem and fondness for each other than ever before.

3

○

○

○

A few days after Sea Diver's arrival in Puerto Plata, Ed bid farewell to the Criles and myself at the airport in Ciudad Trujillo, capital city of the Dominican Republic. From there he hastened to a marine-supply store, where he purchased 140 feet of heavy chain. On this, his second trip to the Silver shoals, he intended to be fully prepared for any eventuality with an absolutely safe anchorage inside the reef harbor.

Before returning to the site of the galleon wreck, however, Ed, Glenn, Vital and Kemp set out for Turks island, where they were to meet Ed's sister, Marilyn, and Mendel Peterson. Marilyn had piloted the two of them from Washington to Nassau in the Widgeon, where they were joined by a Bahamian friend, Leonard Thompson, long-time island pilot and owner-manager of Skyways, Ltd., who was to fly the plane back to Nassau. Ed had arranged for Marilyn and Leonard to bring the plane to Turks island; from there he intended to fly it over the Silver shoals. He wanted to make absolutely certain that the expedition was searching the right area for the Spanish-galleon wreck.

Because of the existence of a U.S. security-guarded guided-missile base at Turks island, they found it necessary to change their seat of operations to the airport on nearby South Caicos island, a part of the Turks island group. From there, a few days later, the men took off in the Widgeon to survey the Silver banks. While Leonard flew the ship, Glenn, the map expert, was to compare the topography of the land and water below with the charts and drawings which we had been using. As soon as they were over the shoals, Ed was to make pictures of the area.

They covered the banks thoroughly. As they flew over the miles of scattered reefs, which looked like icebergs floating in the blue seas beneath them, they were able to locate, in the thickened section on the north edge of the banks, the exact contours of the reefs shown on the early charts, including the open channel to the west of the wreck site and the two half moons to the east. The two yellow buoys which we had left to mark the ballast and the old anchor were clearly in evidence. In the center of the open water inside the reefs could be seen the buoy which marked the mooring we had left.

They took a series of pictures in black and white, some color stills, and some with the motion picture camera before returning to Caicos to prepare Sea Diver for another foray upon this spot, which they now felt certain contained the remains of the wrecked treasure ship.

Leonard returned to Nassau with the Widgeon that same day. The following morning Sea Diver headed for Turks island to pick up the mail, and then, just before sunset, left that anchorage for the Silver shoals.

When they spotted the white line of breakers which marked the northern edge of the shoals, they managed to guide Sea Diver on a path through them to the south side of the reefs. They turned east here, and worked their way along between the coral heads as they searched for the dry rock and the yellow buoys which we had left. It was ten thirty in the morning when they finally dropped anchor in the reef harbor from which we had departed more than two weeks before.

Ed felt that during our previous visit we had made a very thorough survey of the area from the surface of the water, as well as investigating many likely spots on the bottom with the diving equipment and the metal detector. This time he hoped to utilize the magnetometer by towing it behind Reef Diver to seek out any metal remaining beneath the water. This instrument had proved a wonderful aid in times past when it could be kept in adjustment, but there was never any certainty that it would work. He also planned to explore the bottom thoroughly with the help of the Scott equipment.

Ed was surprised to find that in the weeks since our first trip, the general level of the ocean had receded, and now at low tide many of the reefs were revealed slightly above water. By this time the summer trade winds had also appeared and blew every day at velocities of from twenty to thirty-five knots. Even inside the reef harbor, the sea was never calm, while outside it rolled in large waves and broke with a great roar on the edges of the reefs.

Time after time Ed put on his Scott and, with a full tank of air, descended to the bottom, where he swam in a systematic pattern at the base of the reefs, hunting for any sign of a sunken ship or of wreckage from it. Here, fifty to eighty feet beneath the surface, he found a completely different-looking Silver shoals. Viewing these coral cliffs from their base, he was fascinated with the caves, tunnels and mysterious openings which confronted him. He kept the underwater metal detector nearby, and whenever there was any question as to the possible presence of wreckage, he subjected the spot to a careful going over.

After days of systematic search, which covered the

whole area we had previously searched from the surface, he gave up the effort. There was absolutely nothing to be seen of the remains of a lost treasure ship anywhere in these waters, beyond what we had already found on our previous search. The attempt to use the magnetometer was also abandoned. It was impossible to keep it in adjustment or to use it successfully in such a location, where it must be operated in waters the depth of a few inches at one instant and eight to ten fathoms the next.

Ed believes there is not a chance of finding the treasure ship until better electronic equipment is developed than is available today. He feels sure that whatever may be left of the ship is completely hidden in the coral. But it is also his conviction that the Hispaniola treasure was well salvaged, and that Phips's divers erred in their belief that some of the cargo still remained in a part of the hull so encrusted in coral that it could not be reached.

"They were only banging against a coral head that looked like part of a ship," Ed claims. "It would be absolutely impossible for a wooden ship to have survived in these waters any number of years. Whatever broken remains were left are undoubtedly completely hidden and are now an integral part of the reef, for coral probably grows faster and bigger on the Silver shoals than any other place in the western hemisphere.

"Even if the day comes when it would be possible to take electronic equipment over these reefs and actually ascertain the location of the galleon wreck," he maintains, "if the treasure is still there, the explorer will then be faced with the huge problem of dynamiting and dredging into the heart of these coral reefs to secure it. We have already learned what difficulties this will entail."

I asked him about the remains of the old sailing ship we had uncovered close to the spot where the Spanish galleon may have gone down. He said that Mendel Peterson had gone carefully over the blackened bits of ship's rigging, the corroded coins and the broken green bottle. It was his opinion also that the ship could not be the treasure ship, for its anchor was much too small. Secondly, the square-shaped bottle which we had uncovered was of a type that was not made until the middle of the eighteenth century. The ballast stones could have come from almost any part of the known world, he said, and there was no way to trace their origin.

As to the anchors, who could tell? Many anchors had been lost on the Silver shoals over the years. Probably the small one on the inside of the reef had belonged to the ship we had investigated. As to the larger one on the outside of the reef, it might have come from the galleon we were seeking, or it may have come from one of the many vessels which later worked the wreck.

Peterson agreed that if this later wreck could have melted so completely into the reef in what was probably less than two hundred years, it would not take many more years for it to disappear completely, with even the ballast stone buried in the ever-enveloping coral. He pointed out that the Spanish galleon, which had lain there at least an additional century, would undoubtedly be completely concealed by now.

So the mystery of the Silver shoals still remains to tantalize the treasure-seeking adventurer of the future. Somewhere deep within the coral of those reefs on the northern bank exists the last remains of the Spanish plate wreck. Perhaps, in deep concealment, there lie enough gold and silver to supply a modern-day Phips his fortune. Yet there may remain only a few scattered bits which were missed by the combined onslaught of the British expeditions and the hundreds of vulturelike island vessels which followed in their wake.

For the treasure hunter of the future who wants to risk

a gamble—and what treasure seeker does not?—the Silver shoals still offer a challenge. When it is possible to attack these reefs with equipment able to tear them apart and carefully sift the debris, there will still be a chance to uncover treasure. There is little doubt that in the years to come there will be many more forays on the Silver shoals.

On the morning of May twenty-fourth, Sea Diver's crew collected the scattered marker buoys and put Reef Diver aboard the mother ship, preparatory to leaving for Turks island later that afternoon. Pete made a last dive to free the mooring anchor and chain, and shortly after three o'clock they set out. It did not take long to work their way through the now-familiar reefs to the north, and in twenty-five minutes they were in the deep Atlantic.

One would think this the conclusion to a risky undertaking, but actually they were unwittingly entering upon the narrowest escape of the whole expedition. It happened thus.

When Sea Diver had been on a north heading for ten miles in water more than two miles deep, Ed changed her course to 295 degrees to carry her toward the northernmost tip of Turks island, well clear of the Mouchoir shoals, which lay to the west and slightly to the south. The automatic pilot was set on this course, and while Sea Diver plowed her way through a sea roughened by a heavy wind from the southeast, the crew retired, leaving one man on watch every two hours throughout the night. Ed was to follow with the dawn watch.

When he appeared in the wheelhouse at four thirty the next morning, he turned on the radar, expecting to pick up an indication of Turks island ahead and to the south. Instead, he was astonished to see only a few scattered blurs on the uppermost part of the radar screen. Upon orienting himself with the chart, he discovered to his horror that Sea Diver's position was south of Turks island and west of the Mouchoir banks. It was an inescapable fact that Sea Diver had cut a course directly through the northernmost part of the Mouchoir banks, which are strewn with ugly reefs similar to those on the Silver banks.

After verifying his position and putting Sea Diver on a corrected course for her destination at Turks island, Ed turned the watch over to Kemp and set out to discover what had occurred to put Sea Diver in such a near-disastrous position.

The autopilot had acted up several times since the start of the long voyage, and, because the ship was so far from marine service of any kind, Ed had been obliged to repair it himself. So far, he had been able to remedy the trouble each time. He had noted that an iron drive chain had been used in its assembly and wondered at it. While they were on the Silver shoals, he had taken the autopilot apart once again. This time, unknown to him, the iron drive chain had magnetized the compass, causing a fifteen-degree error in its reading.

The more he considered the situation, the more he realized how narrow had been their escape. For, had they plowed upon one of these rocky heads in the dark, Sea Diver would have sunk almost instantly. It would have been impossible to launch Reef Diver from the listing deck, and although there were adequate rubber rafts and escape equipment, the crew would have found themselves adrift fifty miles from the nearest land, with little chance of being rescued in these little-traveled waters.

Fortunately Sea Diver had been spared to carry out the remainder of our plans for the expedition—to revisit Cap Haitien and to trace the course which Columbus may have pursued on his first voyage through the Bahama islands. We were indeed lucky.

*Part
Five*

*On the
Track of
Columbus*

1

o

o

o

Seven long weeks had passed from the time I left Sea Diver at Puerto Plata until school was ended for the summer, and Clayton and I could set out to rejoin her at Cockburn harbor, southernmost settlement of the Caicos islands. During this period, Ed, who had remained aboard, had spent nearly four weeks in the vicinity of the Caicos archipelago, and the rest of the time between Cap Haitien and the Silver shoals.

Now, as Clayton and I headed for Nassau, I looked forward eagerly to my part in Sea Diver's program for the next few weeks, for we planned to complete our investigation of exactly where, in the Bahamas, Columbus had made his first landfall and what track he had sailed from there to Cuba.

Our original idea of following and comparing the two courses championed by Morison and Verhoog was now augmented by another prospect, which had occurred to Ed as he studied a chart of the Bahama area earlier in the year. It promised most exciting possibilities.

When we had first studied the various courses which Columbus might have sailed, we had eliminated all except those proposed by Morison and Verhoog because of obviously untenable arguments. Theirs Ed had traced on a modern chart of the area, measuring off distances and directions as the two scholars had indicated—the one course emanating from Watling, the other from Caicos. Both of these theories seemed to have many good points, but they also contained many discrepancies.

After that, Ed and I pored over every English translation of Columbus's *Journal* that we could get our hands on. We found them all similar, with the exception of a few passages which had been interpreted in slightly different ways. One of these had puzzled us when we first read it, and further study had failed to make it any clearer. This was an entry concerning the admiral's approach to his next anchorage, after leaving San Salvador.

We found that all researchers in the past had come to the conclusion that Columbus had visited and named four islands on his voyage through the Bahamas—first, San Salvador; second, Santa Maria de la Concepción; third, Fernandina; and fourth, Isabella. Yet, as Ed and I interpreted the entries in his *Journal* for October fourteenth and fifteenth, Columbus indicated that he had reached and passed a second island after leaving San Salvador, and before anchoring for the night off a third island, which he had named Santa Maria de la Concepción.

> . . . And as from this island, I saw another, larger, to the west, I clewed sails up to navigate all that day until night, and still was not able to reach the westerly point; this island I named Santa Maria de la Concepción, and, about sunset, I anchored near the said point . . .

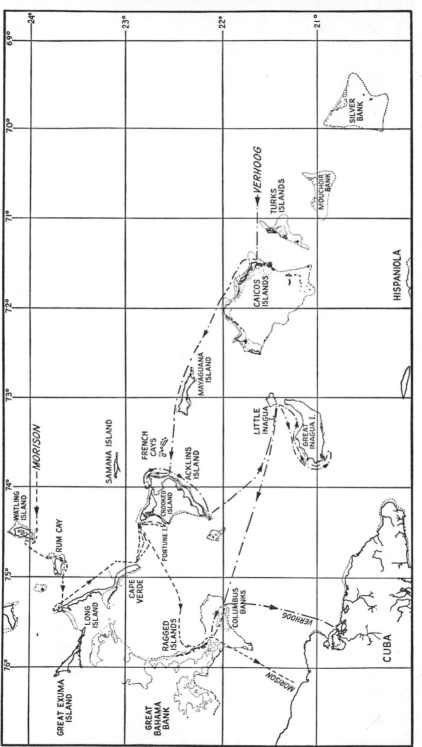

Possible courses of Columbus through Bahama islands to Cuba
as suggested by Admiral Morison and Captain Verhoog.

Where was this additional island, if such there were? It did not fit into the pattern of the chosen courses of either Morison or Verhoog, which encompassed only the accepted formula of four islands. From Watling island it was impossible to fit this unnamed island into the track which Morison had chosen.

As Ed compared the *Journal* entries for this period with the chart showing Verhoog's postulated Caicos landfall, he had an inspiration. After leaving Caicos, could not Columbus have sailed right on past Mayaguana toward Samana and anchored there for the night? Samana then would have been his Santa Maria de la Concepción. From here, then, he could have continued on to Long island, which would have been the third-named island, Fernandina.

Morison had already selected Long island as Fernandina, but we had been unable to reconcile the route he had chosen from Watling with Columbus's descriptions of the shores and distances along the way. Now, by approaching Long island from Caicos and Samana, the questionable pieces of the puzzle seemed to fall into place. From here on we were inclined to agree with Morison that Columbus had sailed to Crooked island, his fourth-named island of Isabella, and from there had continued by way of the Ragged islands to Cuba.

Here are the three suggested courses of Columbus through the Bahamas which we investigated:

Islands named by Columbus	Morison	Verhoog	Link
I. San Salvador (Guanahani)	Watling	Caicos	Caicos Mayaguana) (passed
II. Santa Maria de la Concepción	Rum cay	Mayaguana	Samana

Islands named by Columbus	Morison	Verhoog	Link
III. Fernandina	Long island	Acklin	Long island
IV. Isabella	Crooked	Great Inagua	Crooked

This new route which Ed had evolved also eliminated many of the discrepancies which we had found in Verhoog's chosen track from Caicos by way of Great Inagua. Ed and I became very excited over this new possibility, for it furnished an answer to many of the problems which had hitherto appeared unsolvable.

Again we went over the various translations of the *Journal* which were available. It seemed very necessary to find someone with a thorough knowledge of old Spanish to retranslate this particular section of the *Journal* for us from the most authentic Spanish text available.

Providentially, a few weeks later, while we were in Havana visiting friends, the conversation turned to our pending expedition and some of the problems which it presented. From our host we learned of Armando Alvarez Pedroso, author of a Latin-American prize-winning biography of Columbus,* a man well versed in old Spanish and, necessarily, thoroughly steeped in lore of the Great Discoverer. We were introduced to Dr. Pedroso the next day. He was immediately interested in our project and enthusiastically offered any assistance he might give.

To test our theory of the existence of an unnamed island which Columbus might have passed after leaving San Salvador, Ed asked Dr. Pedroso to read the original Spanish text for October fourteenth and fifteenth and to diagram his interpretation of it. Ed did this without tell-

* *Cristóbal Colón, biografía del descubridor,* Habana, 1944.

ing him of our theory, for he wanted to get Dr. Pedroso's impression direct from the original Spanish.

To our delight, Dr. Pedroso produced a simple sketch of San Salvador and the other islands to which Columbus's course had carried him that included the additional island Ed had visualized. When we explained the reason for our satisfaction at this interpretation, he was immensely interested and offered to write his friend, Dr. Ramon Menéndez Pidal, president of the Royal Academy of Spanish Language in Madrid, to learn what he would infer from a reading of this particular passage. Some time later we received a letter from Dr. Pedroso, stating that the learned Spaniard had been unable to find any fault with our interpretation.

When the time came to make our personal investigation of the islands to which Columbus's fleet may have sailed, we included the possibility that Columbus might have first landed at Caicos, but then, instead of following the course which Verhoog had outlined by way of Great Inagua, sailed past Mayaguana to Samana and then to Long island, where his course joined the one from Watling island suggested by Morison.

I realized as I sat in Leonard Thompson's living room in Nassau the night of June twenty-third, attempting to explain to him and his wife exactly why Ed and I were investigating these possible courses of Columbus, that to brief anyone on such a confusing subject in a short time was no simple task. Leonard, who had accompanied Marilyn and Mendel Peterson when they joined Sea Diver at Turks island a few weeks earlier, was to fly Clayton and me in our Widgeon to join Sea Diver at Caicos the next day, and I wanted him to make some detours from the usual direct route so that we could fly over some of the islands which were included in the three theories we were examining.

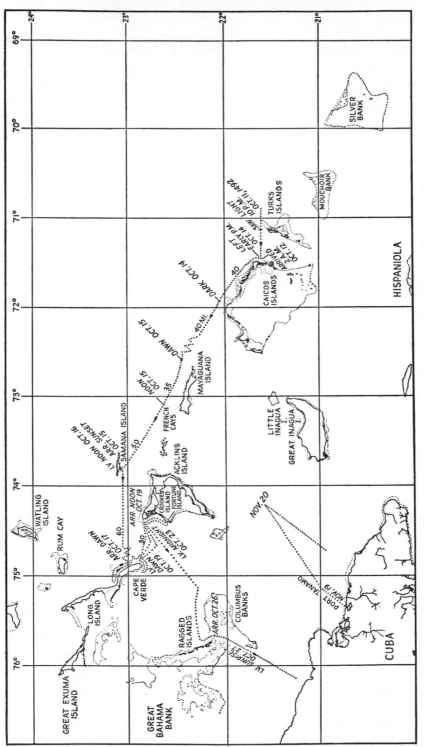

First landfall and track which Columbus's fleet may have followed. This route was evolved by E. A. Link after careful study of other possible courses.

"What! You mean Watling island may not be San Salvador?" he exclaimed, his face a mixture of surprise and dismay, for he, like all Bahamians, was aware that in 1926 the Bahamas Legislature had officially changed the island's name to San Salvador in recognition of its being considered the place of Columbus's first landfall. Now it was difficult for him to adjust his thinking. He became more and more interested as I outlined the three possibilities to him; and when we set out the next morning, he was almost as eager as I to seek out the various islands on our schedule.

When we left Nassau airport, the cabin of the Widgeon loaded with supplies for Sea Diver, it was so early that the sun was still below the horizon. As the sun rose, the lovely panorama of the Bahamas was revealed beneath us, the irregular shapes of countless islands bordering the shallow, greenish water of the banks and the sapphire blue of deeper areas. Carefully following the folded chart in my lap, I was alert for our first glimpse of Watling island. At last it appeared, a dim shape on the horizon. Then, as we closed on it, I saw beneath our wings a diamond-shaped piece of land, so dotted with lakes and ponds it appeared almost half water. At the extreme north end lay a large reef harbor, encased by a string of underwater reefs and a few cays lying just above water.

As we skimmed above the eastern shore I looked down upon a coast of rocky headlands and occasional sand beaches. The water offshore was ruffled with white seas breaking on many scattered coral formations, making it obviously foolhardy for any boat to attempt to reach the rugged shore. There was a slender monument on one of the points, and a white lighthouse that thrust skyward from a higher rise of land. From a distance the western shore appeared more approachable, and there were houses and a road to be seen along its length.

There was not a sign of another island in any direction, even from the height at which we were flying, but soon after we had circled the lower end of Watling and headed on a southwest course toward Long island, we were able to make out Rum cay, the island which Morison believed was Columbus's Santa Maria de la Concepción. It appeared very small in comparison with the other islands we had flown over. It was covered with low trees, interspersed with a few small ponds and the ruins of several old plantation houses.

We continued on the course which Morison had selected for Columbus, picking up the eastern coast of Long island about a quarter of the way from its northern tip. We skimmed this shore almost to its southern point before heading southeast for Crooked island, Columbus's Isabella, according to Morison. Just off its northwest point lay a small, rocky cay, surmounted by a lighthouse which I identified as Bird Cay light. It was in the shelter of this reef harbor that Morison believed Columbus's three ships had spent several days before setting out on the last leg of their journey to Cuba.

All this time I had been staring with intense concentration at whatever was revealed below, checking the topography with the chart in my lap and scribbling hurried notes on my observations. Somehow I had also managed to keep Leonard busy answering a barrage of questions.

He was surprised when I called his attention to a large lagoon near the north shore of Crooked island which did not appear on the chart. This was a good example of the many omissions and inaccuracies on even the best charts of the Bahamas, making it impossible to compare them successfully with the descriptions in Columbus's *Journal*.

Once we had turned east to fly along the north shores

of Crooked and Acklin islands, I discovered that a heavy chain of reefs followed the whole extent of the two islands, more than a mile offshore. As we left Acklin behind, the coral could still be seen, bordering the eastern coastline clear to the horizon. Although Verhoog had picked Acklin as Columbus's Fernandina, it did not appear to suit the description too well, for Columbus had described it as "all of it beach, free from rocks."

We next flew along the north shore of Mayaguana island, Verhoog's Santa Maria de la Concepción. Once again I noted a long, protecting reef the full length of the island, making it impossible to approach from the sea. If Columbus had sailed along this coast, it would not be surprising if he had chosen to go on to the next island without attempting to land.

Then at last the Caicos archipelago was ahead of us. Would this prove to be the first land which Columbus saw after weary months at sea? I wondered. The islands were low and flat, dotted with many shallow bodies of water and separated from each other by narrow channels. There were sandy beaches along the north and west shores and then long stretches of offshore reefs which fringed the islands for miles.

As we flew over the break between Grand Caicos and East Caicos, I looked down upon "a harbour large enough for all the ships of Christendom." Near an opening at the south end of the reefs which formed the outer edge of the harbor was a "piece of land which is formed like an island although it is not one." This could easily have been converted into an island fortress such as Columbus had described. And although a rough sea was breaking on the reefs, inside, "the sea was no more disturbed than water in a well."

We were past so quickly that I had time only to think how perfectly it all answered Columbus's description of the harbor at San Salvador, and then we were flying over Cape Comete and Grassy creek.

Soon I saw beneath us the varicolored pattern of extensive acres of salt flats. Banks of completely dehydrated salt gleamed blindingly in the sunlight as we circled a small town at the end of South Caicos. Below, in the nearby harbor, I spotted Sea Diver. I thrilled with pleased anticipation as I saw a familiar figure drop into the dinghy at her side and start across the water toward town.

We landed on a rough coral strip and taxied back to the end of the runway. Ed arrived soon after in a battered jeep, and we greeted each other happily after a separation of more than seven weeks.

As we drove into town, I was amazed to discover that almost the entire community was built on salt. The road itself was salt, and heaps of salt like snowdrifts banked it on either side. As we neared the docks, we passed large open sheds, inside which black-skinned workers were attacking huge piles of the white crystals with heavy shovels. As they filled sturdy hempen bags, others loaded the bags into little carts hitched behind small, patient donkeys.

At this point the whole tempo of the operation changed, as the drivers set off for the water front with whoops and a flourish of whips, like Roman charioteers charging to the fray. Small sailboats scuttled back and forth between a steamer, which lay at anchor in the open road, and the docks, carrying the heavy bags of salt that had been dumped from the donkey carts at the water's edge.

Ed hustled us into Wee Diver, which put-putted us across the harbor to Sea Diver's anchorage. Three grinning faces looked down upon us from the deck above—Mendel Peterson, Vital and Kemp.

Ed cut the motor and we coasted up to the side of

the larger vessel. As I climbed over the rail, I was startled by a sudden boom almost in my ear. The sound came from a neat, small gun mounted on a handmade carriage on the aft deck. The men eagerly explained that it was a cannon they had picked up from a wreck off the shore of East Caicos, and that Pete had since built the carriage, a perfect model of the original ones of the eighteenth century. It was he who had rammed in some gunpowder and discharged it just as Clayton and I climbed aboard.

I found that Captain Weems was off on a trip in a sailboat with two of the town fishermen, to investigate at first hand the shores and inner waters where Columbus might have preceded him. Pete and Ed were in enthusiastic agreement that Columbus might have landed at South Caicos island. In several trips between Turks island and Caicos they had had every opportunity to check the course which Columbus might have pursued. And in a cruise to the northeast, they had rounded the islands clear to the western side, landing and inspecting various areas as they went.

Attempting to bring the story of Columbus's first glimpse of the New World into focus in my mind, I recalled having read that on the night of October 11, 1492, Columbus's little fleet of three ships was boiling along toward the west with sails full set. For several days the crew had seen evidences of land, including a variety of birds, broken branches, even a carved stick; and the sailors were watching eagerly for their first glimpse of the Indies. They were particularly keen because Columbus had offered a reward to the first one who sighted land.

Columbus, too, was on the alert, and at ten o'clock that night he called Pero Guierrez to verify the sight of a light which he descried on the horizon. Soon after, a sailor on the forecastle called out that he, too, saw a light. They increased the vigilance of their watch, and at two o'clock Rodrigo de Triana caught the first glimpse of the white banks and beaches of Guanahani glowing in the moonlight.

While we sat on the aft deck of Sea Diver that afternoon, sweltering in the extreme heat of the tropical summer, Pete and Ed described their observations as they had followed this same approach with Sea Diver nearly five hundred years later.

Seven miles north of the northernmost point of Turks island, they found that they were able to see the top of its high bluff and the lighthouse surmounting it. Ed said that Columbus, standing on the poop deck of the Santa Maria, could easily have seen the flicker of an Indian campfire on this point as it appeared and disappeared behind the rolling seas.

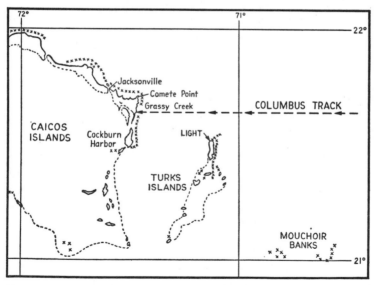

Reconstructed track of Columbus toward first landfall according to Captain Verhoog. The only area along the eastern Bahama islands where it would have been possible to see a light four hours before reaching land.

Or, as Pete said, quoting the *Journal,* if "like a small wax candle raised and lifted up," it had been a torch carried in the canoe of an Indian fisherman a few miles offshore, it would still be possible for those on board Columbus's ships to have seen it five miles away.

In either case, Pete declared, the presence of a light was a good argument that land had to be nearby. And the fact that Columbus claimed and received his own reward of ten thousand maravedis was proof that all were convinced the light was real. He and Ed said this was an excellent argument for the Caicos landfall, for, as we knew, both from the charts and from our airplane reconnaissance, it would have been impossible for the three ships to be near land or in the vicinity of a light if they had been approaching Watling island.

Ed and Pete had then headed Sea Diver toward Caicos, on the same course which they figured Columbus might have followed. At noon, directly ahead, they had sighted Grassy creek with its white sand beach. It could have been on this very spot, they speculated, that Columbus dropped his anchors at daylight and launched the ships' boats to go to shore.

Columbus's description of Guanahani fitted Caicos perfectly, they said: ". . . very large and very flat; with very green trees and much water. In the center of it, there is a very large lagoon; there are no mountains, and all is so green that it is a pleasure to gaze upon it." I had noted during my flight earlier that day that the island also answered Las Casas' description as being bean-shaped and of considerable length.

Sea Diver had then sailed up and down these waters several times, from the harbor at South Caicos around the archipelago to a point beyond the ruins of Fort George, on the western side. The men had explored the large reef harbor at Jacksonville, the very one I had picked out from the air, and were almost certain it was the harbor which Columbus had described.

They said that near Jacksonville they had also come upon a point of land jutting into the sea which answered Columbus's description of where a fort might be built, ". . . a piece of land which is formed like an island although it is not one, on which there were six houses; it could be cut in order to form an island, in two days." Near this piece of land, Pete said, the admiral had recorded the presence of a lovely grove of trees and much water. They had observed a small lake directly behind the point of land.

Captain Weems did not return from his trip until after ten that evening. With his customary exuberance, he reported an interesting two days, during which he had slept on the bare boards of the boat deck with his two guides and subsisted on fish, conch and grits.

They had followed the east shore of South and East Caicos to Jacksonville harbor, hugging the shore so that the captain could examine it in close detail. From Jacksonville they had entered the Going-Through passage to the shallow waters of the inner banks. Beating against the wind and waiting for tides to rise sufficiently to allow them to travel on the second day, it had taken them until this late hour to return to Sea Diver.

Captain Weems described the great stumps which he had seen whenever he went ashore, striking indications of the trees once used by the Indians to fashion their dugout canoes. Wild pigs and donkeys had dashed away as he approached the ruins of old plantation houses and barren stretches of what had once been cultivated farming areas. He said the fishermen had told him that there were Indian carvings on the walls of the caves near Jacksonville, but he had not had time to investigate them.

He said he was sure that the reef harbor at Jacksonville was the one which Columbus had admired. He was much impressed, as he sailed along the shore in its vicinity, at the sight of "many islands" to the west.

"I'm sure Captain Verhoog is right," he said enthusiastically. "Everything indicated to me that Columbus must have landed on Caicos."

At sunrise two days later we set out with Sea Diver from Cockburn harbor to complete our check of the three courses which Columbus might have followed. The moment we were outside the protection of the island, we found ourselves in a heavy, rolling sea which assailed Sea Diver's starboard side as we headed northeast to follow the coastline. Captain Weems climbed the mast to the crow's-nest, and Kemp was stationed on the pulpit at the bow. While Ed steered Sea Diver, meanwhile keeping track of reefs and shore line on the radar, I ran a messenger service from one crew station to the other and, between times, watched the shore line from the pilothouse.

Along this lower part of the Caicos there was no bordering reef, only a scattering of coral heads between us and shore, until we had almost reached Cape Comete. Then, a formed reef which commenced near shore forced us seaward almost a mile before we could safely round the cape. Once past this point and headed northwest along the outer edge of the barrier reef, free of the persistent southeast wind which had kicked up such an uncomfortable sea, I saw that from here on a continuous chain of reefs followed the outline of the shore, forming calm, still waters within its shelter. As I looked toward the western horizon, I was conscious of many islands fading into the distance. It would surely seem that with these glimpses of land to the west, Columbus would have been tempted to lead his fleet in their direction.

Staying well offshore, we followed the islands westward. That evening we anchored not far from the ruins of Fort George, at the north tip of West Caicos, ready to take off the next morning for Mayaguana, some forty miles away, the island which Verhoog had chosen as Santa Maria de la Concepción. We spent the second night in the lee of the northwest point of Mayaguana, in about the same spot Verhoog declared Columbus had anchored before sailing the next day for Acklin island, some forty miles to the west.

It was at this point that we found ourselves differing from Verhoog, for we believed, according to the quotation from the admiral's log mentioned on page 300, that Columbus, following the reef-bound north shore of Mayaguana, had continued on to Samana without attempting to land.

> And as from this island [Mayaguana] I saw another, larger, to the west [Samana], I clewed sails up to navigate all that day until night, and still was not able to reach the westerly point; this island I named Santa Maria de la Concepción, and, about sunset, I anchored near the said point to see if there was gold there.

When we set out the next morning, Ed headed Sea Diver directly north. We were all more serious than usual, for we realized that this new theory of Ed's, which depended on the inclusion of an additional island, would stand or fall by the test we were about to make.

Ed believed that if Columbus's ships had continued on the same course they had followed along the northeast coast of Caicos, they would have bypassed Mayaguana, finally reaching a point where Samana would have been visible on the horizon. He believed that even though Acklin was closer to Mayaguana than Samana, Columbus would have sighted Samana first from this hypothetical spot because of its hundred-foot elevations, whereas the northern part of Acklin was low and flat.

By constantly checking the position of the two islands on our radar screen, Ed was able to pinpoint the section of water where he figured Columbus might have first sighted Samana. Acklin was then twelve miles distant and Samana thirteen, in almost opposite directions. Then Captain Weems climbed to the crow's-nest, for, at these distances, neither island was visible from the deck.

"You're right," he shouted down to us. "There's Samana off the starboard bow." He reported that there was no sign of Acklin, even though we were a mile closer to it.

From there on, the course we had selected led toward Samana and farther away from Acklin. Soon the whole shore line of Samana could be seen from the deck by eye. It covered at least 45 degrees of the horizon, and, with its hundred-foot hills, looked like a large island.

Ed was jubilant at this support of his theory. Even Captain Weems appeared impressed, although he was still unwilling to grant that Verhoog might be wrong. Pete said, "Well, we've got to admit it would certainly be logical for Columbus to have ended up at Samana."

As we turned Sea Diver south to inspect low-lying Acklin island, Verhoog's Fernandina, we argued the merits of Verhoog's choice, which had taken Columbus from Acklin to Great Inagua and then across the Columbus banks to Cuba. Ed and I had felt convinced that Verhoog was wrong ever since spring, when we had sailed past Crooked island to Great Inagua on our way to Haiti. Columbus's colorful description of events and the areas involved just did not tally with Verhoog's selections.

And then before we had sailed for three hours, we saw an island to the east, toward which we steered, and all the three vessels reached it before midday, at its northern point, where there is an islet and a ridge of rocks on its outside, to the north, and another between it and the main island . . . there was a north wind, and the said islet lay on the course of the island of Fernandina from which I had navigated east-west . . .

Yet we had found eighty-seven miles of open sea between Castle light at the southwest point of Acklin and the northeast point of Great Inagua. At Sea Diver's cruising speed of eight knots it had taken us over eleven hours to cover this distance. Although we had left Castle light behind at four thirty in the morning, it was past three in the afternoon before Captain Weems first glimpsed the tops of the hills on Great Inagua from the crow's-nest, and it was five thirty before we finally reached the northeast cape of the island.

"How come Columbus got here before noon in those old tubs of his," Clayton queried disrespectfully, "when it's taken us a whole day with Sea Diver?"

"Yes," returned Ed, "and in order to get Columbus to Cape Hermoso, where they anchored for the night, Verhoog says they sailed another forty-four miles from here to Northwest point, on the other side of the island."

"And what about the direction?" I put in. "Columbus navigated east-west to reach the northern point of Isabella. We've been sailing almost southeast to follow Verhoog's theory."

We cut and slashed at Verhoog's arguments. Before we were finished, we felt we had pretty thoroughly disproved the course he had advanced. Yet his arguments for Caicos as the first landfall still seemed sound. We were impatient to test out if Columbus might have landed at Caicos, and then, by following Ed's suggested track, might have eventually joined up with the one Morison had picked by way of Long and Crooked islands.

Ed and I have since prepared a thorough exposition of our investigations, in which we have attempted to present the arguments both for and against all three theories, so I will not go into the details of the days of search which followed our visit to Samana.*

Briefly, we headed south from Samana toward Acklin, anchoring overnight at Crooked island, close to Bird Rock light. After inspecting the western side of Crooked island the next morning, we sailed north along the coast of Long island to Clarencetown harbor, just a few miles north of the rocky cape that stands out prominently halfway down the lower section of Long island.

Two days later we headed for Rum cay, Morison's Santa Maria de la Concepción, and in the late afternoon dropped anchor in the lee of Watling island. This was the island which tradition said was the place of Columbus's first landfall. Necessarily it was the last to be visited, as it was farthest north on our homeward route. Until we had made a careful comparison of its qualifications with those of the Caicos archipelago, it was impossible to draw any conclusions.

Our anchorage close by the small settlement of Cockburntown was an open harbor formed by an indentation in the shore line. From the chart it appeared to be the only section of the entire island with even partial protection and approaches free from coral heads. We were boarded soon after our arrival, first by the commissioner of the island, and later by a young naval lieutenant and his bride. From them we learned that a U.S. guided-missile base was being established on Watling.

---

* A New Theory on Columbus's Voyage Through the Bahamas. Smithsonian Miscellaneous Collections, Vol. 135, No. 4, published by the Smithsonian Institution, Washington, Jan. 20, 1958, Publication 4306.

This, then, was the explanation of the strange towers and structures on the horizon which had aroused our curiosity as Sea Diver approached that afternoon. For the first time in history, the island had come alive, its lethargic inhabitants startled into unfamiliar but remunerative activity as they labored at roads and pipe lines and the expansive quarters which seem so necessary to American forces overseas.

The next morning we started out eagerly to circle the island with Sea Diver. We planned to inspect Watling carefully from offshore. Another day we would return with one of the small boats to examine whichever locations seemed to require additional scrutiny. We wanted first to determine on what part of the island Columbus might have landed, and second, whether the descriptions in his *Journal* coincided with the geography of Watling.

We headed north along the west shore as Morison believed Columbus had traveled in his long boat when he ". . . went along the island in a north-northeasterly direction, in order to see the other part, which lay to the east, to see what was there and also to see the villages."

As Sea Diver approached the north end of Watling, we came upon a large harbor formed by reefs and cays which carried on for miles to the northeast. We soon discovered that we must navigate carefully, for underwater reefs extended into the sea well beyond the defining line of cays.

As soon as we left the shelter of the island, we began to meet some big seas, and Sea Diver rolled and pitched, occasionally taking water over her starboard bow. It was fortunate that Ed went below just when he did to check the engine room, for a port had been left open, and his workbench, with its valuable tools and machinery, was dripping with salt water. We came about immediately and took shelter in the lee of Green cay, while the men cleaned and wiped each piece with oil before the salt could do any permanent damage.

It was afternoon before we got under way once more. As we skirted the marker at the northern point of the reefs and turned to follow the eastern shore, we came upon a rocky headland at the extreme northeast point of the island which might indeed qualify as "the piece of land which is formed like an island although it is not one" of Columbus's *Journal*. We resolved to return the following day and inspect this cape and harbor with Wee Diver.

By now the wind was blowing stronger than ever, and the pale green of the reef harbor was tumbled with white-capped waves. Sea Diver rolled unpleasantly as she negotiated the tumultuous waters along the eastern shore, well clear of the broken white water which marked the numerous coral heads. There was no protective chain of reefs here, and we were convinced of the riskiness of attempting to reach either the sandy beaches or the alternating projecting headlands which formed the coast.

"Columbus would have had a tough time getting his boats in to that shore," Captain Weems commented. "No wonder Morison had him sail around to the other side of the island."

All day we had been on the alert for some spot in our circuit of the island which might give us Columbus's impression that "I saw so many islands that I could not decide to which I would go first." Unlike Caicos, where the many islands in the distance had been most noticeable, there was not a trace or an illusion of any other islands here at Watling.

As we rounded the southwest point of the island, knowing that Rum cay lay some twenty miles distant, we strained our eyes in its direction. Captain Weems climbed once more to the crow's-nest and swept the horizon with his binoculars. There was not a sign of land anywhere. We headed back toward our anchorage off Cockburntown, convinced that if Watling island was Columbus's San Salvador, he would perforce have landed on its western shore.

Early next morning we set out once more to explore the reef harbor and the point of land which formed its eastern border. We had hoped to enter one of the passages between the reefs with Sea Diver and anchor her in the harbor, but after taking soundings of the approaches to these openings from the skiff, we decided it would be safer to leave her in the open water leeward of Green cay.

A strong wind similar to that of the previous day was kicking up a choppy sea inside the harbor, but we did not realize until after we had set out in Wee Diver to cross the three miles of water between us and the distant point, that it might actually be dangerous to attempt this journey in a small boat.

There were four of us in the skiff—Captain Weems, Pete, Ed and myself—and with our combined weight there was very little freeboard. I sat with Ed on the stern seat while he ran the outboard. The other two sat side by side amidships, busily occupied in bailing the quantities of water which slopped over the bow as Wee Diver caught the tops of the bigger seas. We were soon soaked to the skin from the salt spray which continually drenched us.

We were making scarcely any headway, with wind and sea and tide against us, and Ed would have turned back, I'm sure, had he not feared we would be swamped if we were caught in the trough of the waves. Instead he eased Wee Diver gradually toward shore so that we met the seas on our port bow rather than heading directly into them. Ashore, clouds of white coral dust rose toward the sky as two huge bulldozers dug into the rocky soil.

The sight of small figures moving about the machines comforted me. Should we be swamped, help was not too far away.

I breathed easier when we finally reached the quieter waters in the shelter of the peninsula which was our goal. We drew Wee Diver up on a lovely little crescent of beach beneath white sandstone cliffs whorled into hollow caverns by wind and sea, and followed a steep path up the cliffs. We reached the top only to be assaulted by the same boisterous wind which had plagued us all across the harbor. White spray dashed high into the air against rock bastions which thrust into the ocean, and cascades of white foam enveloped the broken coral rocks offshore. To the south stretched an irregular coast, and on the highest piece of land gleamed the white exclamation point of the lighthouse.

Returning to the shelter of the inner beach, we waded through shallow water to investigate the break which separated this picturesque rocky point, making an island of the outer portion at high tide. At low tide it would indeed be possible to walk across the intervening passage. It was easy to imagine Columbus viewing this spot and envisioning a fortress upon its extremity.

But somehow the harbor itself failed to satisfy his description of a sea "no more disturbed than water in a well." Neither had we found "deep water and a harbour large enough for all the ships of Christendom, the entrance to which is very narrow." And we wondered how, in a limited time, the Santa Maria's longboat would have been able to cover these great distances.

Although we had succeeded in arriving at our destination safely with Wee Diver, we found ourselves in trouble immediately we set out to make the return trip. Salt water had at last worked into the outboard. At first it only sputtered and protested; then it gave up completely.

Using an oar to steer, for we had not yet reached the extremely rough water beyond the shelter of the point, we allowed the wind to carry us toward the naval installation farther down the shore. As Wee Diver grated to a stop in the offshore shallows, we were surrounded by a crowd of curious Navy lads. While Ed and Pete set about removing the outboard to examine it, Captain Weems disappeared in the direction of the encampment in search of tools. He soon returned, accompanied by Commander Redmond, commandant of the base.

As Ed carefully took the engine apart, the men circled about him, absorbed in the mechanics of the operation like all males everywhere. Their response to Captain Weems's questions about the harbor was unanimous. It was nearly always rough, they said. Commander Redmond expressed amazement that the four of us had succeeded in crossing the turbulent harbor in such a small boat. He expressed concern at our attempting to return to the far-distant Sea Diver with wind and sea behind us. He said that it was against rules for the men on the station to venture out on the harbor except on the days when it was calm.

Ed soon had the outboard back in operation, and he and Pete set out to return to Sea Diver. Captain Weems and I accepted the Commander's invitation to take us across the island by car to Cockburntown, where Sea Diver would eventually return.

That afternoon Commander Redmond drove us over the rough, rocky excuse for a road which led to the lighthouse. From its top we could see almost the whole island. I noted particularly the chaotic water off the east shore, and the narrow, rocky point which divided it from the scarcely less agitated reef harbor.

On a neighboring hilltop is the tall shaft which commemorates Columbus's first landfall. I asked Commander

Redmond if we might stop there before returning to Cockburntown. To my surprise he told us that it was impossible to reach it in the jeep, for there was no road part of the way, and it would be necessary to take a boat across one of the inland lakes. I wondered how the monument had been built in the first place back in 1891, and why the Chicago *Herald* had selected such an inaccessible location for it.

The commander left us beside a small marker near Sea Diver's anchorage at Cockburntown. It had evidently been placed there by an enthusiastic yachtsman, for it read, "Christopher Columbus made the first recorded landing in the New World on this beach, Oct. 12, 1492. Yawl Heloise, Feb. 25, 1951."

"At least Columbus would have been able to get ashore at this point," Captain Weems commented, "which is more than you can say about the spot where they put the other monument."

Sea Diver appeared soon after without dropping anchor and the small boat was sent in to shore to pick us up. Ed was eager to get under way immediately, for he planned to anchor overnight off Cat island, the first step on our way back to Nassau.

Our tour of inspection was at an end. Our check of the islands and routes which we had set out to examine was complete. It remained now to digest the information we had gathered and to try to reach a conclusion.

There was no obvious answer. As we had realized from the beginning, each one of the three theories we had studied had its good points and also its discrepancies when viewed from Columbus's *Journal* account. And as there were no existing early charts to aid us, the chief value of our voyage had been in comparing Columbus's word pictures of the islands and waters he had visited with their counterparts as suggested by Morison, Verhoog and ourselves.

At the start Captain Weems had been quite convinced that Verhoog had found the correct solution. Ed and I had at first leaned toward Morison's theory, and later awakened to the possibilities of the Caicos landfall. Pete had remained distinctly neutral, although when Ed had come forth with the idea of the unknown island, thus making it possible to trace Columbus's course by way of Samana, this suggestion had immediately excited his interest.

Now, with our search at an end, as we set out from our overnight anchorage at Cat island, the four of us gathered in Ed's and my cabin below decks, leaving Kemp and Vital to guide Sea Diver across Exuma sound. The time had come to bring together all the information which we had collected, and, if possible, to produce an answer.

Once more we went over the entire problem, using Columbus's *Journal* as our guide. Beginning with the days preceding the landfall, we reread each passage and analyzed it, while I made notes of each person's point of view. We were not satisfied with using one translation, but continually checked with various interpretations as we went along.

By this time Captain Weems's championship of the Verhoog theory had softened, worn down by point after point of unexplainable differences between it and the original text. Morison's arguments made a better showing, for there were fewer obvious discrepancies, but we found it impossible to reconcile the circumstances surrounding the first landfall with Watling island and its environs. Here, we felt, Verhoog had made a good case for Caicos, which we had strengthened by actual investigation.

As our discussion proceeded, both Pete and Captain Weems showed an increasing interest in Ed's theory of the additional island on Columbus's route, which in turn supported the theory that his first landfall had been at Caicos.

All that day we argued, and again that evening, after we had anchored for the night just beyond Ship channel in the Exumas. We did not leave for Nassau until late the following morning, for rain and cloudy skies made it impossible to cross the coral-strewn Yellow banks until there was better visibility. Instead we once again gathered in our cabin to continue our debate. Each controversial point was discussed, summarized and recorded, along with the passage involved, on the dictaphone.

Our final conference took place the next morning at Sea Diver's dock in Nassau. Carefully we rechecked every point. We found that there were a few differences in translation and interpretation which must be cleared up, as well as additional information which could only be obtained when Pete had returned to the Smithsonian. We also listed passages from the *Journal* which we planned to ask Dr. Pedroso to retranslate.

But when all the factors had been carefully weighed, we found that everyone was inclined to agree that of the three theories involved, Ed's revolutionary idea of the unnamed island contained fewer discrepancies, and fitted more completely the descriptions given by Columbus from beginning to end, than either of the other two.

Unless additional original material or charts should be turned up in the future, we concluded there could never be positive knowledge of Columbus's exact route; but we had proved—to our own satisfaction, at least—that he landed first at Caicos and from there followed a course from Mayaguana to Samana to Long island, and from there to Crooked island, the Ragged islands, the Columbus banks and Cuba.

Epilogue

o

o

o

Sea Diver's anchor chain rattled through the riding chock as her anchor spun down through the clear water to the white-sand bottom, less than two fathoms below. We were once more in the lee of Miss Roder cay, on the north Bahama banks. Many months had passed since first we anchored on this spot in our search for the brass cannon on the reefs outside. During that interval Sea Diver had toiled hundreds of dangerous miles throughout the Caribbean. Her once-white hull showed the months of hard labor she had endured, a battle-scarred veteran of Cap Haitien, the Silver shoals, and those long weeks beneath the summer sun while we had sought Columbus's probable track.

We had detoured here on our way to home port, for Ed could not bring himself to return to Miami without one more attempt to locate the brass cannon. This time the Danish salvager, Willy Dahl, who had originally told Ed of the barrels, was also on board. He had been very puzzled at our failure to locate the guns. He was sure Ed had searched in the wrong spot and was confident he could guide us to the right one without any difficulty.

Strong northeast winds and heavy seas had made our last trip to these northern reefs a wild experience. This time, too, the winds were blowing vigorously, but fortunately from the southeast, thereby promising calmer waters in the vicinity of the reefs. We soon had Reef Diver launched and the three of us set out in the compelling heat of the July noon to cross the intervening five miles of water. In place of the terrifying, breaker-drenched reefs which had frightened me so on our previous visit, we now found ourselves approaching innocent-looking patches of brown rock immersed in the clearest of turquoise waters. Ed guided Reef Diver among them, sometimes over them when there was sufficient depth. Soon we were heading toward a scattering of dry rocks which I remembered only as one forlorn coral head that had appeared and disappeared in foaming masses of waves and spray.

Then we were in the open ocean, but this time it was calm, for the reefs behind us acted as a barrier to the southeast wind. We were even able to open the forward ports without danger of a salt-water deluge while Ed and I watched the bottom through the glass plates. Willy, at the wheel, steered Reef Diver straight toward the area we had searched before, a large clear expanse about two hundred yards from the dry rocks, bordered with coral heads just beneath the surface of the water.

Reef Diver circled and circled. Ed and I concentrated our gaze upon the wide ridges of pure white sand which patterned the bottom beneath us. Occasionally, angular edges of coral rock, well decked in living green-brown sea growth, tricked us into imagining cannon shapes, so long and narrow were they. We searched for nearly an hour before concluding that any remains of a shipwreck here could only be buried deep beneath the sand.

So we anchored Reef Diver, and Ed and Willy went

over the side with face masks, Ed carrying the metal detector. Reef Diver's usually dependable engine chugged on as it operated the compressor for the divers. The men had not been down long when they headed hurriedly for the boat. They pulled off their masks, complaining of unpleasant fumes in the air they were breathing. Ed made some adjustments to the compressor and they disappeared again beneath the water.

A few moments later Ed was back again. This time he handed the metal detector over the side to me. It had sprung a leak, he said, and was out of commission. He returned to the bottom. In no time both men were back. The fumes had become most unbearable, and they were concerned as to what was producing them. No use taking chances. They removed their masks and climbed into the boat. This was something that had never happened before. Our equipment was beginning to show the result of its long, hard usage.

So once more Ed and I took our places in the cabin to watch through the glass bottom while Willy guided Reef Diver over and over the same location. The salvager was insistent that we were on the right spot, and that the cannon should be there. Either they were completely buried in the sand, he said, or someone had removed them since he had last seen them two years before. Again he described their appearance, about twenty dull metal barrels scattered in a disorderly pile, half buried in the white sand.

When we returned to Sea Diver at the end of the afternoon, we had not seen a trace of wreckage anywhere. Once again the brass cannon had eluded us. Ever since that first winter, when Robby's and Webby's tales of brass cannon on the north Bahama banks had drawn us there, we had been tantalized by hopes of finding them. Never a year had passed without at least one attempt to follow up the many tales we continued to hear of their existence.

Nevertheless, when we headed Sea Diver into the setting sun later that afternoon on our way back to Miami, it was without any feeling of disappointment. Like solitaire, this was a game which one might expect to win only once in a while. The gamble had been part of the fun. It really didn't matter. We would try again. Someday, perhaps, we would find those brass cannon.

For five wonderful years we had sought adventure in pursuit of evidences of the past. From the time when Columbus first sighted San Salvador through all the exciting days of Spanish conquest, the colorful centuries when buccaneers and pirates dominated the Spanish Main and countless richly laden treasure ships traversed the Florida straits—we had relived the eventful history of the New World.

At the base of scattered coral reefs from the remote Silver shoals to the now-populous Florida keys, and on shallow ocean floors, we had uncovered symbols of a world of the past, meanwhile discovering in this underwater kingdom new horizons of our own, a peace and tranquility seldom encountered on the earth's surface.

But we had made only a beginning. We looked forward to many years of this soul-satisfying life at sea, as well as to the unpredictable and fascinating finds which would undoubtedly be part of it. Next year we would set out with Sea Diver once again, on another voyage of discovery. Life was a wonderful adventure, and we were content.

Bibliography

Beebe, William, *Beneath Tropic Seas* (diving in the Caribbean with some information on photography). New York, Putnam.

Brookfield, Charles M., and Griswold, Oliver, *They All Called It Tropical.* Coconut Grove, the Data Press, 1949.

Burney, James, *History of the Buccaneers of America.* Reprinted from edition of 1816. New York, W. W. Norton & Co., 1950.

Carson, Rachel L., *The Sea Around Us.* New York, Oxford University Press, 1951.

Chapin, Henry, and Smith, F. G. Walton, *The Ocean River.* New York, Charles Scribner's Sons, 1952.

Columbus, Christopher, *Autografi de Cristoforo Colombo in Raccolta di documenti e studi,* Vol. I, Pt. 1, ed. by Cesare de Lollis. Rome, 1892.

Columbus, Christopher, *Journal of First Voyage to America.* Introduced by Van Wyck Brooks. New York, 1924.

Columbus, Christopher, *Select Documents Illustrating the Voyages of Columbus,* translated by Cecil Jane and printed for the Hakluyt Society. London, Argonaut Press, 1930.

Cousteau, Capt. J. Y., *The Silent World.* New York, Harper & Brothers, 1953.

Crile, Jane and Barney, *Treasure Diving Holidays.* New York, the Viking Press, 1954.

Douglas, Marjory Stoneman, *The Everglades:* River of Grass. New York, Rinehart & Co., Inc., 1947.

Etheridge, Harry, *Yachtman's Guide to the Bahamas.* Official publication of Development Board, Nassau, B.W.I. Coral Gables, Tropic Isle Publishers, Inc., 1953.

Hanna, Alfred J. and Kathryn A., *Florida's Golden Sands.* New York, the Bobbs-Merrill Co., Inc., 1950.

Harding, Bertita, *Land Columbus Loved.* New York, Coward-McCann, 1949.

Irving, Washington, *A History of the Life and Voyages of Christopher Columbus.* 4 vols. London and New York, 1828.

Karraker, Cyrus H., *The Hispaniola Treasure,* Philadelphia, University of Pennsylvania Press, 1934.

Link, Edwin A. and Marion C., *A New Theory on Columbus's Voyage Through the Bahamas.* Smithsonian Miscellaneous Collections, Vol. 135, No. 4, Washington, The Smithsonian Institution, 1958.

Mason, F. Van Wyck, *Cutlass Empire* (a novel of Sir Henry Morgan). New York, Doubleday & Co., Inc., 1949.

Morison, Samuel Eliot, *Route of Columbus Along the North Coast of Haiti, and the Site of Navidad.* Transactions of American Philosophical Society, New Series, Vol. 31, Part 4, Philadelphia, 1940.

Murdock, J. B., *The Cruise of Columbus in the Bahamas,* 1492. Proc. U.S. Naval Inst., Vol. 10, No. 3, pp. 449–486, 1884.

Pedroso, Armando Alvarez, *Cristóbal Colón, biografía del descubridor.* Prologue by Clarence H. Haring. Habana, 1944.

Peterson, Mendel L., *History Under the Sea* (underwater exploration of shipwrecks). Washington, The Smithsonian Institution, Publ. 4174, 1954.

Peterson, Mendel L., *The Last Cruise of H.M.S. "Loo."* Smithsonian Miscellaneous Collections, Vol. 131, No. 2, Washington, The Smithsonian Institution, 1955.

Philips, Craig, and Brady, WH, *Sea Pests* (poisonous or harmful sea life of Florida and the West Indies). Miami, Fla., University of Miami Press, 1953.

Rieseberg, Lt. Harry, *Treasure Hunter.* New York, Robert McBride & Co., 1936.

Rodman, Selden, *Haiti, the Black Republic.* New York, Devin-Adair Co., 1954.

Snow, Edward Rowe, *True Tales of Pirates and Their Gold.* New York, Dodd, Mead & Co., 1953.

Verhoog, Pieter, *Guanahani Again* (the landfall of Columbus in 1492). Amsterdam, Holland, C. DeBoer, Jr., 1947.

Verrill, A. Hyatt, *They Found Gold* (the story of successful treasure hunts). New York, G. P. Putnam's Sons, 1936.

Woodbury, George, *Great Days of Piracy in the West Indies,* New York, W. W. Norton & Co., Inc., 1951.